Greece's Pivotal Role in World War II and its Importance to the U.S. Today

Books Published by the American Hellenic Institute Foundation

The Truman Doctrine of Aid to Greece: A Fifty-Year Retrospective (1998, published jointly with the Academy of Political Science)

Modern Greeks: Greece in World War II, The German Occupation and National Resistance, the Civil War (by Costas Stassinopoulos, 1997)

Books Published by the American Hellenic Institute

Handbook on United States Relations with Greece and Cyprus (2000)

Doing Business in Greece (1999)

American Hellenic Who's Who (Fifth edition, 1994)

The Rule of Law and Conditions on Foreign Aid to Turkey (1990)

Cyprus and the Rule of Law (1989)

Cyprus: The Tragedy and the Challenge (by Polyvious G. Polyviou, 1975)

Greece's Pivotal Role in World War II and its Importance to the U.S. Today

Introduction by
General Andrew J. Goodpaster, USA (RET.)
Former Supreme Commander of NATO

Edited by
Eugene T. Rossides

Published by the
American Hellenic Institute Foundation
Washington, DC

Published by
American Hellenic Institute Foundation
1220 16th Street, N.W.
Washington, D.C. 20036

Front and Back cover credit: AP/Wide World photos.

Library of Congress Cataloging in Publication Data

Greece's pivotal role in World War II and its importance to the U.S. today / edited by
Eugene T. Rossides ; introduction by Andrew J. Goodpaster.
p. cm.
Papers presented at a conference held Nov. 22, 1997, Washington, DC.
Includes bibliographical references and index
Contents: Mussolini's decision to attack Greece / James E. Miller—Greek diplomacy in the Greek-Italian war / Constantinos Svolopoulos—The Balkans and the Italian attack on Greece / Victor Papacosma—The Greek-Italian war : the view from the U.S. embassy in Athens / John O. Iatrides—The Greek wartime actions and the national resistance / Andre Gerolymatos—Elements of confusion : Britain and Greece, 1940-1941 / Robin Higham—The role of the Greek merchant marine in World War II / Mathew Los—The economic cost to Greece / James Warren—Rescue in Volos / Yolanda Avram Willis—The American relief effort for wartime Greece / Alexandros Kyrou—The role of Greece in the Eastern Mediterranean / Gregory Demestichas—U.S.-Greek relations from a Greek perspective / Athanasios Platias—The military and geostrategic dimensions of the Truman Doctrine / Photios Metallinos—The importance of Greece to the U.S. today / Eugene T. Rossides.

ISBN 1-889247-03-0
1. World War, 1939-45—Greece—Congresses. 2. World War, 1939-1945—Campaigns—Greece—Congresses. 3. Greece—Strategic aspects—Congresses. 4. United States—Relations—Greece—Congresses. 5. Greece—Relations—United States—Congresses. I. Rossides, Eugene T.

D754.G8 G74 2001
940.53'495—dc21 2001033315

Printed in the United States of America

To the heroic Greek men, women & children of the World War II generation.

TABLE OF CONTENTS

List of Illustrations

1. German anti-aircraft guns in Athens, posted at the Acropolis. Front cover. (AP/Wide World photos)

2. Upon the capture of Athens, German soldiers raised the Swastika over the Acropolis. March 5, 1941. Back cover. (AP/Wide World photos)

3. *German aircraft over Acropolis.*

4. *The struggle goes on at the Bulgarian Front,* 1941. (D.A. Harissiades/ Photographic Archive of the Benaki Museum)

5. *At the banks of Devolis,* 1941. (D.A. Harissiades/Photographic Archive of the Benaki Museum)

6. *Planes Wrecked on Italo-Greek Front.* Greek troops entering Koritza, a big Italian military base in Albania, said they found these wrecked Italian military planes at the airport. Koritza fell to the Greeks in November. January 3, 1941. (AP/Wide World photos)

7. *Italian Prisoners line up for "chow."* Guarded by Greek soldiers, Italian prisoners wait in line for food at their barracks in Athens. Each man in line has his tin dish ready. January 7, 1941. (AP/Wide World photos)

8. *Greeks play with captured weapons.* Greek soldiers amuse themselves with weapons and helmets captured from the Italians on the Albanian fighting front. February 8, 1941. (AP/Wide World photos)

9. *Italians reach Athens as captives.* Columns of Italians, captured by the Greek Army on the Albanian fighting front, march through an Athens street. February 8, 1941. (AP/Wide World photos)

10. *German soldiers on the Acropolis in Athens.* April 29, 1941. (AP/Wide World photos)

11. *Victory parade in Athens.* Victorious German troops paraded past Field Marshal General List in Athens. The photograph shows the units of armored cars passing Field Marshal General List. May 3, 1941. (AP/Wide World photos)

12. *German Troop Carrier Down in Flames.* A German troop-carrying plane that took part in the invasion of the island of Crete falls in flames to the ground near Candia, after being struck by shells from a British anti-aircraft gun. June 23, 1941. (AP/Wide World photos)

13. *Liberation of Athens.* October 12, 1944. (Voula Papaioannou/Photographic Archive of the Benaki Museum)

14. 210 Jewish children (Greek citizens) whose parents were killed by the Germans were collected throughout Greece and sent to families in Palestine which were going to adopt them. The work was done by UNRRA which provided transport, the Joint Distribution Committee and the Greek Jewish Agency. The photograph was taken in Piraeus, Greece by Voula Papaioannou prior to August 1, 1946. (Voula Papaioannou/Photographic Archive of the Benaki Museum)

Preface

Tens of thousands of books have been written about World War II, yet relatively few have dealt with Greece's pivotal role in that historic war. While many of the battles in World War II deserved the coverage they have received, few compare in importance to the outcome of the war as the battles fought on the Albanian front in the Italy-Greece war in 1940-41.

With Europe under the heel of Nazi Germany and with Britain fighting the Axis powers alone, Greece's courageous reply on October 28, 1940 of OXI (No!) to Mussolini's surrender ultimatum echoed throughout the world and gave support to Britain and the forces of freedom. General Andrew J. Goodpaster, former Supreme Commander of NATO, has characterized Greece's actions as pivotal in World War II.

OXI day, October 28, is a national holiday in Greece. It could also be celebrated in Europe, in Russia, in the United States and indeed throughout the world for its significance to the outcome of World War II.

This volume stems from a conference on the subject and is designed to illuminate Greece's efforts in World War II and to set forth the reasons for Greece's importance to the U.S. today. It is my hope that this volume will stimulate much additional scholarship on Greece's historic role in World War II and in the 20th Century as well as Greece's importance to the U.S. in the new millenium.

Conference coordinators Dr. Van Coufoudakis, Dean, School of Arts and Sciences, Indiana University-Purdue University, and Dr. John O. Iatrides, Professor of Political Science at Southern Connecticut State University, were instrumental in developing the conference program and in recommending and obtaining outstanding speakers.

I am pleased to acknowledge the distinguished speakers at our conference on Greece's role in World War II. They brought to life the dramatic events of the time. Their names and biographies are listed in the appendix.

I am most grateful to General Goodpaster for his perceptive and thoughtful introduction on Greece's pivotal role in World War II. The conference and this publication were made possible through the generous contributions of the Hellenic Bank Association, the Atlantic Bank of New York, the Hellenic American National Council, the Pan Cretan Association of America and the following American Hellenic Institute Foundation members: Gregory Demetrakas, Dennis Georges, James H. Lagos, Dr. Spiro Macris, James Pedas, Theodore Pedas, Eugene T. Rossides, Ted G. Spyropoulos and Steven G. Yeonas.

My thanks to Evanthia Allen who copy edited the manuscript, to Chrysoula Economopoulos for her research assistance and a very special thanks to Yola Pakhchanian for her editing and overseeing every step of the publication of this volume.

Eugene T. Rossides
President
American Hellenic Institute Foundation

Introduction

As the years pass, it becomes more and more necessary to recall and record for new generations just how the people of Greece, alone or with allies, gained and held for their country for a century and more the independence and democracy it possesses today—and how in one special moment in history Greece at heavy cost and sacrifice and with great courage and determination played a pivotal role in World War II in defying the forces of tyranny and Axis aggression that were arrayed against not only Greece but the whole of Western civilization. It is an inspiring story.

The essays in this volume tell in vivid detail the story of Greece in World War II and in its aftermath. They take note as well of the collective response to the common threat of the Cold War and review the problems as seen by Greece today, focusing on the relationship with its neighbor Turkey, and with the issues over Cyprus that continue to exist unresolved. The cooperation and mutual support of Greece and the United States is one key strand—a major one—throughout the whole period and in the changed world we now live in.

Never to be forgotten is the valiant role of Greece against the Axis nations that were on the march in Europe. Brought into the war by Mussolini's attack in October 1940—at a time when Britain stood alone against the Axis partners—Greek forces in defense of their homeland brought the Italian forces to a standstill, and in fact threw them well back into Albania by the end of the year. When Hitler, to support his humiliated partner, launched his attack against Yugoslavia and Greece in April 1941, he did so with massive forces that were capable and sufficient to overwhelm the Greek and supporting British forces. The delay that resulted, however, is widely held to have been a vital factor tipping the scale against decisive victory by Hitler in Russia.

It was a fearful cost to Greece, brought under occupation for the remainder of the war. But, as these essays make clear, the Greek Resistance and the continued participation of Greek shipping were continuing contributions vital to the overall Allied effort. In preserving and presenting the history of the Greek wartime role, the authors make an enduring contribution to future understanding. But the trauma for Greece did not end with the allied liberation in 1945. As Western Europe, including Greece, lay nearly prostrate and in ruins, the new threat of Soviet Communist domination quickly arose. By early 1947, Britain—itself in grave straits from the war's devastation, distress and financial demands—found itself unable to continue its support to Greece and Turkey against postwar privation and Soviet pressures and brought the problem to the United States. The decisive action by President Truman—a new departure in American policy—was a turning point in Euro-Atlantic affairs. Followed by the Marshall Plan, and then by NATO, his action set a course by which its European partners and the United States, all working together, were able to achieve recovery, security and peace then and for the rest of the century.

Throughout the Cold War, the role of NATO was primarily focused on a single clear mission—to hold a threatening Soviet Union in check, by peaceful means if at all possible, by collective defense if actually attacked. It was this aim of preserving the freedom and sovereignty of the participating nations and their people that drew and held the nations together in the collective commitment and collective effort of NATO.

Five principal working objectives guided the common effort of the Alliance as it earned its place as the most successful alliance in all of recorded history.

The first of these was *deterrence*—the prevention of aggression and attack. Second was *defense,* the building of collective military capability, which gave reality to deterrence and could halt aggression and punish the aggressor if it nevertheless should come. The third was *solidarity,* standing and working together, to achieve, in the words of General Eisenhower, a state of security that would be beyond the reach of any or of all if they had to act separately. The fourth was *détente,* correctly seen as reducing armed tensions through reducing the primary causes of tension—Soviet expansionism backed by its massive military power. And the fifth was *equity,* a fair sharing of the overall risks and burdens. The going was not always by any means smooth or easy. But with the North Atlantic Council providing a deliberative forum giving political direction and a military command structure welding, as it was said, a collection of forces into a collective force, with an integrated top-level command structure, its central purpose was well served.

NATO proved to have great internal values as many deep-seated, often ancient clashes and grievances were subordinated to the overriding purpose and commitment to shared security throughout the duration of the Cold War. The final success for the security objective came with the collapse of the Soviet Union, and the historic achievement in peace of the freedom of the Warsaw Pact nations previously held by force.

The NATO nations, till then faced with mortal threat, were now faced with new challenges and new uncertainties. What would be NATO's role? How, and how well, would it be achieved? There was even question on the part of many as to whether NATO would indeed have a future. Such were among the questions that faced both Greece and the United States at that time as NATO members, just as they faced their NATO fellow allies. It was soon confirmed, however, by the NATO member nations that their common defense commitment in support of collective security would be continued, with work initiated to revise the basic NATO strategic concept in response to the new security environment. Beyond this, however, the response of the NATO nations can best be regarded as unfinished business—a "work in progress" that still goes on today. The NATO "Partnership for Peace" was extended to a wide range of additional nations, including former members of the Soviet Union. It has achieved a considerable degree of success, though strengthening of its role is very much needed. Relations with Russia, however, have not yet been satisfactorily developed to the extent needed, and much more constructive effort is required.

But all in all the international post-Cold War framework that has emerged, with all its limitations and all the sovereign reservations that exist—a framework that includes as its main elements the United Nations, NATO and the OSCE (the Organization for Security and Cooperation in Europe)—is furthering the peaceful security and well-being of the nations and their people in a Europe generally whole and free, with continuing beneficial ties between Europe and the United States. It is a Europe which is striving to deal with new issues of profound policy significance, including—crucially important—resolution for such questions as intervention by force within sovereign countries to bring ethnic genocide and humanitarian violations to an end.

Knotty and deep-seated problems—especially in the Balkans and the Eastern Mediterranean in which Greece is deeply concerned—will continue to engage and test the international framework, with ethnic challenges and bi-national discord foremost among the issues no longer suppressed and overshadowed by the Cold War. The United States, we can be confident, will continue to offer its good offices and be ready, should the occasion demand it, to consider cooperative action. The international institutions can be of great help, but national leaders—such as Truman in his time as well as Marshall and Eisenhower from the United States, Schumann and Monnet in Western Europe and, in the Eastern Mediterranean, Venizelos and Ataturk (as one outsider believes)—will make the difference between success and failure. Whether such statesmen will arise with the vision and leadership abilities needed to resolve and settle these issues remains a crucial question. In all of this, as we look to the future, the many issues on which the United States and Greece share a wide range of security interests and common objectives give assurance of the importance of their mutual cooperation, friendship and well-being in dealing with the problems the new century will bring.

General Andrew J. Goodpaster, USA (Ret.)
Former Supreme Commander of NATO

Greece Stands Alone:
The Diplomatic Setting

Mussolini's Parallel War: Italy Attacks Greece, October 1940

James E. Miller

Fascist Italy's October 1940 attack on Greece was a national tragedy for both states. For Italy, defeat in the mountains of Greece and Albania led to submission to the dictates of Nazi Germany, invasion, occupation, civil war, a punitive postwar peace and difficult years of postwar economic and social reconstruction. For victorious Greece, Nazi invasion and occupation, mass starvation, multiple civil conflicts, and massive reconstruction followed its triumph over Mussolini's forces.

It takes nothing from our admiration of the courage of Greek soldiers in defense of their homeland to state that the war was the product of the muddled geopolitical and personal ambitions of a "gang that couldn't shoot straight." For sheer incompetence and breathtaking short-sightedness, few aggressors have ever matched Mussolini and his collaborators. Italy went to war with little psychological or military preparation and only the vaguest of plans. Nevertheless, the war had both long-term and proximate causes. This essay will attempt to clarify the causes of a war that quickly became a national disaster for Italy but also, fortuitously, a major step in the collapse of Fascism.[1]

Italy's "Megali Idea"

Italy's penetration of the Balkans had roots in its nineteenth century political and economic development. Forty years after Greece began its national revolution against Turkish rule, a united Italian kingdom emerged from a series of diplomatic maneuvers and wars against the Austro-Hungarian Empire. Unification was carried out by a small elite of upper- and middle-class patriots with a minimum of popular participation. The leaders of the new state had ambitious plans for national development, which were

---

JAMES E. MILLER is Professor at the Department of History, John Hopkins University, Washington, DC.

1. The best general interpretations of the war from the Italian perspective are Mario Cervi, *Hollow Legions* (New York: 1971) and McGregor Knox, *Mussolini Unleashed* (New York: 1982).

quickened by a sense of exposure to the designs of more powerful European states and by a corresponding desire to see Italy play the role of a great power. During the first decades of national existence, Italy's leaders concentrated on creating the economic sinews of power, particularly building an infrastructure of roads, canals, and railroads. They promoted capital formation through a regressive taxation policy and by encouraging the creation of investment banks. The new state actively sought foreign investment. The Italian government attempted to build security through alliance with the powerful German *Reich* and the former enemy and occupier of Italy, the Austro-Hungarian Empire.[2]

Late nineteenth century Italy's security needs were extensive. In addition to the challenges posed by a hostile France and still unreconciled Austria, the new state faced serious threats within its own borders in the form of the Roman Catholic Church and a growing mass of discontented peasants and workers. The Church, which lost both its political independence and territorial control of central Italy during national unification, refused to accept the settlement offered to it in 1871 (the Law of Guarantees), insisting that it had to possess a distinct international identity that resulted from an accord negotiated by juridical equals. The Roman Church would never accept the role of Italian national church. At the same time, however, it insisted on a major role in the internal life of the new state. While ostentatiously refusing to permit Catholics to participate directly in the political life of Italy (Pope Pius IX's so-called "non-expedit" policy), the Vatican supported efforts by Italian bishops and laity to build a structure of cultural, labor, and mutual support organizations with the ability to mobilize mass political pressure on the Italian state.[3]

Meanwhile, a regressive taxation policy was bearing its fruits. Italy was industrializing and simultaneously creating a powerful new threat to the interests of its ruling elite. Industrial development pulled peasants from the land into the cities and, by concentrating masses of poor and exploited workers in urban centers, offered radical political idealists the chance to organize and educate the working classes in the gospel according to Karl

2. On the general issues of Italian political and economic development, see Giorgio Candeloro, *Storia dell' Italia moderna,* vol. 6 (Milan: 1970). For the classic interpretation of its post-unification foreign policy, see Frederico Chabod, *Storia della politica estera italiana* (Bari: 1971).

3. Two older but still useful syntheses of the "Catholic problem" in unified Italy are A. C. Jemolo, *Chiesa e Stato in Italia* (Turin: 1961) and Giorgio Candeloro, *Il Movimento cattolico in Italia* (Rome: 1972). A more recent study is G. B. Guerri, *Gli italiani sotto la chiesa* (Milan: 1992).

Marx. Union organizational activities accelerated in the late 1880s, and in 1892 the Italian Socialist Party held its first congress at Genoa.[4]

Imperialism was the logical outcome both of the successes and threats facing Italy's ruling elites. Successful entrepreneurs, already accustomed to support from the state, looked to their government to open new markets through diplomacy and, where necessary, force. Italian leaders, such as Francesco Crispi, had fought with Garibaldi in creating Italian unity in 1860. They either forgot or ignored that Italy's national hero and his teacher, Giuseppe Mazzini, both insisted that a peaceful and prosperous Europe had to be built on respect for the rights of other national groups. Instead, Italy's leaders built a small empire in Africa, promoted economic penetration in the Balkans, and actively looked for more imperial opportunities. Italy, like nineteenth century Greece, was guided by an irredentist *Megali Idea* (Great Idea) rooted in a romantic reading of its past that stressed imperial glory. While nineteenth century Greeks looked to the glories of the Byzantine Empire (and to unredeemed Greek populations living in the Ottoman Empire) to justify plans for a great state, Italians invoked Imperial Rome and the Renaissance Venetian state to provide a historical justification for colonial adventures in Africa and the Balkans.

Its dangerous imperialist policy offered the Italian Right a useful tool for dealing with the internal socialist threat. One of the frequently proclaimed objectives of African colonization was to offer a "promised land" for Italy's surplus population of poor peasants as well as greater prosperity for its workers through the creation of a protected area for the export of industrial goods. Finally, the evocation of past national glories was an ideological counterweight to Marxist ideas of the unity of the international proletariat. At critical moments of internal tension from 1890 onward, the nationalist Right sought to use imperial expansion as an antidote to internal economic and social conflict. In 1914-1915, the conservative Salandra-Sonnino government abandoned its thirty-year-old alliance with Austria and Germany and maneuvered the nation into war on the side of the Triple Entente of England, France, and Russia, in order to achieve a major territorial expansion in the Balkans and Anatolia.[5]

4. Among a number of fine books on the rise of socialism, immodesty suggests James E. Miller, *From Elite to Mass Politics* (Kent, Ohio: 1990).
5. Richard Drake, *Byzantium for Rome* (Chapel Hill: 1980) and John Thayer, *Italy and the Great War* (Madison: 1964) on imperial ideology. Richard Webster, *Industrial Imperialism in Italy* (Berkeley: 1975) is the classic study of the connections of industry and government.

Although largely frustrated by Woodrow Wilson at the Versailles Peace Conference, Foreign Minister Sidney Sonnino's "sacred egotism" of alliance switching succeeded in winning territory in Istria, and in establishing for Italy an effective protectorate over Albania. Italian ambitions in Anatolia played a role in fueling Greek intervention in Asia Minor. Moreover, the conflicts that erupted over a postwar peace settlement clearly established that Greece and newly created Yugoslavia were the major obstacles to increased Italian influence in the Balkans.

A dangerous witch's brew of imperial nationalism passed into the hands of Benito Mussolini in 1922. In consolidating his power, the Duce quickly seized upon the psychological value of successful Balkan involvement. In 1923, utilizing the flimsiest of pretexts, Italy bombarded and occupied Corfu, with the clear intent of taking this one-time Venetian imperial possession from a Greece that was still in the throes of the Anatolian catastrophe. Only international action coordinated by the League of Nations forced the Italians to withdraw.

Thereafter, Mussolini found many good reasons for better international behavior, but even American stabilization bank loans and favorable relations with the era's two great status quo powers, Britain and France, were unable to completely restrain the Fascist state's disruptive policies in the Balkans. Throughout the 1920s and 1930s, Italy actively sought to damage and dismember the Yugoslav state. It supported IMRO (Internal Macedonian Revolutionary Organization) terrorists operating out of Bulgaria. The October 1934 assassination of King Alexander of Yugoslavia and French Foreign Minister Barthou by an Italian-financed terrorist was the fruit of this policy.[6]

The brutal friendship

In the mid-1930s Mussolini dramatically reversed his international alliances. The Great Depression of 1929 speedily removed one of the major factors in Italy's general pattern of international moderation: U.S. bank loans were no longer available to stabilize the regime. Mussolini substituted policies of economic autarchy for Italy's former reliance on international finance, and at the same time accentuated the regime's imperial objectives in the Mediterranean, bringing Italy directly into conflict with Britain and France.

---

6. Nancy Barker, *The Macedonia Question* (London: 1949) remains a useful summary of Italian involvement in the Balkans. See also H. James Burgwyn, *Il revisionismo fascista* (Milan: 1979). See James Barros, *The Corfu Incident of 1923* (Princeton, NJ: Princeton University Press, 1965) on that aspect of Greek-Italian relations.

The Fascist attack on Ethiopia (1935) and Italy's subsequent participation in the Spanish Civil War (1936-1939) drove wedges between Mussolini and the democratic powers. Meanwhile, relations between the Duce and the new Nazi Party regime in Germany went from cold to warm. After blocking Hitler's ambitions in Austria (1934), Mussolini began to see the German dictatorship as a natural ally in Italy's conflicts with the British and French. Hitler, who genuinely admired the Italian leader, was anxious to cement a relationship of cooperation. Mussolini, ever the Machiavellian, was considerably less intrigued with Hitler. He was, however, very impressed with Nazi power. A 1938 visit to Germany for the Maifeld celebration dramatically underlined both Hitler's control over the German people and the rapid progress of his remilitarization. Mussolini returned both awed and intimidated by the German leader.[7]

The immediate fruit of this new relationship was a freer hand for Hitler. *Anschluss* with Austria became easier with Italy on the sidelines. During the 1938 Great-Power confrontation over Czechoslovakia, Germany enjoyed active Italian diplomatic support. Mussolini, in turn, began to vaunt the power of the Pact of Steel to remake Europe and spoke of an "axis" around which future international politics would rotate. However, the reality was scarcely one of coordinated power politics. Hitler never took the Italians into his confidence when major decisions were made. He made his pact with Stalin (August 1939) and launched the invasion of Poland (September 1, 1939) without alerting his ally. Germany conducted the early stages of its war against the Western "plutocracies" with only the most minimal coordination with its erstwhile Italian ally. German indifference enabled Italy to avoid immediate involvement in the war, to the great relief of most Italians, including many senior Fascists. Germany's actions also revealed, however, how secondary a power Italy really was, a fact that was bound to play a role in Mussolini's subsequent calculations.[8]

By June 1940, with Germany triumphant in the West, Mussolini determined to enter the war on the side of his indifferent ally. Correctly calculating that France was on its last legs, the Italian dictator declared war on June 10, hoping for a share of the spoils of German victory.

Italy's brief French campaign was a foretaste of national disasters to come. In September 1939, the Italians had avoided entry into the war by presenting Germany with a huge (and purposely undeliverable) list of armaments and supplies needed to support their military effort. In the nine

7. On the psychological relationship of the two men, F. W. Deakin, *The Brutal Friendship* (New York: 1966) remains the best.
8. Galeazzo Ciano, *The Ciano Diaries* (New York: 1946), pp. 263-274.

months that passed little had been done to cover the gaps in Italy's preparations. Poorly equipped, poorly trained, poorly led, and poorly motivated, Italian troops quickly bogged down in their first military offensive. The French counterattacked and soundly defeated their would-be invaders. In the armistice talks that followed Germany's triumph, the French were able to resist most Italian demands for concessions. Hitler's support for his ally was lukewarm.[9]

Italy's "parallel war," 1940

The failure of the French attack, although partially masked by the enormity of German success, was a stinging rebuff for Mussolini and his collaborators. The dictator's son-in-law and foreign minister, Count Galeazzo Ciano, who had maneuvered to keep Italy out of the war, abruptly shifted position as he recognized the depth of Mussolini's embarrassment (and the fragility of his own position). From an opponent of war, he suddenly became one of the prime motivators of the concept of a "parallel war" that Italy would wage in the Mediterranean in pursuit of long-standing national objectives: expansion into the Balkans and the conquest of an African colonial empire at the expense of Great Britain.[10]

The first issue to settle was the choice of a Balkan victim. Fascist leaders were pulled by the lure of an attack on Yugoslavia as well as the prospects of an invasion of Greece. Their indecision helped to postpone an attack, but the time lag did not noticeably improve the level of their military preparation. Instead, provocative Italian actions permitted Italy's potential victims to hasten their own defensive preparations. As a result, Greece was in a better position to confront Italy in October 1940 than it would have been in the summer of that year.[11]

The driving force behind the Italian decision to attack Greece rather than Yugoslavia was neither military nor geostrategic calculation but the ambitions of three members of the governmental hierarchy: Ciano, Marshal de Vecchi, the military governor of the Dodecanese, and Visconti Prasca, the chief of military forces in Albania. Having committed himself to a parallel war somewhere, Ciano simply decided that the Greek looked to be the more inviting target. De Vecchi fed the war fever in Rome with a series of inaccurate reports on hostile Greek actions and intentions.

---

9. Knox, *Mussolini Unleashed,* pp. 125-137.
10. Dino Grandi, *Il mio paese* (Bologna: 1985), pp. 589-600.
11. See the reporting in *Foreign Relations of the United States, 1940,* vol. 3, pp. 525, 541. Hereinafter, volumes in this series will be abbreviated as *FRUS* with volume and page.

Visconti Prasca campaigned for an invasion in order to secure the glory of a successful military campaign.

Meanwhile, the Italian military acted in an uncoordinated and provocative manner. The unprovoked sinking of the former cruiser Helle on August 15 by an Italian submarine was a locally ordered initiative, not a decision taken at the highest levels of national policymaking. The timid Greek response to this and other provocations had the effect of reinforcing the conviction of the war party in Rome that Greece would be an easy target.[12]

Ioannis Metaxas, Greece's dictator, emerged from the 1940 crisis and his subsequent (well-timed) death as something of a national hero. However, this authoritarian ex-army officer badly misjudged the Italians, and his weak diplomatic response to repeated Italian provocation ranks as a major Greek blunder.

Metaxas, who adopted many of the outward forms of Fascism-Nazism to cover his ideologically threadbare authoritarian regime, and King George II, his collaborator, ignored or brushed off signs of the threat posed by Fascist Italy in the apparent hope that they would go away. Trusting to Germany's clear opposition to any Italian adventures in the Balkans, the Greek government attempted to placate Mussolini's regime. While Metaxas was fatalistically ready to confront Italy on the battlefront, his diplomacy was less than forceful. Earlier and stronger signs of a will to resist might have aided the efforts of various Italian officials to avert a war with Greece.[13] Among these officials were the head of the military staff, Marshal Pietro Badoglio, the service chiefs, King Victor Emanuel III, and the Italian commander on the North African front.

Italian public opinion, as measured by embassies and other foreign observers, was decisively opposed to any military adventure. The institutions that were the main props of the regime—the military, the monarch, big business, the Church—all feared being yoked to Hitler's war machine. Mussolini's decision to wage war in Greece put the regime's narrowing base of support on the line. The subsequent Italian defeat was a critical step toward the collapse of Fascism.[14]

In mid-October, following discussions with Hitler at the Brenner Pass (October 4), the Duce made his decision for war with Greece. He

12. Knox, *Mussolini Unleashed,* pp. 172-77. *FRUS* , vol. 3, pp. 530, 534. Ciano, *Diary,* pp. 272, 274, 284.
13. *FRUS,* vol. 3, pp. 528, 531, 540, 542, 546. Knox, *Mussolini Unleashed,* p. 139.
14. On the state of Italian public opinion, J. Miller, "Carlo Sforza e l'evoluzione della politica americana verso l'Italia," *Storia contemporanea* 7 (1976) and Aurelio Lepre, *L'occhio del Duce* (Milan: 1992).

announced it to his military subordinates on October 13 and reconfirmed his decision the following day. This miscalculation was made despite the wealth of information that Italy was, in fact, in no position to launch a successful attack. The Italian dictator knew that his forces on the ground in Albania were unprepared for an offensive; that supply was a serious problem both for the Greek project and for military operations in North Africa; that his generals had serious misgivings about command responsibilities; that given the late start of the offensive, Italy would have to carry out a fall and winter *blitzkrieg* in the rugged mountains of Greece.[15]

Faced with these insurmountable difficulties, Mussolini and his generals engaged in surrealistic planning. The Duce insisted on an offensive. The generals set aside their professional objections and began to create optimistic scenarios to meet the dictator's demands. By October 15, they were able to project an offensive that would immobilize Thessalonike and lead to the capture of Athens by December. Visconti Prasca cheerfully rearranged Greek geography to meet the Duce's desires. He ignored the reality of port bottlenecks in Valona and claimed that speedy reinforcement by three extra mountain divisions would enable the Italian army to meet its objectives. Amazingly, Badoglio, who knew better, failed to object to his subordinate's flights of fancy. Mussolini, who had imposed his will in Hilter-like fashion on his subordinates, withdrew to plan his triumphant entry into Alexandria, Egypt after the expected success of Italian forces in North Africa. Left alone, the military chiefs began to show signs of reassessing the entire plan. Mussolini, however, quashed their outburst of common sense with a series of tirades (October 17-18).[16]

The Greek government, meanwhile, having abandoned all its illusions about Italian behavior, was speedily mobilizing. When Italian diplomacy failed to entice Bulgaria into a joint attack on Greece, the Italians faced a new reality. Their intended victim would have more troops at his disposal than the attacking forces, would have reserves massed, would possess better lines of communications, and would face the initial Italian attack from Albania with only slightly fewer front-line soldiers than Visconti Prasca. Added to this, of course, was the psychological boost that the Greeks would enjoy as the angry victims of Fascist aggression.[17]

15. G. Ciano, *Ciano's Diplomatic Papers* (London: 1948), pp.389-91. Knox, *Mussolini Unleashed,* pp. 203-13.
16. Knox, *Mussolini Unleashed,* pp. 212-217.
17. Ibid., p. 218.

Nevertheless, Mussolini unleashed his "parallel war" on October 28, 1940. Italy quickly paid the price of its leaders' folly. Italian attackers needed a miracle to succeed and as usual miracles were in short supply.

Why?

In assessing the proximate causes for Mussolini's massive miscalculation, a number of factors are evident. In the first place, the Italian dictator felt he had to score a major prestige success independent of the already victorious Hitler. Greece, which turned all its diplomatic efforts to avoiding war, appeared weak, and seemed to offer the opportunity to establish Italy's independent role within the Axis on European soil. Success in the Balkans, in turn, would vindicate Mussolini's claims to Italian dominance in the Mediterranean. If combined with a victory over the British in North Africa, the triumph over Greece would open the whole region to exploitation and might even convince the British to end their resistance. Such a smashing geopolitical triumph would put Italy's leader on the same level as Hitler as warlord and enable Mussolini to play an equal role in settling the postwar international map.

Furthermore, a triumph in Greece would enable Mussolini to subordinate completely all the powerful groups that opposed his war plans: dissident Fascists, the military, the monarchy, the business elite. Fascism and its leader would finally become the dominant force that he had always claimed it should be in a totalitarian state.

Defeat fundamentally altered the Duce's position and that of Italy. Italy's decades-long pretensions to the role of a great power collapsed in the mountains of Greece. Its relationship with Germany moved from unequal partnership to subordination. Its Mediterranean ambitions came apart as Germany, however unwillingly, took control of the war effort in this strategic sector. At home, Fascism began to disintegrate. Public concern about war moved to apathy and outright resistance to the regime. The crown, military, and elites began to look for ways to dislodge the regime. By late 1942, as Fascist defeats mounted, the replacement of Mussolini and negotiation of a separate peace with the Anglo-Americans became the primary objective of a ruling class that saw its only survival in ridding itself of Fascism. Defeatism infected the Fascist Party and its senior leadership, which began looking for ways to unload its founder and survive.

Italy survived. Neither Fascism nor its founder would. Mussolini was executed by his own people at war's end. Ciano, another of the authors of the 1940 disaster, had already succumbed to a firing squad at his father-in-law's order. The Italian people paid the price of the 1940 invasion: military defeat, German and Allied occupation, a civil war, a bloody resistance to Nazism, the humiliation of the peace settlement, territorial losses, and a slow, difficult economic reconstruction. The parallels with the wartime and postwar fate of Greece are striking. The war of 1940-1941 was a calamity for both peoples. ✦

The Greek Decision to Resist the Axis Invasion, 1940-41

Constantine Svolopoulos

The Greek government's refusal to succumb to the demands of Fascist Italy and to give away its sovereign rights over a significant part of its territory—a decision enthusiastically endorsed by the Greek people—had repercussions beyond Greece and even beyond the regional setting of the Balkans and the Eastern Mediterranean. The repulsion of the Italian attack, the victorious drive of the Greek army into Italian-occupied Albania, and then the strong resistance that the Greeks put up against the German invasion both in the mainland and on Crete affected the course of the Second World War on the political, diplomatic, and strategic levels.

It is self-evident that the determination of the Greeks to resist Axis aggression was the main factor that shaped their attitudes in 1940-41. In studying this period, it is interesting to assess how and by whom the decision to resist was made and what considerations and feelings lay behind it.

In 1939 both the political leadership and public opinion were strongly opposed to the country's participation in a general international conflict. The irredentist motives that had led Greece to enter the First World War—that is, the Megali Idea policy of recovering unredeemed territories from Turkey—were no longer there in 1939. Since World War I, some of the nation's irredentist ambitions had been realized, while others were no longer relevant after the collapse of the Greek campaign in Asia Minor in 1922 and the 1923 Greek-Turkish compulsory exchange of populations. Some aspirations based on the principle of self-determination had survived, however. The Dodecanese islands, Cyprus, and Northern Epirus were territories in which Greeks formed the majority of the population. Nevertheless, Athens did not link its policy vis-à-vis the warring parties in World War II with the fate of these lands.

CONSTANTINE SVOLOPOULOS is Professor at the Department of History, University of Athens.

After the conclusion of the Lausanne Treaty of 1923, the main aim of Greek diplomacy was the protection of the country's territorial integrity and independence.[1] Former Prime Minister Eleftherios Venizelos himself, the man who had advocated Greece's intervention in the Great War as a means of realizing its territorial claims, had become, after 1923 and until his death in 1936, a fervent supporter of a policy that would ensure that the country would not be drawn into a war again.[2] The Metaxas regime of the Fourth of August, 1936 [the day King George suspended constitutional liberties and dissolved parliament without fixing a date for new elections] had also accepted this view. This was significant, since it was during Metaxas' rule that such a general war was beginning to seem possible.

It is indeed instructive to assess whether it was possible for a small country as strategically situated as Greece to adopt an attitude of strict neutrality. In the late 1930s, the government's fervent search for a territorial guarantee kept Athens within the British sphere of influence, although this policy failed to give Greece an alliance with Britain.[3] Still, while always striving to preserve close relations with London, the Greek government, after the outbreak of the war, generally respected—at least formally—international rules on neutrality. The Italian Ambassador in Athens, Emanuele Grazzi, noted in his memoirs that "neutrality was respected until the last moment by the Greek government with care and with all means at its disposal."[4]

It was in 1928-29 that Venizelos managed to balance Greece's relations with the three Great Powers—Britain, France, and Italy—which influenced the course of events in the Mediterranean.[5] But beginning with Italy's aggression against Abyssinia in 1935, a process started of dramatic changes

1. Constantinos Svolopoulos, *Ελληνικη Εξωτερικη Πολιτικη, 1900-1945 (Greek Foreign Policy, 1900-1945)* (Athens: 1992).
2. Constantinos Svolopoulos, *Το Βαλκανικον Συμφωνον και η Ελληνικη Εξωτερικη Πολιτικη, 1928-1934. Ανεκδοτον Κειμενον του Ε.Βενιζελου (The Balkan Pact and Greek Foreign Policy, 1928-1934.* An unpublished text by Eleftherios Venizelos (Athens: 1974).
3. On Greek-British relations, see John Koliopoulos, *Greece and the British Connection, 1935-1941* (Oxford: 1977).
4. Emanuele Grazzi, *Η Αρχη του Τελους: Η Επιχειρηση Κατα της Ελλαδος (The Beginning of the End: the Operation against Greece)*, translated from Italian (Athens: 1980), p. 132.
5. Constantinos Svolopoulos, *Η Ελληνικη Εξοτερικη Πολιτικη μετα τη Συνθηκη της Λωζανης: Η Κρισιμη Καμπη (Ιουλιος—Δεκεμβριος 1928) (Greek Foreign Policy after the Lausanne Treaty: The Turning Point, July-December 1928)* (Thessalonike: 1977). See also Constantinos A. Karamanlis, *Ο Ελευθερος Βενιζελος και οι Εξωτερικες μας Σχεσεις 1928-1932 (El.Venizelos and Greece's Foreign Relations 1928-1932)* (Athens: 1986).

in international relations in Europe, placing the Greek government in an uncomfortable position; Greece might now have to side either with its traditional Western allies, or with the powerful bloc which was being formed under the leadership of Hitler's Germany.

Motivated both by international and internal factors, Greece chose the Western allies, and this preference became increasingly apparent in the country's foreign policy in the late 1930s. At the same time, however, Athens also tried to avoid any move that could be taken as a provocation and might trigger the reaction of the other bloc. Italy's 1940 attack on Greece certainly was not motivated by the sense of a threat against Rome because of Greece's diplomatic orientation—especially since Athens did not have an alliance with Britain and France. The explanation for the Italian attack lies primarily in the desire of the Fascist leadership to achieve its expansionist goals.

The territory of Greece, a crossroads of strategically important sea and air communication routes, attracted Mussolini's attention. Indeed, his powerful German ally had accepted that the Mediterranean was a region of Italian interest, and this had encouraged the Italian dictator's opportunism. As he put it just before the attack on Greece, "this [was] an operation which I have thought over for months and months before my entry in the war, even before the outbreak of the war." The Fascist coup in Albania in April 1939, the outbreak of the war in Europe and Italy's involvement in June 1940, and the subsequent intensification of Italian pressure on Greece, all these events gave Mussolini ample opportunities to put into practice his aggressive policy toward Greece.[6]

In 1939-40 the attitude of the Greek government toward Italy was careful but firm. Athens denied any involvement in the unilateral declaration of guarantee offered by Britain and France on April 7, 1939, in the aftermath of Albania's occupation by Italy. After Mussolini entered the war, Greece had reaffirmed its intention to maintain strict neutrality, strongly disclaiming Fascist accusations about alleged use of Greek ports or airfields by British forces, or about maltreatment of Albanian citizens. Last but not least, Greece refrained from protesting when provoked, even after the sinking by an Italian submarine of the light cruiser Helle, on August 15, 1940 at the port of Tenos, during an annual religious ceremony.

6. *Βασιλικον Υπουργειον Εξωτερικων* (Royal Foreign Ministry), *Διπλωματικα Εγγραφα: Η Ιταλικη Επιθεσις κατα της Ελλαδος* (Diplomatic Documents: "The Italian Attack on Greece") (Athens: 1940).

Nevertheless, immediately after the first signs of Italian pressure, as early as August 1939, Metaxas emphasized to the Italian ambassador that "Greece has no desire to act against Italy and make war with it, unless Italy violates vital interests of Greece and especially its territorial integrity." He concluded: "In that case, please cable [to Rome] that Greece will defend its honor and integrity to the very end."[7] This position, which was then reaffirmed repeatedly, has been summarized, in two dramatic phrases, by the Greek prime minister in a minute he wrote in his own hand on September 2, 1940: "Determined to make war to the end in order not to succumb to the Italian demands...[Greece's] decision to defend itself to the end and to sacrifice itself, rather than succumb."[8] The rejection, at dawn of October 28, 1940, of the Italian ultimatum confirmed Greece's persistence in this position.

Greece maintained its determination to fight even in the face of the threat of an attack by Germany. Up until the end of March 1941, the allies did not know of Hitler's decision to invade the Soviet Union.[9] It was important for him to consolidate his control over southeastern Europe prior to turning toward the U.S.S.R. Hitler's intentions became clear after he approved the operational plan "Marita," and especially after the descent of German troops, through Romania and Bulgaria, into the south of the Balkan Peninsula. It then became obvious that it was not possible to form a peripheral front in an effort to block Germany's invasion plans.[10]

The Greek proposal for a common front of Balkan countries was realistic, since the Italians had been defeated in Albania. It was killed, however, because of the desire of Greece's neighbors to avoid the most immediate danger, and to obtain gains at Greece's expense.[11]

Throughout the period from October 1940 to the German attack in early April 1941, Greece repeatedly affirmed its decision to resist even an inva-

---

7. Ibid.; 31. This position was repeated, equally firmly, by Greek diplomats in Rome, and Grazzi mentioned that the Under-Secretary for Foreign Affairs, M. Mavroudis, said as much to him on August 13, 1940. (Grazzi, op.cit., p. 182).
8. Minute by Metaxas on the text of a report by Rizos-Ragavis from Berlin, September 2, 1940. Greek Foreign Ministry: Historical Archive.
9. See Mavroudis (Athens) to Simopoulos (London), March 11, 1941, *Υπουργειο Εξω-τερικων*, 1940-41 *Ελληνικα Διπλωματικα Εγγραφα* (Foreign Ministry, 1940-41 Hellenic Diplomatic Documents), edited by Constantinos Svolopoulos (hereafter *Ε.Δ.Ε.*,) (Athens: 1974).
10. On the German decision, see D. Kitsikis, *Η Ελλας της 4ης Αυγουστου και οι Μεγαλες Δυναμεις* (4th August Greece and the Great Powers) (Athens: 1974).
11. Constantinos Svolopoulos, "Greece and its Neighbours on the Eve of the German Invasion of the Balkans," Balkan Studies 28 (1987), pp. 355-371.

sion by the *Wehrmacht*. On December 20, 1940 Metaxas stressed to the German minister in Athens that his country's rapprochement with Britain was an inevitable consequence of the Italian attack and was not directed against Berlin, but if the Reich confronted Greece in the Balkans, the Athens-London relationship would take on an anti-German flavor.[12]

On their part, the British were convinced that Greece was determined to go all the way. As Michael Palairet reported from Athens, Metaxas intended to reject any German threat or ultimatum, as he had done with the Italians on October 28. The Greeks, he continued, had already made clear that although they did not want to provoke Germany by words or deeds, they would not succumb.[13] On January 18, 1941, a few days before he died, Metaxas outlined his position in a cable to London, following a crucial meeting with the commander of the British forces in the Middle East, General Wavell: "We are determined to resist the German attack, if it comes, with any means at our disposal and every sacrifice, but we do not want to provoke it in any way, unless the help that Britain would be prepared to offer in Macedonia were sufficient to this end."[14]

Metaxas' death did not lead to a change in the Greek position regarding a possible German attack. The arrival in Greece of a British expeditionary force was contrary to the initial decision not to accept anything less than sufficient British forces to repel a German attack, but it took place after Berlin's decision to move.[15] Even before the 8th of February, the new Greek Prime Minister Alexandros Koryzis had assured the British government that his country would resist a German attack by any means at its disposal.[16] This decision was confirmed in the next months, and in early April it was put into effect.

Was the Greek decision to resist the Axis invasion motivated only by a sense of national pride and the moral obligation to defend the country's honor? Were there other, more rational political considerations? Two pieces of evidence confirm the second hypothesis.

---

12. Minute by Metaxas, December 20, 1940. E.Δ.E., pp. 40-42.
13. Foreign Office 371/29855, Palairet to Foreign Office, December 31, 1940.
14. Minute by Metaxas, January 18, 1941. E.Δ.E., p. 62. However, British forces were just sufficient for the front in North Africa. The issue of massive British assistance had in fact been addressed in mid-November 1940, after the Greeks had pushed the Italians back to Albania. At that time, the Greek government had proposed to London to undertake joint operations in the Balkans, see E.Δ.E., Minute by Metaxas, November 17, 1940.
15. See, for example, E.Δ.E., pp. 55-59, Minute by Metaxas on a meeting with Palairet and Wavell, January 15, 1941.
16. Minute by Koryzis, February 8, 1941, E.Δ.E., p. 75.

First, on September 2, 1940, in a hand-written minute with reference to Minister Rangavis' report from Berlin, Metaxas explained the reasons that, in his view, had led Hitler to prevent an Italian attack against Greece at that time:

Mr. Rangavis errs if he thinks that Hitler's attitude (toward Greece) was dictated by sentimental philhellenism...Germany made its decision when it became convinced by Athens that Greece is determined to make war to the end, rather than succumb to the Italian demands...Greece was saved mainly by its determination to defend itself to the end and to sacrifice itself, rather than succumb.[17]

Unable to get an alliance which would strengthen the country's security, Metaxas had reached the conclusion that the resolution to defend national territory was the ultimate means to deter an invasion. Since powerful states relentlessly imposed their will on weak ones, if Greece were to show weakness, or signs of pulling back, it would encourage, rather than deter, aggression.

This attitude seems to have been combined in Metaxas' mind with other more specific considerations, which he outlined on October 29, 1940 during a secret meeting with the editors of the Athenian newspapers, and providing the second piece of evidence:

To avoid war, we should have volunteered to become slaves and pay for this "honor" by reaching out Greece's right arm, to be cut by Italy, and its left arm, to be cut by Bulgaria. Of course, it is not difficult to predict that the British themselves would then cut off Greece's legs. And the British would be right to do so. Rulers of the Seas, they would not omit, defending themselves after such self-enslavement of Greece to their enemies, to occupy at least Crete and our other islands...

According to the same view, disgrace and partition of the national territory would then inevitably bring a new rift and the collapse of Greece's home front.[18] With his experience of the 1917 National Rift and its disastrous results, Metaxas seemed to believe that even if the country were defeated in battle, it was important to preserve unity of the national territories during the war, even if occupied; after the end of the conflict, national sovereignty would be restored.

This perspective, in the long term, was probably linked with Metaxas' belief in an allied victory. Of course when Metaxas chose sides, the outcome of the war was not obvious. And in turn his choice illustrates how

17. See note 6.

18. *Ιωαννης Μεταξας: Το Προσωπικο του Ημερολογιο* (Ioannis Metaxas: His Personal Diary), volume d' (Athens: 1960), pp. 523-4.

deeply he believed that Greece's national interests would be served by a victory of the Western allies.

Having studied at the Berlin Military Academy, his views were determined, during the First World War, by the conviction that German arms would prevail. In the ensuing years, however, he had acquired additional experience. His ideas had gradually changed and he believed that Greece's geopolitical position was the most important factor which should determine its stand. He had thus come to the conclusion that the country's territorial integrity—which was paramount—was largely dependent on Britain's assistance. As he put it during a meeting of political leaders on February 28, 1934:

Greece is not a peninsula surrounded by sea, but a sea surrounded by land. Therefore, due to its geographical position, it cannot confront a naval Great Power. This is something that Greece cannot even afford to think of... Greece may adopt as a political doctrine that in no case can it find itself on a side opposite that which Britain has joined.[19]

Up to the beginning of the Greek-Italian war in 1940, Metaxas did not manage to acquire a treaty of alliance with Britain, which would have put teeth in the Anglo-French guarantee of Greece's territorial integrity; but the war had linked his country's interests even closer to British ones. Moreover, Metaxas was in full agreement with Greek public opinion when he looked forward to Greece's participation, together with the Western allies, in the peace conference after the final victory.

One must not exaggerate the importance of British influence in the shaping of Athens' position in the war. Greece was primarily concerned with the preservation of its territorial integrity, and this, for geopolitical reasons, was going to be achieved by taking the side of Britain. In view of this priority, Metaxas disregarded any common ideological ground between himself and Fascist Italy, and didn't take advantage of economically beneficial deals with Nazi Germany. He doggedly tried not to compromise the possibility of having a free political choice, obviously in favor of Britain.

To be sure, London could have exerted strong and decisive political and economic pressure on Greece in order to secure its influence in the country. Despite appearances, Metaxas' dictatorship was, in fact, vulnerable to external pressures, which could easily be combined with activity by the suppressed democratic opposition. Such pressures would have come mainly from London and could have proven fatal for the regime. It should not, however, be assumed that close relations with London were

19. Panayotis Pipinelis, *Ιστορια της Εξωτερικης Πολιτικης της Ελλαδος*, 1923-1941 (A History of Greek Foreign Policy, 1923-1941) (Athens: 1948), p.198.

basically due to the British potential to destabilize the Metaxas regime. When all is said and done, it is beyond any doubt that the Greek government, on its own initiative, decided to seek a common fate with that of Britain, and that this decision was dominated by the Greeks' understanding of how they could best serve what they perceived as their country's vital and permanent interests.

At this point one may ask if Greece's refusal to succumb to Axis pressure was due only to the attitude of a leading group in the country. What, in fact, was the role of public opinion in this decision-making? What were its long-term effects on internal politics? On this level, the course of events speaks for itself. In fact, the government's decisions were implemented effectively not due to any oppressive measures of the Metaxas regime, but because the government's policy corresponded to the expectations of the Greek people.

Metaxas himself, in his diary, referred to the disagreement of certain of his officials to a confrontation with Italy; after his death, even more of them were skeptical about the decision to resist the German attack to the bitter end. But they never had important influence on the government and were always outnumbered by those who favored resistance.

In a wider context, the acceptance of Metaxas' policy of "defense and sacrifice" was always strong. The demonstrations of public enthusiasm on the morning of October 28, 1940, when the Italian invasion and mobilization were announced, and the performance of the Greek army on the battlefields are evidence of the unanimity with which the Greeks greeted the war. Nationalists, conservatives, liberals who supported the struggle of the Western democracies against totalitarianism, citizens angry at the Fascist provocations, all moved to the same position. It is ironic that Metaxas, at the end of a lonely political career during which he was always deprived of wide popular support, now expressed the entire nation's determination to engage in a war to the end.

The decision to resist seemed to drastically alter the relationship between leadership and people, which had been formed under the dictatorship. Deeply rooted patterns and ideas, linked to the historical traditions of Hellenism, seemed to signal a new start for the country, through the trial of war. "*Νικη Λευτερια*" (Victory-Freedom) was not a mere propaganda slogan, but a frank expression of deeper aspirations and principles, guiding an effort which acquired the proportions of an epic. It could be said that the Greek people rediscovered the dynamic of their historical presence and consciously oriented themselves to a common future with the European peoples who aspired to freedom and peace. In those critical hours, it was proved that Greeks would not be puppets of the totalitarian powers. Consequently, any slogans or symbols of the regime that would remind the populace of some ideological connection with Fascism could no longer survive.

After eight months of war, and having already made a considerable contribution to its outcome, Greece fell to the combined attacks of the Axis powers, after having strongly resisted on the mainland and on Crete. At that moment, during the inter-allied conference held in London in early June, the Greek government of Prime Minister Emmanuel Tsouderos confirmed the nation's determination to continue the struggle against the enemy:

For our independence and freedom, we sacrificed everything. Our land has been conquered, but we will go on fighting to the end, with every means we have, together with our allies, until the prevalence of freedom, and the establishment of peace and free cooperation of the peoples, in a free Europe. ✦

Dead-End Diplomacy: Greece and the Balkan States in the Path of War

S. Victor Papacosma

Conditions in southeastern Europe at the close of World War I hardly augured well for the development of stability and cooperation. Too many unresolved issues and grievances among the region's peoples remained, and, despite the attention given to the Wilsonian precept of national self-determination at the Paris Peace Conference, its application to the ethnic hodgepodge in the Balkans could never be complete nor totally fair-in large part, because there were victorious and defeated states coming out of the war. The victorious would naturally be inclined to pursue maintenance of the new status quo and the defeated would seek revision of the newly determined borders and settlements.

For Greece, the fighting associated with World War I did not end in the fall of 1918. Prime Minister Eleftherios Venizelos had guided Greece into the war on the side of the victorious Entente in the summer of 1917, and now sought to reap rewards. With strong historical and ethnic claims to Smyrna and the area around it, Venizelos welcomed the opportunity to land troops there in May 1919. Sent to Smyrna to enforce the will of the victorious powers as final peace terms for the defunct Ottoman Empire were being drafted, the Greek army and accompanying Greek administrators arrived at the port anticipating the eventual annexation of Turkish territory. But dramatic changes in Greece's political leadership in late 1920 and shifts in the policies of the former Entente powers combined to produce a different conclusion: defeat and the flight of thousands of Greek and Armenian refugees in 1922. The Greco-Turkish War had precluded implementation of the Treaty of Sèvres (August 10, 1920), which was quite favorable to Greek interests, to be replaced by the Treaty of Lausanne (July 24, 1923), which reordered settlements and conditions in the eastern Mediterranean. Greece gave up much that it had recently gained, and Turkey retrieved some territory and rights lost in the Treaty of Sèvres.

S. VICTOR PAPACOSMA is Professor of History at Kent State University and Director of the Lemnitzer Center for NATO and European Community Studies.

With the demise of the *Megali Idea* and a plethora of domestic problems to contend with, Greek governments pursued restrained foreign policy initiatives during the remainder of the decade. Britain and France no longer manifested their previously strong concern in Greece and Turkey. The one great power displaying a heightened interest in the region was Italy, on the winning side during World War I but dismayed at its limited gains and, since October 1922, under the aggressive leadership of Europe's first fascist leader, Benito Mussolini. Opportunities would surface that would allow Italy to exert its influence in southeastern Europe.

As a newly created union of South Slavs, the Kingdom of Serbs, Croats, and Slovenes (the official name of Yugoslavia until 1929) from its first days experienced problems among its ethnic groups, particularly the Serbs and Croats, who disputed constitutional and other formulas for sharing authority. In its program to extend its influence on the eastern side of the Adriatic, Rome would exploit these differences by covertly aiding Croat extremists (Ustasa) against the Serb-dominated Yugoslav government. Albania, small, backward, and weak, soon fell under the sway of Italy, upon whom it depended for aid. Bulgaria, defeated in the Second Balkan War and on the losing side during World War I, never forsook its claims to Greece's Western Thrace and to Macedonian territory that had fallen under the control of Belgrade and Athens; here too Italy cultivated the revisionist aspirations of Bulgaria. Allied with the Entente and despite a dismal performance on the battlefield, Romania emerged from the war significantly enlarged by the acquisition of Hapsburg and Russian territories, but insecure because of neighbors with revisionist aspirations.

The singular instance of bold diplomacy came in the rapprochement between Greece and Turkey in 1930, when Eleftherios Venizelos and Mustafa Kemal shelved centuries of enmity and signed treaties of friendship and commerce. Otherwise, the presence of minorities in the respective Balkan states played an important and, in many instances, dominant role in regional diplomacy by hindering efforts at greater cooperation. Minority disputes linked with territorial claims had divided the Balkan states into hostile camps after the First Balkan War (1912-13), a division that persisted throughout the interwar period. Thus, even within the context of the Balkan Conferences (semi-official meetings from 1930 to 1933, organized by visionaries seeking regional rapprochement and exploring the possibilities of an eventual confederation of Balkan states), minority issues intruded to block advances even in nonpolitical areas. Bulgaria insisted that the Slav Macedonians in Yugoslavia and the Slavophones in northern Greece should be granted minority status as Bulgarians and receive benefits stipulated in League of Nations minority treaties. Albania spoke out in similar terms for its countrymen in Yugoslavia and Greece. The gap between those states supporting the maintenance of the regional status quo-Greece, Romania, Turkey, and Yugoslavia—and those pursuing its revision-Bulgaria and Hungary, in particular, but also Albania—would widen in the 1930s.

Quite early, apprehensions over the revisionist intentions of Hungary and Bulgaria had led to the formation of the Little Entente of Czechoslovakia, Yugoslavia, and Romania in 1920 and 1921. France supported these efforts in Europe's east to maintain the status quo and followed by signing separate treaties with like-minded states. Concerns over the need for collective security started heightening during the 1930s with the shocks of the depression, the League of Nations' evident weakness in the face of Japanese aggression, and the coming to power of Adolf Hitler. Sufficiently motivated, Bulgaria's neighbors determined to arrive at an agreement among themselves. Signed on February 4, 1934, the Balkan Pact pledged Greece, Romania, Turkey, and Yugoslavia to mutually guarantee the security of their existing frontiers. With the hope that Bulgaria and Albania would choose to join them in the future, the agreement was to be open to all Balkan countries, whose adherence would be "the object of favorable examination by the contracting parties."

From its inception, however, the Balkan Pact (which became the Balkan Entente in October 1934) proved not to be an impenetrable shield. Because none of the four signatories was willing to see the pact applied against a Great Power, it became little more than an expression of solidarity in favor of the maintenance of the regional status quo, which really meant that it was directed against Bulgaria. Thus, the Soviet Union's ambassador to Ankara hypothesized that in a conflict between Romania and the Soviet Union, Bulgaria might decide to join Moscow, thereby obligating Turkey to support Romania against the two foes. Such action would go against the Russo-Turkish Treaty of Neutrality (1925). To avert such a circumstance, Bucharest issued a written declaration that it would not expect Turkish support during a conflict with the Soviets. A related situation surfaced in Athens when the political opposition, led by Venizelos, protested that the Greek government should be assured that Greece would not be involved in a war with Italy as a result of obligations to protect Yugoslavia's frontiers. The other three signatories pledged that under no conditions would the requirements of the pact involve Greece in a war with a Great Power. The Balkan Entente, therefore, had value only should one of the states be attacked by Bulgaria, and there was little likelihood that Sofia would adopt an offensive policy without Great-Power backing.

In developing a foreign policy that sought to normalize relations as much as possible with Greece's neighbors, Venizelos had signed in September 1928 a treaty of friendship and arbitration with Mussolini's Italy, the one Great Power with evident ambitions in the Eastern Mediterranean. Greece's relations with Turkey became closer during the 1930s, as both states increasingly shared regional security concerns. Athens supported Ankara in its program to revise policy governing the Straits in return for Greece's right to remilitarize Lemnos and Samothrace, and in the aftermath of the signing of the Montreux Convention in June 1936, Turkey's foreign minister stated to the Greek ambassador that Greece's attitude "was not that of a simple allied country but indeed of a brother-state."[1]

The frailty of Balkan security arrangements, apparent by the mid-1930s, differed little from the shaky patterns evident in the relations among the Great Powers. Britain and France, adherents of maintaining the status quo, did little with their fault-ridden appeasement policy to thwart the revisionist proclivities of Hitler and Mussolini. Nor did London and Paris actively seek to bolster their presence and policy in southeastern Europe or to cultivate trade relations during this economically depressed period. Balkan agricultural resources formed a natural complement to the expanding German industrial plant. Deprived of other markets by the world economic crisis, the Balkan states had few options but to be drawn into the German trade orbit.

Italy, on its part, continued to cultivate its relations with disaffected Bulgaria and Hungary and with extremist parties in Yugoslavia, concurrently increasing its influence in Albania. Left on its own, Greece, sharing an insecurity with its regional allies, sought to avert conflict not through multilateral solidarity but with cautious diplomacy. These states essentially wished to avoid commitments toward other nations that would involve war beyond their borders. Ultimately, the Little and Balkan Ententes never withstood the challenges that they were devised to combat, in part because they had no substantive support from Britain and France. Developments in 1938 associated with the *Anschluss* of Austria and the Munich crisis intensified these patterns.

Prime Minister Ioannis Metaxas, despite his authoritarian regime and earlier associations with Germany, sought through quiet diplomacy to solicit backing from Britain for Greece. Historian John Koliopoulos has concluded that "the British underestimated the real as well as the potential value of Greece, while the Greeks overestimated Britain's ability and

1. Quoted in Domna Dontas, *The Regime of the Straits, Lemnos, and Samothrace* (Athens: G. C. Eleftheroudakis S.A., 1987), p. 144.

willingness to come to their assistance."[2] Additionally, the British believed that an alliance with Athens would offend both Italy and Germany, a price London was not yet ready to pay.

Seeking to emulate the expansionist gains of Hitler after his partitioning of rump Czechoslovakia in March 1939, Mussolini sent his forces into Albania on Good Friday, April 7, and incorporated it into Italy. The response from London and Paris came in the form of unilateral guarantees of the independence of Greece and Romania that amounted to little more than a promise of support in the event that these two states became victims of aggression.

When war did break out in early September, with Germany's invasion of Poland on the heels of the signing of the Nazi-Soviet Treaty of Non-Aggression, Greece, like the other Balkan states, remained neutral. The four Balkan Entente states had been unable during peace to establish a firm common policy on mutual defense, and it was hardly likely that in the more perilous time of war they would be able to reverse this pattern. Largely because it was not then in the immediate interests of the belligerents to extend hostilities to the Balkans, the war was still relatively distant from the region. Meeting in Belgrade in early February 1940, the Balkan Entente leaders, rather expectedly, could not agree on effective mutual aid in case of attack coming from outside the region and instead sanctioned that it remained the prerogative of the member-states to deal individually with the Great Powers in the quest to maintain their neutrality. Although Greece was declaring its neutrality, largely because of its military unpreparedness, Italy nonetheless perched menacingly on Greece's northwestern border and posed the major threat to it (as it had for some time). During these months Greece's neutrality tilted benevolently toward Britain, while Athens concurrently tried not to respond to Italian provocations.

Conditions in southeastern Europe shifted markedly after Germany's 1940 springtime offensive and conquests in Western Europe that left Britain alone to confront the Axis. Italy exploited the situation to enter the war formally, and hardly courageously, by moving into southern France on June 10. On that occasion, Mussolini announced: "I declare categorically that Italy has not the slightest desire to draw into the conflict any

2. John Koliopoulos, "Metaxas and Greek Foreign Relations," in *The Metaxas Dictatorship: Aspects of Greece 1936-1940*, ed. Robin Higham and Thanos Veremis (Athens: Hellenic Foundation for European and Foreign Policy and Vryonis Center for the Study of Hellenism, 1993), p. 95.

other nation....Let Switzerland, Yugoslavia, Greece, Turkey and Egypt mark my words."[3]

Such, of course, would not be the case, as other belligerents too now looked in the direction of the Balkans. Thus, the Soviet Union sought to bolster its position in the Balkans in the immediate aftermath of German victories in the West. A late June ultimatum to the Romanian government forced it to cede Bessarabia and northern Bukovina to Moscow. The Axis then mediated disputes between Romania and its revisionist neighbors, Bulgaria and Hungary, that resulted in further dismemberment, with the partitioning of Transylvania with Hungary in the so-called Vienna Award on August 30 and the cession of southern Dobrudja to Bulgaria on September 7. Bucharest had received no diplomatic support from Balkan Entente states and drifted into the Axis camp in order to protect its remaining territory.

It was now Italy's turn to move-against a Greece that appeared weak and without the prospect of substantive support from any quarter. The Greeks responded to the Italian invasion of October 28 in heroic style and, in time, with limited help from Britain.

The two remaining Balkan Entente allies stood by and watched developments from a distance. Belgrade, unwilling to venture with open support for Greece, nevertheless turned down German offers of Greek territory. Turkey stood aloof, despite agreements with Greece and a treaty of mutual assistance with Britain and France signed on October 19, 1939. Indeed, Turkey maintained neutrality until the last weeks of the war, exasperating the opposing sides separately with the same tactics of elusiveness. Ankara dickered with the British and the Germans in an attempt to receive territorial awards for involvement. It volunteered to occupy eastern Aegean islands and the Dodecanese islands and showed interest in acquiring control of Thessalonike. At various junctures Turkey also asked for compensation in Bulgarian Thrace, Albania, Cyprus, Iraq, and Syria.[4] Although nothing came of these diplomatic forays, specifically, in the case of Greece, they did indicate an evident willingness on the part of Turkey to seek gains at the expense of a professed ally during its period of extreme hardship and vulnerability.

3. Quoted in L. S. Stavrianos, *The Balkans since 1453* (New York: Holt, Rinehart and Winston, 1958), p. 750.
4. Frank Weber, *The Evasive Neutral: Germany, Britain and the Quest for a Turkish Alliance in the Second World War* (Columbia, MO: University of Missouri Press, 1979), pp. 59-60, 81-82.

With Hitler's earlier decision to invade the Soviet Union, Axis control of the Balkans became paramount. Germany had bullied Romania to join it and succeeded during the winter of 1941 in adding Bulgaria, which, in any case, had been nurturing longstanding claims to Greek Macedonia and WesternThrace. The Yugoslav government yielded to German pressures and signed the Tripartite Pact on March 25, but on their return to Belgrade from Vienna, the prime minister and foreign minister confronted a military coup against them. Despite protestations of neutrality by the new government, Hitler decided to deal once and for all with Yugoslavia and Greece. Yugoslavia succumbed quickly after the Axis invasion began on April 6, while Greece, with the help of British forces, resisted against overwhelming odds for nearly two months.

The insecure strategic environment of the Balkan Peninsula once again had witnessed war, and its inhabitants once again found themselves caught up in the struggles of stronger forces. But as this analysis has attempted to emphasize, local disputes during the interwar period ultimately allowed stronger powers to exploit and manipulate regional conditions and animosities to their advantage. Various diplomatic initiatives on the part of Greece all ran into obstacles, a veritable dead-end, in securing its national interests against the aggressive designs of rival states.

The remarkable story of Greece at the time of the Italian invasion is that, despite the crushing victories of the Axis juggernaut in Western Europe, it stood its ground with no prospect of victory in the longer run. The Greeks reacted thus because they believed, unlike the response of many other Europeans during the spring of 1940, that a short-run success had much to offer them and those fighting the sinister forces of fascist aggression. Metaxas summed up such sentiments when he stated:

Greece is not fighting for victory. She is fighting for glory, and for honor. She has a debt to herself to remain worthy of her history...There are times in which a nation, if it wishes to remain great, gains by being able to fight, even if it has no hopes of victory.[5]

When Britain stood alone, it was Greece that provided a first victory against the Axis. ✦

5. Quoted in Bobby John Macris, "The Foreign Policy of the Metaxas Regime, 1936-1941" (Ph.D. diss., Indiana University, 1979), p. 343.

The Greek-Italian War: The View from the U.S. Embassy in Athens

John O. Iatrides

In the summer of 1938, as the storm clouds of the approaching war gathered over much of Europe, tension and uncertainty quickly spread to the Balkans. Fascist Italy's brutal occupation of Ethiopia, followed by the seizure of Albania, were widely regarded as the first steps in an aggressive march into the Eastern Mediterranean. Greece appeared to be next on Mussolini's list of conquests. Accordingly, for foreign observers on the scene, the intentions of the Greek government were a matter of intense debate. Traditionally strong ties to England, the reputation of King George II as an Anglophile, and its vulnerability to superior naval power seemed to dictate that the place of Greece was on the side of the Anglo-French coalition. On the other hand, the dictator, General John Metaxas, was an avowed admirer of Fascism and of Hitler's Germany and had modeled his regime after Mussolini's. German economic interests were strong in Athens, where many prominent personalities in and out of government were openly pro-German. Moreover, Greece was too small and weak to stand up to the Axis. Accordingly, many foreign commentators believed that in the end Greece would try to stay out of harm's way by remaining neutral.

In the 1930s the United States maintained a very small diplomatic presence in Athens. American interests in Eastern Europe, including the Balkans, had traditionally been limited to modest trade activity, which in the aftermath of the Great Depression had declined precipitously. The administration of President Franklin D. Roosevelt appeared unwilling to involve itself in any attempt to oppose Mussolini's aggressive designs.

But if the United States remained detached from the drama unfolding in the Balkans, its embassy in Athens became a remarkable listening post for political, diplomatic, economic and military developments across the region and beyond. This was due to the steady stream of reports reaching Washington and written by Lincoln MacVeagh, the political appointee who had arrived in Athens in 1933 as Roosevelt's minister to Greece. A linguist,

---

JOHN O. IATRIDES, Ph.D., is Professor of International Politics at Southern Connecticut State University.

student of the classics, history, and literature and a former publisher, MacVeagh was also a friend of the Roosevelt family and of prominent Democrats in his home state of Connecticut. In Athens he had developed excellent contacts with the country's political leaders, including Metaxas and King George, as well as with the local representatives of the major European powers. He was without doubt one of the most knowledgeable, perceptive, and literate diplomatic observers in Greece and the Balkans. His frequent dispatches, his "Dear Franklin" letters to the president, and the daily entries of his private diary have preserved for the student of those turbulent years a remarkably detailed, lively, and informed chronicle of historic events.[1]

Only days before the start of the Second World War MacVeagh had a long conversation with Metaxas and reported to Roosevelt (letter of August 21, 1939) the dictator's words: "We are with the Western Powers, because it is to our own interests, and because of our allies [the Turks]....Greece will defend her independence to the last man." Yet despite Metaxas' categorical statements MacVeagh remained skeptical that Greece would stand up to the Axis, and his skepticism grew stronger after the Nazis' rapid advances against the French in 1940. He wrote to Roosevelt on May 24, 1940:

People in government still maintain that Greece will resist if attacked...but one senses more than a little bravado in what they say, while the man in the street is at least more honest. You can hear it said in the cafes that all Greece's expenditure for defense, which is enormous for so small and poor a country, has been just so much money thrown away.... Greece may yet play the part of Leonidas, but at present I am betting on Ulysses. More than once in the last few days I have caught Greek thoughts turning to the possibility of remaining non-belligerent in case Italy goes to war with England and France and even Turkey....Recent events have made the Greeks acutely aware of their own helplessness and exposure.

On August 13, 1940 MacVeagh recorded in his diary:

The Italians have started a violent press and radio campaign against Greece, alleging complicity in the murder of an Albanian so-called patriot, and also maltreatment of the Albanian minority in Epirus. All without any grounds whatever....I got Passakay, the Turkish Military Attache, to come. He was pessimistic and predicted that the war would soon come to the

---

All passages quoted in this article are taken from John O. Iatrides, ed., *Ambassador MacVeagh Reports: Greece, 1933-1947* (Princeton: Princeton University Press, 1980).

Balkans....He thought the Germans are giving the Italians a free hand here. Also that the Turks would go no further than to keep Bulgaria from profiting from the occasion, and that Yugoslavia would not help Greece either. Thus he saw Greece practically facing Italy alone at this time.

And two days later:

The axe may have fallen on little Greece today, or at least the Axis seems to have done so!....[T]he Greek cruiser Helli...was sunk this morning at Tinos by an unidentified submarine....No Greek seems to doubt that the Italians are responsible.

Diary, August 20, 1940:

Called on Mr. Metaxas in the forenoon. Found him looking fairly well. He said at once, when I asked him about the "situation," that Greece isn't putting her faith in any more assurances; that tension has lessened but the Greek Government is remaining vigilant, and if attacked will fight "to the last man, the last woman, the last child." When I asked him whether he might not be invited soon to Vienna to settle the Albanian problem, he said such a conference would have to consider all minority claims involving this country, and asked me in return if I thought the Italians would care to discuss the Greek minority in Albania or the Dodecanese. His attitude appeared to me to be pessimistic and intransigent at the same time.

Diary, October 28, 1940:

I was waked up at 4:15 this morning by a call from [Athens correspondent of the New York Times] Shan Sedgwick who said that at 3 o'clock the Italian Minister handed Mr. Metaxas an ultimatum, expiring at 6 a.m., demanding the right to occupy strategic points in this country because of Greece's unneutral attitude in favoring Great Britain and fomenting troubles in Albania....When Metaxas asked Grazzi what points Italy demanded the rights to occupy, the latter replied he did not know. Unless Greece yielded, the Italian troops were under orders to advance at 6 a.m.... I have learned later from other sources close to the Premier that Mr. Metaxas said also "It is now 3:30 and this ultimatum gives me till 6. Why, Mr. Minister, I couldn't turn over my house to you in that time, much less my country." Bravo!.... Actually the Italians began firing on the Albanian front at 5:30. Evidently, from the manner of the ultimatum, the Italians wanted to give no chance to the British to bolster Greek courage, and counted on the Greeks caving in if they had to make a decision of their own at once. But again their psychology was at fault. At 6 a.m. the Greek Government declared general mobilization and later martial law was proclaimed throughout the country.... It became evident during the day that more men were reporting than there was equipment or transportation for, and there were jams about all the barracks and army parks....

Diary, October 31, 1940:

Greek morale is still high, but if England delays to put in an appearance, at least much longer, it may begin to sink. Also if the BBC gets in many more of its bloomers! This morning [Britain's Air Chief Marshal] Joubert said over the broadcast that Greece is very far away, but the Greeks are a brave people and though they can't win, will go down fighting!....But what does London know or care about the psychology of the Greeks?

If MacVeagh was critical of Britain's apparently passive response to Italy's attack on Greece, he was no more pleased with the attitude of his own government.

Diary, October 31, 1940:

I cannot imagine why there has as yet been no pronouncement from the USA regarding the aggression against this country which is surely one of the most arrant monstrosities of even this war. Yesterday the Department cabled "You are instructed to inquire of the Greek Government whether it considers itself in a state of war," and I got an immediate reply from Mr. Mavroudis [of the Foreign Ministry] that Greece considers itself at war since 5:30 a.m. on October 28, at which time she was subjected to an unwarranted attack by Italy....Let us pray "for all good souls lost in the dark" of red tape! If I had been the President, and Greece had been invaded as she has, I would have gathered my cultural tags and rapped out a manifesto to shake the world.

MacVeagh followed the progress of the war day by day, hour by hour, and his messages to Washington convey the highs and the lows of the unfolding drama. Exactly one month after the Italian attack (on November 28, 1940) he wrote to Roosevelt:

The army has done excellently and appears to have established a moral superiority over the enemy, but its equipment is inferior and it particularly needs pursuit planes and antiaircraft ammunition. The British were cautious about coming here at first, but are now giving some valuable assistance to the Greeks in the air and exploiting the opportunity afforded to them themselves to bring the war home to the Italians....[According to the British officer coordinating British-Greek military cooperation] it is impossible to overemphasize the importance of the Greek success [in Albania] since "after all it is the first and only success of the Allied armies on land." ....Local political affairs have taken an amazing turn. When Italy began menacing this country, politicians of all shades of opinion rallied behind the government, instituting a kind of "era of good feeling" for the duration of the emergency. But when General Metaxas accepted the Italian challenge so simply and fearlessly in the dark hours before the dawn on October 28, he spoke words which have positively endeared him to the Greek people. He now represents the whole country as perhaps no one has ever done at any time in its history ancient or modern. The "era of good feeling" has become a "union sacrée." As I have cautioned the Department, this condition may not survive a long and hard struggle calling for solider qualities than enthusiasm, but it represents an unexpectedly good start and should help tremendously no matter what the future holds.

Diary, December 6, 1940:

The Greek advance threatened now north of Premeti toward Klissoura and Tepeleni makes the Italian position at Argyrocastro precarious and if pushed still further may spell the doom of Valona. But how long can the Greeks keep up the pressure, and will their ammunition hold out?

Diary, December 7, 1940:

I had a talk with Mr. Metaxas, at his request. He asked that I forward pleas to Washington, and to the President personally, for credits for war purchases and for airplanes. In regard to the first of these matters he said that Greece must go on driving the Italians hard in order, if possible, to get them out of Albania this winter. "Let us not fool ourselves," he said, "the Germans will attack in the spring, undoubtedly. If we can get through with Italy in Albania by that time, we can reform to protect ourselves, and Yugoslavia, Turkey, and perhaps even Bulgaria will be encouraged to resist the German pressure. If not, the whole Balkans are likely to collapse. Thus the present war may be a turning point, and it may even be the turning point in the whole war. But our supplies of munitions are not sufficient to last us over an unremitting offensive lasting many months. Nor can the British supply us with enough. We must apply to America, where the material can be bought. But our dollars are low. I believe it is in America's interest as well as our own that supplies should be sent here to help us be victorious."

[Due to a variety of problems nothing came of Greek requests for American airplanes and military supplies.]

Writing to President Roosevelt on Christmas Day 1940, MacVeagh took stock of the situation once again and concluded:

The Greeks, after advancing for the better part of two months over territory which an American observer with the Royal Air Force described to me as resembling the worst parts of the Rocky Mountains, are now facing reinforced Italian resistance on the last and best strategic line covering Valona and the coastal plain....Of course I have been as much surprised as anyone by the Greek successes. Explaining miracles is perhaps a thankless business, but it is human to try one's hand at it....Something has released an energy in these people of which none of us had any suspicion. Patriotism may be part of this something, as well as hatred of the Italians, and resentment over their insults and threats. But more important than these, I believe, has been the consciousness of unity which the nation suddenly achieved in the dark dawn of October 28th. The history of ancient Greece is at least 50 percent discord, and there was plenty of it in the Greek Revolution, while the whole life of the Modern Greek State has been factious almost beyond belief. But from the moment Mr. Metaxas rejected the Italian ultimatum, there has been only one party, one class, one purpose in the whole of this small land. Such unity is in itself a force, but the realization of it by a people which has never known anything like it has created a kind of national intoxication to which the traversing if not the removal of mountains is a thing to be taken in one's stride.

As MacVeagh had predicted, the euphoria and sense of national unity could not last indefinitely.

Diary, January 9, 1941:

The first flush of enthusiasm having worn off, the Greeks are back at their game of criticism and politics, and German propaganda is busy spreading the evil, so as to undermine morale. There is dissatisfaction over the amount of assistance rendered by the British, and over the superior feeding, lodging, and clothing of the British troops; over Metaxas's failure to form a coalition government and taking all the kudos of Greece's resistance for himself and his regime; over the turning over of so much relief work to the fascist and incompetent Neolaia; over the dismissal of Generals at the front, etc., etc., The "era of good feeling" is a thing of the past—though doubtless all this doesn't spell disaster yet awhile. Morale will continue good as long as the Greek troops can go on advancing—and they are still doing a little of this. But the regime has failed to endear itself to the people, though it had a grand chance to do so after winning admiration and respect in the first days of the war. Now we can expect, even if Greece wins, to revert to the old internal struggle; and if there are reverses, the position of the Government, and the dynasty too, may become very difficult.

And in a letter to Roosevelt on January 19, 1941:

Neither bad weather nor difficult terrain, nor enemy reinforcements, nor inferiority of equipment, nor deficiency in transport, nor lack of airplanes has yet halted the Greek advance. But those things have, taken all together, slowed the advance down, and it now seems definitely out of the question that the Italians can be ousted this winter. All the more reason for the Greeks to dread the future, with their flank and rear exposed to possible German onslaught!

Diary, January 29, 1941:

Poor Mr. Metaxas died at 7:00 a.m. His illness had too many complications for his fighting spirit....[T]he last three days were hopeless, but the old man fought on, and everyone hoped for a miracle....The King acted quickly to keep the government going, and by nine o'clock Mr. Koryzis had taken the oath as Premier.

MacVeagh wrote to the President on February 23, 1941:

[Greece] is certain to find herself handicapped by the recent death of General Metaxas, her one available "strong man." His passing has, as it were, decapitated the state. The King is now the dictator, or rather, all the dictator that there is....The King's policy is now to carry on from where Gen. Metaxas left off....The latter had planned to resist any German aggression exactly as he resisted the Italian, in the belief that honor requires it and that, in any case, England is bound to win the war with America's help....Greece is still in her heroic mood. But the King's character is hardly the kind to keep a volatile people united in a long struggle against odds....I am afraid Greece is in for some bad days whatever happens....

A month later, on Greece's Independence Day (March 25, 1941):

Dear Franklin: Yugoslavia has joined the Axis today....Turkey's attitude...has become increasingly offish and timid as regards helping Greece and Great Britain, and Yugoslavia's action is likely to make it more so.... It is expected here that German demands will be made on Greece very soon, probably in the form of an ultimatum....Indications...confirm what the King told me some time ago, namely, that it is the intention of the British and Greeks to make their principal resistance in the Olympus region.

Diary, April 6, 1941:

The balloon has gone up!....[The German Minister to Greece] phoned the Premier at about 5 and was received at a quarter to six. He read Mr. Koryzis a statement declaring that Germany considers Greece to have been unneutral ever since the war began, but especially since she allowed the debarkation here of large numbers of British troops. Consequently Germany must put aside the Greek forces on the border and enter Greece to strike at the British, though this does not mean that she is inimical to Greece or to the Greek nation....

Diary, April 9, 1941:

I talked with [British Minister to Greece] Sir Michael [Palairet] and learned the amazing fact that the British forces here consist of no more than 1½ [one and one-half] divisions, plus a mechanized brigade and some anti-aircraft units. Of course there is also a lot of transport, and hospitals and labor troops etc. But all this hardly makes an "Imperial Army" such as the British radio has been speaking of!....I have pooh-poohed the idea that [Generals] Wavell and Wilson would let themselves in for another Dunkirk; but if they haven't done just that, they will be running things pretty close....

Diary, April 10, 1941:

The Germans have taken Monastir and made contact...with the Italians in the region north of the lakes....The Greeks must now try to draw back their right flank in Albania and establish a line with the British. This may involve giving up Koritza and Florina, and running the line from near Moschopolis to Edessa, using high ground, and leading thence along the Vermion range to Verria and Katerini....However, the Germans have crossed the Vardar in a swift move from Salonica and are reported already in Verria!....The Greeks have just shown themselves great fighters...far surpassing on the Metaxas line [against the Germans] what they have already done against the Italians. Perhaps they, in the plenitude of their amazing spirit, are the finest fighters of all. But again, how few!...The hordes of the mechanized barbarians are too numerous for the few free peoples brave enough to fight for their freedom. The men in the Metaxas forts all knew they must die—like the Spartans of Leonidas—and they were all volunteers....

Diary, April 14, 1941:

I wrote to the President some time ago of the likelihood of a "succession of Thermopylaes" here, and it looks as if I was right. A Salamis, and even more, a Plataea, can hardly be hoped for.

Diary, April 24, 1941:

Greece has been having a pretty hard time of it these past weeks: in fact we have been assisting at the death pangs of a wonderfully brave little nation, and we Americans have been in the midst of it all, and shall be sufferers from the consequences, but at no time has the Department of State indicated by so much as a word that it even knows what is going on (it daily sends us messages to relay to Salonica!) let alone that it is interested. I would never have thought it possible to work faithfully for anyone for eight years and then be so thoroughly ignored with all my people in trouble as I have been by Uncle Sam.

Diary, April 27, 1941:

"Athens was captured by the Germans....I saw the swastika flag hoisted on the Acropolis, and a rocket fired...."

MacVeagh left Athens on the 5th of June 1941 and returned to the United States for reassignment. His final analysis of the Greek situation contained the following observation:

...the flight of King George and his crew has marked the end of a strange and remarkably interesting period in Greek history, during which a temperamentally constitutional monarch tried to govern the world's prime democracy through the medium of a dictator, and saw that dictator die in a blaze of glory whilst he himself lived on to reap the reward of dislike and failure. Whether what the future holds for immortal Greece includes another try for King George II it would be foolish to attempt to predict, but those who are interested in that country of restless political change might do well to keep in mind a growing itch to try a Republic on the American model. ✦

The Military Struggle

Greek Wartime Actions: From the Albanian War to the Battle of Crete and The National Resistance

André Gerolymatos

The Albanian War

On October 28, 1940 Benito Mussolini issued an ultimatum to the Greek government, demanding concessions that would have brought Greece under Italian occupation. The government of General Ioannis Metaxas, without hesitation, simply said "No." For Greece this one-syllable statement meant a leap into the unknown, for ever since September 1939 the Axis powers had enjoyed victory after victory until they had conquered most of Europe. Only Great Britain stood as the sole obstacle in the way of an ultimate Axis victory.

Metaxas' decision to defy Mussolini, which was fully supported by the Greek people, came at the worse possible time in the history of Greece. The country had suffered a traumatic defeat in Asia Minor in 1922, followed by a series of coups and counter-coups, and was just barely emerging from the ravages of the Great Depression. Yet despite these serious handicaps and the military superiority of Fascist Italy, the decision to fight placed Greece on the side of Great Britain and what appeared to be the losing side in the Second World War. Metaxas was under no illusions that his country was ready for a major war, and he knew that at best the British could provide only token support. He had little choice, however. Acceptance of the Italian demands would have placed Greece within Italy's sphere of influence and under military occupation.

When Mussolini decided to add Greece to his empire the Italians had, as a consequence of their occupation of Albania in 1939, direct lines of communication to the Balkan peninsula. Initially Mussolini had chosen to annex Yugoslavia into his new Roman Empire, but Hitler had emphatically

---

ANDRÉ GEROLYMATOS is Associate Professor, Department of History, Simon Fraser University, (SFU) at Vancouver, B.C.

vetoed that plan. In the summer of 1940 Hitler was planning the invasion and conquest of the Soviet Union, and it was essential that his right flank in the Balkans remain undisturbed. In addition, the German war economy depended on uninterrupted supplies of Balkan oil, chrome, manganese, copper, aluminum, lead, nickel, and tin. Indeed, the Germans had established their economic hegemony over the region and Romania, Bulgaria, and Yugoslavia had joined the Axis tripartite pact. With the exception of Greece, Hitler's Germany had succeeded, through economic ties and the threat of invasion, in securing the Balkans and the raw materials necessary to sustain Germany's war industry.

Mussolini could not and would not accept the unending string of victories secured by Hitler, who had been the Italian dictator's junior Fascist partner in 1933. The junior had now eclipsed the senior dictator. For Mussolini, Greece represented an easy and cheap victory and one that would reestablish Fascist Italy as a major player in the division of the new world order after the war. Most significantly, Mussolini decided that the attack on Greece should be executed without Hitler's knowledge, in effect to pay him back for all the times that Mussolini had had to learn from the newspapers of Germany's latest invasion. Hence Mussolini's often quoted comment to his son-in-law, Count Galeazzo Ciano: "Hitler always confronts me with a *fait accompli.* This time I am going to pay him back in his own coin."

In his desire to demonstrate to Hitler and the world that he could achieve success on his own, Mussolini had underestimated the Greeks and overestimated his own forces. In Albania the Fascist dictator had assembled nine divisions, almost 100,000 troops, although his own generals had advised an army of at least twice that size. Mussolini compounded his blunder by committing Italy to the Greek front despite the fact that his armies were already barely holding their own against the British in the Middle East and North Africa. To make matters worse, Mussolini gave his generals two weeks to complete the conquest of Greece, and picked the 28th of October, 1940 for the invasion in order to celebrate his successful march on Rome on that date in 1922.

The Italian invasion of Greece unfolded in a three-prong attack against Epirus and the Pindus Mountains of northwestern Greece. The northern Italian army was to capture the town of Florina and then move on to Thessalonike, Greece's largest port on the northern Aegean Sea. The southern advance was to move along the coast of the Adriatic, while the center army, consisting of two columns, was to attack in the direction of the Pindus Mountains toward Metsovo, and capture the vital pass that controlled the main road leading to the southwest and east. From Metsovo the Italians, enjoying overwhelming air power and superior armor, would easily break into central Greece.

But the Greek army was not as ill prepared as the Italians believed. Metaxas was certainly aware of the military build-up on Greece's western frontier and had quietly begun mobilizing the Greek army. A few months before the Italian invasion, the Greek General Staff had secretly called up three reserve divisions and part of a fourth. Even the Greek public was not aware of the size or the nature of the mobilization. By October the Greeks had more than two divisions on the Albanian front. Another vital factor that worked in favor of the Greeks rather than the better-equipped Italians was that the Greek forces enjoyed the advantage of shorter lines of communications and supply; they also had the psychological advantage of defending their country.

As the three-pronged Italian attack advanced into Greek territory, the Greek forces avoided frontal assaults and used the narrow mountain passes and jagged uplands to their advantage. Very quickly the Italian armor bogged down on the narrow and winding mountain roads, while the Italian air force was rendered ineffective by low cloud cover over the Pindus mountain range. As the Italians faced insurmountable logistical problems, the Greeks concentrated their strength on the higher slopes. About fifteen miles from the vital pass at Metsovo, the middle prong of the Italian advance quickly ran into difficulties. Although spearheaded by the elite 3rd Julia Alpine Division, a unit of 10,800 men, the resistance confronting the Italian forces grew progressively stronger, forcing the Julia Division to slow down and then stop. On November 3 the Italian unit found itself under attack by the Greek army on three flanks. The Julia Division began to fall back.

In the meantime the Greek forces, using the high-ridge lines to their advantage, continued to harass the Julia as it retreated slowly along the valleys below. The Greek units, supplied by local peasants and equipped with light guns, would from time to time descend on the Julia Division in coordinated assaults, taking elements of the division by surprise and forcing them to surrender. Within a few days the Julia Division broke and ran. In the process it lost one fifth of its strength and most of its equipment. By November 13, 1940 the Greek forces had regained all the territory lost to the Italians and on the 14th the Greek army went on the offensive and invaded Albania all along the northwestern front. The Italians fell back and within a short time were retreating so rapidly that cargo planes sent in to supply them fell into Greek hands. On November 22 the

Greek army captured Koritsa, an Italian base twenty miles inside Albania, and by the end of the year Greek forces had occupied more than one quarter of Albania, including the port of Saranda on the Adriatic coast.

The German Invasion

The Greek victories were a spectacular embarrassment for Mussolini and the Axis as a whole. Despite the failures and great casualties, Mussolini persisted in his determination to conquer Greece. By March 1941 the Italian forces were increased to twenty-eight divisions; under Mussolini's personal oversight they launched an offensive along a twenty-mile front, only to face another failure. The political and strategic repercussions represented a major setback for the Axis. For the British and the rest of the free world the Greek army had demonstrated, for the first time in the war and despite overwhelming odds and the technical superiority of Hitler's ally, that at least one of the Axis powers could be defeated.

The strategic and political consequences of the Greek victory were not lost on Hitler. The German dictator was livid over Mussolini's blunder, but he could not afford to let his only ally go down in defeat. Equally relevant, the Greek success exposed the German army's southeastern flank in the Balkans just as Germany was preparing to attack the Soviet Union. Although Metaxas had made every effort to assure the Nazis that Greece wished to avoid a conflict with Germany, Hitler assumed it was only a matter of time before the British would send reinforcements to Greece and use Greek airfields to bomb the vital oil fields in Romania. As early as the middle of November Hitler ordered plans for the invasion of northern Greece; after the coup in Yugoslavia in March 1941, he decided to occupy all of the Balkan peninsula.

On April 6 the German army invaded Yugoslavia and Greece and within twelve days the Yugoslavs capitulated. The collapse of the Yugoslav forces exposed Greece's northwestern flank, which the Germans exploited, along with their advance from Bulgaria. The Germans quickly isolated the Greek army in Macedonia and the Greek forces in Albania. The 50,000 British troops sent by Winston Churchill to support the Greeks found themselves outflanked; they began a series of withdrawals, but each time failed to establish a solid line of defense and kept falling back until most of these forces had to be evacuated by the Royal Navy.

The Greek army fought under the most trying circumstances and with woefully inferior numbers. In the east, one hundred and fifty volunteers defended the Metaxas Line, which was intended to protect Macedonia and Thrace from invasion. A few days before the German invasion, they sent their belongings home and took their last communion. On the 6th of April the vanguard of the German Panzers, supported by hundreds of sorties from the air force, pounded the Greek fortifications for two days. The volunteers fought back and held their ground to the last man.

When the advance formations of the German army broke through and occupied the ruins of the fortifications they found nothing but corpses. In a rare display of chivalry the Panzer commander ordered a military burial for the Greeks and as the gunfire from the honor guard rang out, it signaled the beginning of the dark days of occupation. Nevertheless, the sacrifices of the Greek army were not in vain: Hitler's attack on Greece and the willingness of the Greeks to fight laid the groundwork for Germany's defeat in the Soviet Union.

The Greek Campaign and the German Defeat in the U.S.S.R.

It is becoming increasingly evident that the battles of Greece and Crete were fundamentally a prelude to Operation Barbarossa, the German invasion of the Soviet Union. In this context Hitler's Balkan campaign was not only a diversion; strategically, the attack against Greece is inextricably linked to Germany's defeat on the Eastern front in the winter of 1941. For the last fifty years historians and even some of the participants have debated whether and how the German invasion of Greece affected the conduct of the German offensive in Russia.

In considering the impact of the German invasion of Greece upon Operation Barbarossa, military historians have essentially adopted two positions. One is that Operation Marita (the German attack on Yugoslavia and Greece) caused some delay but not enough to change the course of events on the Eastern front. The second position is that there was a four- to six-week postponement that made a critical difference to the outcome of the battle for Moscow and, in turn, was a direct contributor to Germany's defeat.

These interpretations are based almost exclusively upon German primary sources and accounts, and although they are informative and analytical they do not offer an unequivocal answer as to which position is the correct one. The most competent professional voices, the German military themselves, are also divided into two camps on this issue, with several intermediary positions. In his survey of Hitler's generals, B.H. Liddell-Hart[1] quotes from both schools. Thus Field Marshalls von Kleist and von Rundstedt accepted the delay version as correct. In their account, although the German troops used in the Balkans were only a small fraction

1. B.H. Liddell-Hart, *The German Generals Talk,* (New York: W. Morrow 1948).

of the invasion force foreseen for Operation Barbarossa, their technical specialization, particularly the armored units, was essential to Barbarossa's success. The time taken for their withdrawal from their advanced position in the Peloponnese to the Eastern front forced a delay in the timetable. This view was also shared by the German admiralty, which was, however, not involved in Operation Marita.

Other generals, such as Eric von Manstein or the Chief of Staff of the German army, General Franz Halder, and the military historian Mueller-Hildebrand recognize a certain plausibility in these arguments but maintain that weather conditions in any case would not have allowed a significantly earlier date. According to them, the spring of 1941 had been unusually wet, the river Bug and its tributaries had very high water levels, which overflowed wide areas, making them swampy and difficult to traverse. Some contemporary historians, such as John Keegan and Peter Calvocoressi,[2] argue that the weather was the most decisive factor in delaying the German invasion of Russia. Heinz Guderian, Germany's best tank commander, took an intermediate position: he gave credit to the effect of weather conditions, but also attributed the additional delay to the Balkan campaign.[3]

The above debate was carried out in the 1950s and was essentially limited to depositions (testimonials) provided by different German "experts." Since they relied almost exclusively on one or another of the German sources, British historians were also divided into two camps, either denying[4] or affirming[5] the Balkan reason for the delay. Four subsequent decades of historiography have failed to settle this dispute, whether by adding to the sources of information or by providing new arguments.

During this period the only new but rather ambiguous source has been Hitler's so-called *Testament,* dating back to February 17, 1945. In it Hitler

2. John Keegan, *The Second World War* (Toronto: Key Porter Books Limited 1989), p. 174; Peter Calvocoressi, et. al., *Total War: The Causes and Courses of the Second World War* (London: Penguin Books 1989), p. 179.
3. Heinz Guderian, *Panzer Leader,* trans. C. Fitzgibbon (New York: Futura Publications 1974), p. 145.4. Francis de Guignand, *Operation Victory* (London: Hodder and Stoughton 1946), p. 67.
4. Francis de Guignand, *Operation Victory* (London: Hodder and Stoughton 1946), p. 67.
5. This group, which accepted rather uncritically the version of four or more weeks of delay, included several of the official war histories: "June 1941–August 1942" Vol. III, ed. J.M.A. Gwyer, and J.R.M. Butler in *Grand Strategy: History of the Second World War: United Kingdom Military Series, 6 Vols.*, ed. J.R.M. Butler, (London: HMSO 1956-1976), p. 72; "The Initial Triumph of the Axis", *Survey of International Affairs 1939-1946,* Arnold and Veronica M. Toynbee, eds., (London: Oxford University Press 1958) p. 19.

expressly linked the failure of the Russian campaign to the previous and unwanted Balkan adventure. The projected ten-volume edition of *Germany and the Second World War* by the German government-sponsored Research Institute for Military History pays scant attention to the relationship of the Balkan to the Russian campaign. In the fourth volume, dedicated to the first phase of Barbarossa, in more than 1100 pages, there is not a single reference to this issue. Similarly the third volume, referring to the early events in the Mediterranean theater, contains only three sentences (on page 487)[6] on the subject, relying instead almost exclusively on Mueller-Hildebrand's time-honored appreciation. It should, however, be emphasized that Mueller-Hildebrand's published as well as unpublished conclusions, although skeptical, varied as to the net delay due to the Balkan factor. Apart from some vague and unspecific references, his estimates vacillated from one to two weeks to less than three weeks.

To determine the relationship of the German invasion of Greece to Operation Barbarossa, two factors have to be considered. First and foremost is how much of a delay was caused, and was it a result of the Balkan operation or of the weather? Secondly, did the delay have any impact on the Battle of Moscow? Beyond that it is almost impossible to speculate. We can safely assume that the arithmetic argument, i.e. subtracting the weeks between the initial planning and the final date of Barbarossa, is much too simple. Staff officers are accustomed to playing around with the dates of projected operations, which are frequently changed.

The most remarkable example of such changes was the date planned for the attack against France, which a year earlier had been changed not less than nineteen times. Accordingly, the end of May as the initial date for the invasion of Russia is in itself rather vague and far from final. What is known for certain is that the decision to postpone Barbarossa was made by Hitler on March 27, and the order was issued on April 3. From this point on Hitler kept his options open. On June 11 he issued Directive No. 32, which included additional provisions for Barbarossa and a working date of the 19th; three days later the German armies invaded Russia.[7] It was characteristic of Hitler to keep his own counsel and announce operations

6. Also *Germany and the Second World War*, Vol. III, The Mediterranean, South-East, and North Africa 1939-1941, eds. Gerhard Schreiber, Bernd Stegemann and Detlef Vogel trans. Dean S. McMurry, Ewald Osers and Louise Willmot translation editor P.S. Falla, Research Institute for Military History Freiburg im Breisgau, Germany (Oxford: Clarendon Press 1995) p. 487.
7. H.R. Trevor-Roper, ed., *Hitler's Directives* (New York: Holt, Rinehart and Winston 1966), pp. 129-134.

as late as possible, partly for reasons of security and partly because he was prepared to wait on events and act quickly if a new opportunity presented itself. The new date for Barbarossa was not only dependent on the weather but also on the timing of the Balkan campaign.

As far as the impact of the weather on the delay is concerned, it must be kept in mind that it would have been very difficult for German meteorologists to predict weather conditions almost two months in advance. Alfred Jodl offered some insight on the problem of weather prediction during his testimony at the Nuremberg trials:

The meteorologists failed completely in this. At times they thought they could predict such a state of weather, and then all preparations would be made for the attack. Then they would cancel their weather forecasts again, and the final preparations for the attack would be discontinued once more. That is why we so often prepared for the attack and then refrained from carrying it out.[8]

According to Andrew Zapantis, who has provided a comprehensive study of meteorological conditions in Poland and western Russia, the weather factor is not as decisive as it seems.[9] The data provided by Zapantis indicate that the western Bug River freezes at the end of December and the ice breaks up during the second week of March. He adds that although the *World Weather Records* for 1941-1950 do not contain information on Brest, a city on the western Bug, they do include detailed information on Vilnius, a city about two hundred miles north of the western Bug.[10]

The World Weather Records for 1941-1950 indicate that the mean temperature in Vilnius in April 1941 was 2 degrees Celsius (above the melting point), whereas in May the mean temperature rose to 9.4 degrees Celsius and in June it reached 15.2 degrees Celsius. Total precipitation in Vilnius in April was 48 units (mm. hr: 2m) slightly above the mean precipitation of 44.5 for April during 1918-1950; in May 1941, total precipitation was 50 units, below the mean precipitation of 59.1 for the same decades; while in June it was 31 units, well below the mean precipitation of 78.1 for the same month between 1918-1950.[11] Meteorological reports on eastern Poland, compiled for Zapantis from the *Deutscher Wetterdienst* (Zentramt) for the period of April 15 to June 15, indicate that during the entire two-

8. *Trial of the Major War Criminals before the International Military Tribunal,* Vol. 15, Nuremberg, 1947-1949, p. 125.
9. Andrew L. Zapantis, *Greek-Soviet Relations, 1917-1941* (New York: 1982), pp. 564-580.
10. Ibid., pp. 564-565.
11. Ibid., p. 565.

month period the ground of Warsaw (near which the western Bug River joins the Narev and flows into the Vistula) was not affected by freezing, ice, snow, or slush.[12]

Furthermore, during the same period the ground around Warsaw had flooding only once, during part of one day (in the morning of May 30), but by the evening the flooding had disappeared. Most of the time, from mid-April to mid-June 1941, the ground of the Polish capital was dry.[13] Zapantis also has compiled information on the weather from the Polish and Soviet meteorological services, which confirms the German data.[14] Consequently, the information compiled by Zapantis and the fact that the German meteorologists could not provide accurate weather predictions two months in advance effectively eliminates the weather as a factor for the delay in launching Operation Barabarossa.

The other point of consideration is the impact of the Balkan campaign (Operation Marita) itself on the timetable for the Russian invasion. According to the German Order of Battle, the Twelfth Army was diverted from Army Group South to take part in Operation Marita. After the coup in Belgrade, Hitler also diverted the Second German Army to facilitate the conquest of Yugoslavia. The entire force committed to the Balkan campaign was comprised of fourteen infantry divisions; four mountain divisions; six Panzer divisions; two motorized divisions as well as several independent regiments.

According to Martin van Creveld, many units used in Operation Marita could have been re-deployed to the Russian front much sooner than they were, a fact which van Creveld argues proves that whatever delay was caused to Barbarossa did not result from the Balkan campaign.[15] Due to the swift collapse of Yugoslavia, according to General Franz Halder, some units were transferred north as early as April 14, but some also had to be used against Greece.[16] Indeed, as reported by General Gunther Blumentritt, two Panzer divisions missed the start of the invasion of Russia because they required overhaul and partial re-equipment after their march across the Greek mountains.[17]

12. Ibid., p. 567.
13. Ibid., p. 568.
14. Ibid., pp. 5.9-580.
15. M. L. van Creveld, *Hitler's Strategy 1940-1941: The Balkan Clue* (Cambridge: Cambridge University Press, 1973), pp. 182-183.
16. Franz Halder, *The Halder War Diary, 1939-1942*, C. Burdick and Hans-Adolf Jacobsen, eds. (Novato, CA: 1988).
17. Gunther Blumentritt, "Moscow," *The Fatal Decisions: The Battles of Britain, Moscow, El Alamein, Stalingrad, France-1944 and the Ardennes*, S. Freiden and W. Richardson, eds. (New York: 1956), p. 48.

Perhaps more significant was the role of the German air force during the Balkan campaign. From April until the end of May the Germans were forced to deploy over one thousand of their planes in mainland Greece and Crete.[18] This represented close to forty percent of the air force units employed in the initial assault against the Soviet Union (2,770); these forces, it should be noted, consisted of bombers, dive bombers, and fighter planes. For the operation against Crete an additional five hundred and thirty Ju 52 transport aircraft and one hundred gliders were committed.[19] Significantly, most of these units, including Fliegerkorps VIII, were part of Army Group Center and after the battle joined the Army Group on the Russian front.[20] During the course of Operations Marita and Mercury (the attack on Crete), twenty percent of the planes were damaged beyond repair, and an almost equal number required extensive maintenance.[21]

Lost Opportunities: The Battle of Crete

The Battle of Crete was both a strategic blunder on the part of the British and a tragedy for the island's population. Although General Bernard Freyberg had advance notice of the pending attack from Ultra, the British decipherment of the German secret codes, he was ordered not to take any measures that would compromise the greatest secret of the war: the fact that the British had broken the codes.

Despite evidence to the contrary, Freyberg was convinced that the Germans were to mount a naval attack against Crete and thus prepared the defense of the island in anticipation of a seaborne invasion. (a) He did not fortify the airfields, especially Maleme, although he was fully aware that the main German attack would be concentrated on the airfields and that the first twenty-four hours would be crucial to the outcome of the battle. Once the Germans captured Maleme they would be in a position to airlift considerable reinforcements and the outcome would be a foregone

18. *The Rise and Fall of the German Air Force, 1933-1945*, Air Historical Branch, Royal Air Force (London: HMSO 1983), p. 127.
19. Ibid., p. 124.
20. Ibid., pp. 131-133. Just about all of the air force units employed in the attack against the Balkans were transferred to the Russian front. To provide air cover for the Eastern Mediterranean, Fliegerkorps X was transferred to Greece. The units left in Greece after the Battle of Crete included only two hundred and forty bombers, dive-bombers, and reconnaissance planes; an additional one hundred and fifty planes were sent to North Africa.
21. According to Halder (*Diary*, p. 395), one hundred and seventy planes were damaged beyond repair during the Battle of Crete. The total number of planes lost or seriously damaged was approximately three hundred and fifty.

conclusion.[22] (b) It is evident now, from the release of previously classified documents, that Churchill was not made aware that the Ultra information would not be used to undermine the German attack against Crete.[23]

As far as the British prime minister was concerned, the use of Ultra was a major advantage to the coming battle. His only instructions were that every precaution be taken to mask the original source of information by spreading rumors that the British had a highly placed spy in the German high command. Freyberg, however, following orders from Cairo, not only failed to make use of Ultra but inexplicably removed a Greek regiment from the defenses of Maleme in order to protect the Ultra secret. At the same time the British commander, in spite of evidence to the contrary, harbored a strong suspicion that the main German thrust would come by sea.

Equally catastrophic for the inhabitants of Crete and the remnants of the Greek armed forces, the British refused to arm volunteers from the general population. In considering the defense of the island Freyberg adopted a traditional attitude toward the conduct of the war and placed little reliance on the effectiveness of Greek civilians or even the Greek military. Although he commanded 40,000 troops, most of these were demoralized and consisted of cooks, mechanics, orderlies, and other non-combat personnel. The few units that comprised regular formations were used to buttress the odd assortment of units that made up the Allied forces in Crete.

Hitler, for his part, was at first reluctant to use Germany's elite paratroopers for the assault on Crete, but General Kurt Student, with Goering's

---

22. Anthony Beevor *Crete, the Battle and the Resistance* (Boulder, Colorado: Westview Press, 1994) p. 87-89.
23. According to Anthony Beevor in *Crete, the Battle and the Resistance* (Boulder, Colorado: Westview Press, 1994) pp. 89-91, Freyberg misread Ultra intelligence. He cites a letter Freyberg sent to Wavell on May 13 and concludes "F. appears to have preserved the secret of Ultra better by having misunderstood the contents than by his painstaking preservation of secrecy." Peter Calvocoressi in the authoritative history of World War II, *Total War: The Causes and Courses of the Second World War*, 2 Vols. (London: Penguin Books 1989) p. 178, however, states that Freyberg was prevented from deploying his forces to anticipate an airborne attack based exclusively on information from Ultra by his commanding officer Field Marshal Archibald Wavell. The German report on the Battle of Crete, *Gefechtbericht XI Fl. Korps—Einsatz Kreta*, is another example of this view: "One thing stands out from all the information gleaned from the enemy (prisoners' statements, diaries and captured documents) that they were on the whole very well informed about German intentions, thanks to an excellent espionage network, but expected that the bulk of the invasion forces would come by sea."

support, convinced the German dictator that with the element of surprise the operation was feasible. Unknown to Student, of course, almost as soon as the orders were issued, the British were not only fully apprised of the plan but had the details of the German order of battle. On May 20, 1941 the German attack was preceded by a devastating air bombardment of the British defenses, followed by hundreds of Stuka dive bombers and fighters that bombed or machine-gunned the troops on the ground. By 7:30 A.M. the sky was filled as four hundred ninety-three Junkers transport planes towing another seventy gliders practically covered the sun. In a few minutes thousands of paratroopers began their descent, while the gliders crash-landed near their targets.

Initially the battle was turning in favor of the British. The Germans had made several critical mistakes, first by underestimating the strength of the British and Greek forces and second, most of the German units missed their primary objectives and often fell on top of the British defenders. As a result, the paratroopers suffered devastating losses. Entire battalions were wiped out and in the first couple of days thousands of German soldiers were killed as they fell from the sky or immediately upon landing. However, a few units managed to survive and began consolidating their position at the edge of the Maleme airfield.

In other parts of Crete the fighting was equally hard, particularly in the interior of the island. In many instances the Germans, as much as the British, were surprised and often perplexed by the ferocity that the Cretans, both men and women, displayed against the invaders. Using out-dated rifles, knives, pitchforks, daggers and even rocks and axes, ordinary villagers threw themselves against the paratroopers and inflicted serious casualties. For the Cretans, the German attack brought back memories of the Ottoman occupation and the war they had fought to end Turkish rule.

It is uncertain how many men and women took part in the battle against the Germans, since most of the fighting on the island was not characterized by major engagements but by hundreds of small encounters, often isolated duels. What is certain is that the Cretans made a considerable contribution to the high casualties suffered by the paratroopers. Yet the very courage of the armed irregular Cretan fighters exacted a heavy price on the unarmed civilians. After the battle the Germans executed two hundred males in the town of Galatta in reprisal. Other Cretan men and women faced German firing squads as retaliation for daring to oppose the Nazis, and would continue to do so throughout the occupation.

In any event the bravery of the Cretans, New Zealanders, and Australians could not compensate for ineffectual leadership and the determination of General Student to overcome almost impossible obstacles and sustain the attack. In addition, the endurance of the German soldiers to continue fighting under difficult conditions gave General Student a slight tactical advantage. Despite a casualty rate of almost ninety percent, the handful of German troops near Maleme gained control of the airfield, which enabled German pilots to land successfully with reinforcements. Freyberg ordered counterattacks to recapture the vital airport, but these were uncoordinated and ultimately failed.

The loss of Maleme made the British position in Crete untenable. In a matter of days the paratroopers were supplemented by fresh battalions of the 5th Mountain Division, which pushed the British forces from the other two airfields at Rethymnon and Irakleon, thus sealing the fate of the island. Once again the Royal Navy had to execute a difficult evacuation of the British army and suffer the loss of irreplaceable ships sunk by German warplanes. Although the navy rescued thousands, at least 12,000 Commonwealth forces were taken prisoner.

The Germans also paid a dear price for Crete. Most of their elite paratroop battalions were decimated and a high percentage of officers and noncommissioned officers were either killed or severely wounded. During the course of the battle the Germans suffered 4,000 killed and 2,594 wounded out of a force of 10,000. Crete effectively served as the graveyard of the paratroopers, both literally and figuratively.

Hitler, exasperated at the high losses, decreed that in the future there would be no further attempts at airborne assaults and that the day of the paratrooper was over. Indeed, for the duration of the war the German High Command avoided any major use of airborne troops, and with a few minor exceptions Germany's elite hunters from the sky were employed as regular infantry. Thereafter, the Germans abandoned the use of paratroopers, which they had pioneered, and no longer made use of this flexible and effective element of their armed forces.

In terms of grand strategy, the battles of Greece and Crete must be understood within the context of the major arguments put forth by the British and the Germans. Fundamentally, there are two critical considerations that cannot be dismissed. First, the weather argument is not relevant since the delay for Barbarossa came as a result of Hitler's order on March 27, 1941 and at that time it was not possible to predict weather conditions in eastern Poland and western Russia. Furthermore, Zapantis has proven that ground conditions in these regions were relatively normal. Second, in addition to the diversion of the vital armored divisions almost forty percent of the German air force had to be deployed in the Balkans.

Even if we assume that the army units could have joined in the attack at a later date, as has been proposed by some historians, it is highly unlikely that Barbarossa could have proceeded without a substantial part of the German air force. Hitler had fixed the original date for the invasion of Russia for the 15th of May, but after he was forced to commit substantial army and air force units to the Balkan campaign he had no choice but to delay Barbarossa. Had Greece collapsed without putting up a fight in April and had Crete followed suit, it may have been possible to advance the date of the invasion.

It was certainly possible for the German High Command to re-route units almost from the midst of battle in the Balkans back to the Eastern front. This was the case with the transfer of some units after the immediate collapse of Yugoslavia to the northwest Greek frontier in order for them to take part in the battle for Greece. Yet the units were not transferred to the East because of the resistance offered by the Greek army and the British Expeditionary Force on the mainland and in Crete. Therefore, we must consider what impact an immediate Greek collapse would have had on Barbarossa, in addition to the delay caused by the resistance of the Greeks.

The most plausible comparison is the situation in Yugoslavia. The Yugoslav forces were overrun in a matter of days, thus freeing almost half the German forces to concentrate on Greece. If the Greeks had followed the fate of the Yugoslavs, the Balkan campaign could have been over in a week. The Germans then would have been able to commence their invasion of Russia by the middle of May. The consequences of this are difficult to calculate but it is conceivable that the Germans could have achieved the conquest of Moscow, thus psychologically providing a tremendous boost to the German army and may even have brought down Stalin's government. At the very least such an outcome would have prolonged the war on the Eastern front.

The Resistance

For the Greek people the elements of grand strategy were superseded by a new reality-occupation, starvation, resistance, reprisals, and the almost complete destruction of Greece's infrastructure. The Germans lost little time before initiating a campaign of plunder and terror. Most of Greece's food stocks were confiscated and sent to Germany. All motor vehicles were appropriated by the Axis authorities, as were villas, apartments, furniture, and the entire public transportation system. In addition, a ban was imposed on fishing, which accompanied by the expropriation of most boats, left the Greeks with practically no means to sustain even a minimal level of subsistence.

Part of the harshness of the occupation policies was a direct result of the Battle of Crete. The Nazis, in their typical narrow-minded, self-delusional mindset, were angered because, during the course of the battle, the Greeks on the mainland had the temerity to cheer the victories of the Allies and the Greek forces fighting on the island. The Axis authorities had assumed that the Greek population would accept the occupation and even display a degree of gratitude toward their oppressors.

Another consideration was that Germany faced food shortages and any excuse was sufficient to plunder Greece to feed the Germans at home. The problem of basic survival was further compounded by the embargo the British imposed on occupied countries. Greece, which depended on imported foodstuffs, oil, coal, and other necessities, was hit very hard. Within a few months of the occupation the daily toll of death by starvation increased dramatically. By the winter of 1941-1942 it was not uncommon for the streets of cities such as Athens and smaller towns to be strewn with hundreds of bloated corpses.

Yet despite the deterioration of daily life, it did not take long for the development of resistance. At first, opposition to the occupation was spontaneous and spasmodic. People cheered British prisoners of war as the Germans drove through the streets of Athens to the P.O.W. camps. The Athenians showered the defeated Allies with whatever food they had, with chocolates, cigarettes, and any other bits of what had become precious commodities. Shortly after, popular resistance manifested itself in more concrete and at the same time dangerous activities.

One easy and substantive means of striking back at the enemy was through the writing of slogans on walls and buildings. Another example of the mass resistance to Axis rule was the offering of refuge to those wanted by the Nazis. This included hiding escaped Allied soldiers and also Greek Jews, whom the SS and Gestapo were quickly attempting to round up. In both cases the penalty for harboring "enemies" of the Axis was death or the concentration camp. These attempts at intimidation had less impact than the more practical problem of securing sufficient food for the British soldiers and Jewish families who found refuge in the homes of Greek families.

These early resistance activities were supplemented by the creation by 1944 of over two hundred underground newspapers, which maintained a constant flow of information about the war and conditions around the country. Later the problem of securing an escape route for their hidden guests brought many Athenians into a world of clandestine work; those who survived initiated a rudimentary underground. This was no mean feat considering the state of almost total collapse of the Greek state.

The phenomenon of resistance to German and Italian occupation took many forms during the course of the war. The Greek Resistance cannot be characterized by a single organization or even a group of organizations, but must be defined within the context of an entire population carrying on a war against the Axis. Those who participated in the Resistance included the trained saboteur, the gifted amateur, and the average citizen who in a split second had to decide whether to accept the pleas of an Allied soldier or just walk away. As the testimony of hundreds of British, New Zealand, and Australian soldiers indicates, it was a rare occurrence that any were denied a safe haven from the Axis security services.

While the drama of mass starvation was playing out in the cities, organized resistance began to form in two directions. Over the next eight months, as the demobilized soldiers of the Greek army returned home, many made their way to the mountain regions of Greece and linked up with guerrilla bands that had formed over the course of the winter of 1941-1942. The large number of officers and junior officers provided the guerrilla fighters with a degree of discipline and military skills. Although lacking sufficient arms, the various bands assembled a motley collection of hunting rifles, knives, and an assortment of stolen Italian weapons.

In the fall of 1942 the British intelligence services in the Middle East sent a commando team to the Greek mountains; together with the guerrilla bands, the commandos mounted the first major act of sabotage in occupied Europe. The target for the British was the Gorgopotamos viaduct. The destruction of this bridge meant that the critical supplies for Rommel's Africa Corps, which were carried by train from Germany through Central Europe to North Africa, had to travel along the single rail line connecting Thessalonike and Athens. On the night of November 25 the British commando team planted the demolition charges while the Greek guerrilla bands fought off the garrison; within a few minutes the bridge was destroyed.

The Gorgopotamos operation was a tonic for the Greek people and served as a lesson for the Allies and the Axis that resistance was possible and that the guerrilla war could be coordinated with Allied strategy. Within months of the operation additional guerrilla bands took to the mountains and the High Command in the Middle East established British military missions to the guerrilla bands. Between 1942 and 1944, eighty such missions were set up and served as the coordinating bodies between the Greek Resistance and the Allied planners in Cairo and London. During the same period the numbers of guerrilla bands increased from a few groups of a couple of hundred in the fall of 1942 to over 70,000 by the end of the occupation.

In the early summer of 1943 Greek resistance bands took part in one of the major deception operations of the war. After the defeat of Rommel's Africa Corps, Allied planners decided to invade Sicily. In order to launch the enterprise, which the Germans expected, it was necessary to convince Hitler that the proposed target was Greece and not Sicily. One part of the deception included floating the body of a British officer (the officer did not exist and the body belonged to a vagrant who had died in London), near the coast of Spain; on the body were planted documents that indicated an invasion of Greece. The other part of the plan required that all the Greek guerrilla bands mount a widespread series of attacks against Axis fortifications, bridges, railway lines, and other military installations in order to create the appearance of imminent liberation. The ruse worked; the German High Command transferred seven divisions to Greece and kept some of those units there even after the Allies landed on the beaches in Sicily.

The use of deception was a key element of Allied strategy, but it required the cooperation of the guerrilla forces and clandestine cells in the major Greek cities. After 1943, with the plans for the invasion of Normandy, the Greek Resistance was instrumental, along with the Yugoslavs, in tying down twenty-eight German divisions in the Balkans. It is almost impossible to calculate the outcome of the D-Day invasion if even half of those divisions were present in France.

The success of the guerrillas exacted a gruesome levy on the unarmed civilians of the mountain villages and cities. Each act of resistance resulted in reprisals that left hundreds of villages destroyed and thousands executed. In the major cities each act of sabotage also exacted a grim toll. The Axis security services, along with the SS and Gestapo, rounded up thousands of innocent men, women, and children for the firing squads, irrespective of their victims' role or proximity to damage inflicted by the Resistance.

The fury of the Axis was in reaction to the damage inflicted by the Resistance between 1941 and 1942. During the course of the guerrilla war, the Greeks, with the aid of the British and later the Americans, mounted an impressive campaign of destruction:

- Three thousand subversive operations, averaging ninety-four per month, a record that peaked at three hundred from April to November of 1944.
- Thirty-four thousand six hundred and fifty enemy casualties, of which 20,000 were German.
- Two thousand one hundred operations were carried out against the Axis communication system, leading to the destruction of: two hundred locomotives, 1,154 train cars, one hundred and seventeen trains, sixty-seven railway bridges, and five tunnels.
- The rail lines were cut in one hundred and fifty-seven locations and at least 28,000 meters of rail line were destroyed.

- Two hundred operations were carried out against roads, destroying one hundred and thirty-six bridges and eight hundred and fifty-four military transports.
- Approximately forty operations were carried out against enemy stores and equipment, resulting in the elimination of seventeen ammunition and fuel sites and the destruction of:
  —1,000 tons of petrol
  —1,000 shells
  —two hundred bombs
  —eight hundred and forty cases of ammunition
  —five aircraft
  —sixteen tanks
  —five chrome and nickel mines.

Remarkable as this record is, it is by no means the only contribution of the Greek Resistance. In Athens and the other major cities and towns of Greece another war was taking place. This struggle was fought in the shadows, back streets, and basements. By its very nature it was kept secret and remained secret until recently. The espionage and sabotage campaign implemented by the Greeks remains almost unparalleled in the annals of military history.

Hundreds of clandestine cells mushroomed during the occupation and provided the Allies with hundreds of thousands of strategic and tactical information reports on the Axis. The range of activities included keeping track of German units moving in and out of Greece through the use of workers on the Acropolis, who kept a record of the army units by identifying them from their shoulder patches.

Others infiltrated the Italian and German security services and procured the lists of wanted or suspected individuals. Many more groups concentrated on Axis shipping and sent frequent messages to Cairo on the movements of the German and Italian convoys to North Africa. In one instance, thanks to the efforts of one team, an entire German convoy of fifty ships was intercepted by the Royal Navy, which proceeded to sink all the ships. One agent even managed to photograph the plans of the German V1 and V2 rockets.

The complete story of the Athenian clandestine networks has yet to be written. Suffice to say that there were over 3,000 Greek operatives who matched their wits against the SS and Gestapo. These men and women are responsible for the destruction or sabotage of over two hundred and fifty-three ships and contributed to the sinking of over 68,000 tons of enemy shipping. Unfortunately, many of those who participated in espionage and sabotage against the Axis have remained anonymous, their activities shrouded in the closed archives of the British Public Records Office.

Even more unfortunate, many of these brave men and women did not survive the occupation, but faced the firing squad or underwent unspeakable torture at the hands of the SS and Gestapo. Their contribution represents a significant element of the history of the Greek Resistance and a critical chapter in European history. These unsung heroes are, to a great extent, part of the thousands of ordinary Greek citizens who chose to fight rather than passively accept defeat on the battlefield.

Indeed, the remarkable legacy of the Greek Resistance is common to all who lived during Greece's darkest time. Yet the monuments are few and certainly outside of Greece little is known about the extraordinary efforts of a small nation that remained loyal to its past and did honor to its Allies. One reason is that the literature of the Greek resistance has not penetrated the English language. The other important factor is that the post-war period was as cruel to Greece as was the occupation.

After 1944 the Greek people were struggling to survive and there was little time to write about the sacrifices of the past when new sacrifices were required in the present. The war left Greece a desolate country that only recovered at the beginning of the 1950s. Perhaps in the fullness of time, and before it is forgotten, the valor and the horror of the occupation will find its place in history.

In the final analysis, Greece's contribution to the Second World War must be addressed in relation to the role it played in defeating the Axis. In this consideration certain salient points must be taken into account. In 1940 Greece was the only country to defeat and humiliate one of the Axis powers. Less than a year later the Greek army, after an unequal campaign against the Italians, had to face the Germans, whose army had not tasted defeat and had walked across Europe smashing army after army. It was only in the Greek mountains that the Germans encountered a foe who displayed single-minded determination not to be overwhelmed by the myth of German invincibility.

The Greeks, although ultimately defeated, never surrendered. It is one of the few occasions in the early phase of the war that the victorious Germans faced such opposition. The process was repeated during the battle of Crete, and once again the remarkable aspect of the battle was the role of the general population, which also refused to accept defeat. When the British began to fail, the Cretans stepped in to inflict a death toll on the Germans that proportionately would not be equaled until almost the end of the war. The occupation also failed to break the morale of the Greek people, and they responded by implementing one of the most successful resistance movements in the Second World War.

How relevant were these contributions of the Greeks? Looked upon in another way the question to ask is what would have been the outcome of the war if Greece, like Turkey, had chosen neutrality? For one thing, it is certain that Hitler's legions would not have encountered any delay in the Balkans and may have achieved their goal of capturing Moscow before the winter. Furthermore, the additional twenty-eight divisions that the Germans kept in the Balkans would have posed a serious threat to the Allied armies in Normandy, as would have been the case earlier in North Africa and Sicily. ✦

Elements of Confusion Britain and Greece, 1940-1941

Robin Higham

British policy and actions toward Greece a half century ago were driven by several myths. Upper-class Englishmen like my father, who left Harrow School in 1914, wrote and spoke classical Greek. He and the then Prime Minister in 1940, Winston Churchill, had been brought up not only on the history and myths of classical Greece, but also on the story of Hellenic independence. Lord Byron (whose portrait still hangs in the British Ambassador's residence—the former Venizelos house on Vasilisis Sofias in Athens)—was still a household hero. But though the Duke of Kent had recently married Princess Marina of the Hellenes, Englishmen in the 1930s thought of Greece as a colony somewhere in the Balkans or the Levant, they really were not quite sure which or where.

Thus the moment that the Italians attacked on October 28, 1940 the Greeks were seen, like the Spartans of old at Thermopylae, as the heroic last free people still fighting the Axis on the continent of Europe. In 1939 Britain and France had given Greece guarantees of her sovereign territory. But that was before Poland fell in September of that year, thus depriving Greece of her second arms supplier, the first having been Czechoslovakia, which by 1940 was also in Hitler's hands. In the spring of 1940 the situation had changed even more radically. The Germans had swept into Norway, the Low Countries, and most importantly of all, into France. On June 10 Italy had belatedly joined in the Axis war by attempting to attack Gaul. But the Italians had been defeated in the Alps, where their own unpreparedness and stubborn French resistance had given them frostbite.

The fall of France and Italian entry into the war had not only vitiated the guarantee to Greece, but had closed the Mediterranean to peaceful British shipping and lengthened the route from Britain to the Suez Canal from 3,000-odd miles to 12,000-odd miles. The air route across France and North Africa was closed. And as of June 10, 1940 the Middle East became a theater of war, something which had never been envisioned prewar.

ROBIN HIGHAM is Professor at Kansas State University. He received his Ph.D. from Harvard in 1957 and the Samuel Eliot Morison Prize of the American Military Institute for his contributions to the field of military history.

The Egyptian base was unprepared and unequipped for war. The Commander-in-Chief, General Sir Archibald Wavell was *primus inter pares* with the Air Officer Commanding-in-Chief (AOC-in-C), Air Chief Marshal Sir Arthur Longmore, and with the Commander-in-Chief of the Mediterranean Fleet, Sir Andrew Browne Cunningham. The latter was often absent from the councils of war owing to being at sea with the fleet.

There was very little infrastructure in Egypt. The army had a few garrison stations, and once the war with Italy began it was fully occupied with the East African campaign to turn the Italians out of Ethiopia, which they had been allowed to seize in 1935-1936. That campaign lasted into 1941 and was conducted with few resources and a lot of South African and Indian help. Its successful conclusion safeguarded the Red Sea and the route from England around the Cape of Good Hope to Suez at the south end of the Canal.

The Royal Navy did have a major base at Alexandria at the mouth of the Nile, but its principal Mediterranean home port had been at the island of Malta. This was only sixty miles south of Sicily and subject to brutal air attacks, and so was now untenable as a fleet base. Moreover, the British had lost control of the sea; all convoys had to reach Egypt via Cape Town, reducing the round-trip voyages *per annum* to two, a tremendous lowering of cargo capacity. This vitally affected Greece, since coal for railways and ships operating out of Hellenic ports came from Cardiff in Wales, the best steaming coal in the world in the days before the discovery of coal at Ptolemais in northern Greece.

Because the Middle East had not been seen as an operational theater but as a training base in the interwar years, Longmore had very few air assets and these were largely obsolescent or suffering from teething problems. Moreover, not only was the AOC-in-C plagued by a shortage of aircraft, spare parts, and the necessary handtool kits with which to undertake repairs, but there was no infrastructure of workshops, salvage units and the like in theater. Of crucial importance for what happened in 1940-1941 was the lack of understanding of these matters in London. Nor did those in Whitehall, at the center of the best railway system in the world at the time, comprehend the High Command in the Middle East's difficulties in regard to transport and distances. The theater was roughly 1,000 miles wide from the Libyan border to Aden and eventually would be some 2,000 miles long, from Nairobi to Thessalonike. None of the commanders had transport aircraft for their personal use.

In addition to the campaign in East Africa, Wavell had to guard against the further advance into Egypt from Cyrenaica of the Italians, who had merely made a token crossing of the border before sitting down. The truth was that the Italians had already reached their economic pinnacle before the war began, as demonstrated in the story of their development of tanks which had peaked in 1938.

During the summer of 1940, while the Battle of Britain was being fought in the skies over England, the Middle East was quiet. It was starved for support because of the twin fears in Britain that the Germans might actually launch Operation Sealion (the invasion) and that the *Luftwaffe* was so much larger than the RAF (Royal Air Force).

The daytime Battle of Britain was over by October and the nighttime one rumbled on as the Blitz into the spring of 1941. It was only in March of that year, when Hitler was well along with his preparations to invade the U.S.S.R., that Prime Minister Winston Churchill in London got the report of Mr. Justice Singleton, recently appointed to look into RAF estimates of the strength of the German Air Force. His conclusion was that far from having more than 14,000 aircraft, the *Luftwaffe* actually had only about 5,000. Once this was realized and the fear of invasion ended, there was a dramatic shift in British grand strategy. It became possible to begin to match means to ends. But there was a significant lag of some nine months. For instance, it was only at the time of the fall of Greece in May 1941 that someone in London realized that of 1,786 aircraft allocated to the Middle East since the autumn of 1940, only three hundred had actually arrived in theater and that all of these had needed to be erected and tested or overhauled before they could become operational. One of the basic facts of aid for Greece was that there was very little to spare, as we shall see.

The minute that the Italian declaration of war against and invasion of Greece was known in Cairo, Longmore at once dispatched one squadron of Blenheim medium bombers to Eleusis via Crete, where a British presence had been established in September. London soon ordered the AOC-in-C Middle East to send more from his almost non-existent forces. It was this paucity of vital air assets that created a lot of ill-feeling between the ebullient, bellicose, imaginative Winston Churchill, a former hussar who had marched with Kitchener to Khartoum in 1898, and the former Royal Naval Air Service AOC-in-C and his commander-in-chief, the silent, one-eyed but brilliant Wavell.

One of the principal problems in Greece and Crete, and one largely neglected by historians until very recently, was the lack of all-weather airfields, let alone of runways suitable for modern aircraft. At the time the Royal Hellenic Air Force (RHAF) not only lacked the funds to develop runways, something just being laid down in Britain, but also it scarcely needed more than dry, flat ground off which to operate its Polish and French aircraft.

From November 1, 1940 the Royal Air Force began to operate in Greece with Blenheim twin-engined medium bombers and Gloster Gladiator single-engined biplane fighters.

The commander of the RAF sent to Greece, AVM John d'Albiac, was given detailed instructions as to his role in helping the Greeks. He was also authorized to evacuate upon his own recognizance should the situation warrant. Apart from the shortage of aircraft, spare parts, and tools, d'Albiac was burdened with an ineffective doctrine and concern about the VD rate in Athens.

What the RHAF and the Greek troops in Albania needed was tactical air support. What d'Albiac had in mind was the standard RAF deterrent doctrine—destruction of the enemy's war-making capacity, a task well beyond the power and range of his force. Moreover, as Greece lacked all-weather aerodromes, when the rains came in December most of the RAF were evacuated to the Western Desert, where General Wavell had just opened a reconnaissance in force against the Italians that would turn into a successful drive all the way across Cyrenaica to El Agheila.

D'Albiac was imbued with the British deterrent doctrine for the defense of the home islands. This meant that the enemy's capital city would be attacked to destroy the will of the people, and his armaments industry hit to destroy the sinews of war. Unfortunately, the RAF at home was incapable of these tasks since it could not effectively reach Berlin and it had neither the navigational ability, the bombsights, nor the carrying capacity to be effective. D'Albiac's force could not reach the Ploesti oilfields in Romania, nor could the Blenheims do much damage to the Italian supply ports of Valona and Durazzo on the Albanian coast, nor could they reach Rome. Eventually the AOC, British Air Forces Greece, had under his command some Fleet Air Arm Swordfish biplane torpedo bombers of the type which had crippled the Italian fleet in Taranto harbor on November 11, 1940. These carried ship-killing weapons and could rumble in with their wheels banging the wave tops to launch torpedoes and sink supplies. But that was not too often.

What the Greek Commander-in-Chief, General Alexandros Papagos, really needed was a tactical air force to supplement his own gallant Royal Hellenic Air Force in repelling the Italian thrust from Albania into Epirus. But the lack of advanced landing grounds west of Larisa limited the front-line time of the Gladiators; furthermore, bad weather and mountains caused the loss of a number of aircraft and aircrew. Those British aircraft which did make successful forced landings at some other place than Paramythia lost their tailwheels or were otherwise unable to be repaired on the spot and flown out. Nor, at this stage of the war, did the RAF have the necessary recovery vehicles, so wastage was higher than it needed to have been.

The situation in Athens in the early winter of 1940 was interesting since the Germans were neutral, and thus free to transmit any intelligence they gathered to Berlin for onward transmission. It was rather like CNN in Baghdad in 1990-1991. At times there were tensions at Zonar's, where Germans and British ate at adjoining tables. As the Greeks became more hard-pressed, so the contents of the man- and woman-power barrel dropped. By December the situation was critical enough that it was agreed that the British would take over the defense of Crete, so as to release the Cretan division for service on the Albanian front.

Geography played an important role in this. Crete was the natural right-wing bastion of the British position in the Eastern Mediterranean. It contained a potential naval base at Suda Bay and the possibility for a number of airfields both along the northern coast and in the Mesara valley. The former had ports, but the latter did not. Internal transportation was primitive, as Crete in 1940 was still largely undeveloped. Any British shipping to Heraklion, Chania, or Agios Nikolaos had to steam north through the Kos passage at the eastern end of the island. The danger of this route, and the one to Athens, was that the Italians held the Dodecanese Islands, had airfields on Rhodes, and their main shipping route from the Dodecanese to the Italian mainland passed through the southern Aegean between the north shore of Crete and the Morea on the mainland. The Battle of Cape Matapan (March 28, 1941) took place just to the northwest of Crete.

Given the later fate of Crete, it must be noted that at this stage of the war the British lacked a grand strategy for the theater. In part this was because of Churchill's own character and his dominance of his Cabinet, in part because of the parlous state of Britain at home, and in part because the Eastern Mediterranean had never been envisaged as a theater of war in which the Royal Navy would not have had unchallenged control of the seas. That British policy was unsettled can be seen in the indecision over the deployment of a Marine Naval Base Defense Force for Suda Bay with full recognition of the geostrategic impact of air power on the area.

Geostrategy was also visible in the matter of the Greek economy. London's attitude toward what was regarded as a colonial entity was that the Greeks had little with which to pay for coal and capital developments in a depressed world, and that they had been buying their arms mainly from French, Czech, and Polish firms. This general attitude, in spite of RHAF and RHN (Royal Hellenic Navy) ties with Britain, meant that London was not much interested in Athens.

As a result, not only were Greek army officers trained in Germany (General Ioannis Metaxas) or France (Alexandros Papagos), but that, far more importantly, the Greek economy was aligned with the Danubian axis that led to Germany. For a variety of reasons then, the doughty Greek Premier Ioannis Metaxas had to be carefully realistic in his dealings with all concerned.

Metaxas was aware of Italian desires for aggrandizement to take the Italian people's eyes off the troubles that Mussolini's government was having at home and in Africa. Metaxas did not want war because he was well aware of the fragility not only of his political situation, but more importantly of the economic and military one. With all of his arms suppliers knocked out of the war, Greece's supplies of military materiel were limited. He hoped, therefore, to maintain the neutrality of the Hellenes. That was why he played down the reaction to the sinking of the destroyer-minelayer Helle on August 15, 1940 at Tinos, even though the remnants of the torpedoes found were clearly Italian. Put to the challenge of the Italian ultimatum of October 28, however, Metaxas could only respond with "Ochi" (No). His determination was to beat the Italians, and this made him an ally of the British in the Mediterranean war.

At the same time, Metaxas was aware of the way in which the Germans were infiltrating and intimidating the Balkans and especially of renewed German relations with Bulgaria, Greece's long-standing enemy, against whom a miniature Maginot, the Metaxas Line, had been constructed north of Thessalonike. Metaxas was also cognizant of the Allied army that had been immured about Thessalonike for the better part of two years during World War I, and how it had suffered from malaria and other diseases.

Once the year 1941 commenced, the Greek tragedy of the Second World War began to march to its inevitable conclusion: the collapse that led to German occupation.

Early in the new year Churchill, always anxious to be on the attack, and with his schoolboy memories of the classical Greeks victorious at Marathon and Salamis, continued to see Greece's King George as the leader of the only freedom-loving force still fighting the evil Axis Xerxes on the mainland of Europe. Churchill desired to help. Thus he ordered the Commander-in-Chief in the Middle East to Athens to discuss support. In this Churchill had been abetted by the British Minister, Sir Michael Palairet, who had been constantly clamoring for more aid. Wavell had already recalled Major-General M. D. Gambier-Parry for making indiscreet remarks which could be interpreted that British military support was just around the corner.

Wavell spent several days early in January in Athens talking to Metaxas. In the course of these conversations he offered what he could, which was not much at all, certainly not the nine divisions which Metaxas and Wavell agreed would be the minimum needed. These, and the shipping to transport them to Thessalonike, were simply not available outside of Britain. Moreover, Wavell's medical officers, with previous experience of the Macedonian campaign of 1916-1918, would advise him against sending troops to what was still, in their opinion, a highly diseased country—malaria and cholera as well as dysentery being endemic before the draining of the marshes around Pella.

Metaxas' response to Churchill's offer was to tell Wavell that the English general had spoken like a commander-in-chief and to politely decline to accept a pigless poke. A memorandum of understanding was concluded on January 18, and Wavell returned to Athens believing that he had done his duty and that fate would run its course.

And everything probably would have run its course, but for a number of factors. First, in spite of heroic efforts by the Greeks in advancing into Albania and of the women and old men in the support corps in bringing supplies forward (see the statue in Thessalonike), terrible winter weather prevented the Hellenes from being victorious in spite of the defeats that Mussolini was also suffering in East Africa and the Western Desert.

Second, the Greek infrastructure was being sucked dry of everything from donkeys to shells, and the railways were being forced to burn olive wood in place of coal (which meant that they could run trains to Florina that were only half as long as they would have been with coal).

Third, Hitler was preparing to go into the Soviet Union and wanted to set the Balkan house in order after Mussolini had made a mess of the attack on Greece. Hitler also wanted to thwart Italian ambitions in the Balkans before Germany's eastern campaign started. That offensive, Operation Barbarossa, was eventually delayed by the late spring thaw as much as by other factors.

For the Greeks, the future looked grim. Metaxas had told Wavell that he hoped to defeat the Italians; in fact, he was determined to do so, but he knew that the Greeks could not fight both the Germans and the Italians. So if the Germans attacked, even if they simply supported the hated Bulgarians, the premier saw no other course than to save Greece by capitulation. It may be that it was this crushing burden of command that ultimately propelled Greece further along the road to tragedy. Certainly it is one of the myths that has since confused the story to think that either Metaxas or Papagos believed that Greece could resist the Germans. As we shall see, by March 1941 the Greek Army did not have the troops to man any line longer than the one on the Epirus front.

Less than two weeks after the Wavell-Metaxas agreement, diabetic complications, age, and the burdens of command, caused the death of the premier. Metaxas had come to power in 1936 in a political vacuum. At a time when many countries were reeling under an economic depression, he was only one among several leaders to adopt dictatorial methods in order to save his country. President Franklin Delano Roosevelt's New Deal actions were remarkably similar to Adolf Hitler's domestic programs, though without the latter's anti-Semitic and expansionist agendas. Once the war broke out, the "little Moltke," as Metaxas was known, became a national symbol and hero in spite of the fact that he did not look the part.

The death of Metaxas deprived Greece of a vital asset, a leader who had military training and experience, who understood politics, and who could manage the king as well as the war.

Once the premier was gone, the king appointed Alexandros Koryzis to succeed him. He was a banker, president of the Greek Red Cross Society, an upright and honest man, but one entirely unprepared by experience or inclination to conduct a war fraught with such danger for Greece. His forte had been helping to solve the disruptions caused by the 1923 exchange of populations between Greece and Turkey.

Not having been in the Cabinet, one of Koryzis' first actions on taking up the reins of power was to ask Palairet, unaware of the agreement of January 18. This set Koryzis' foot on the next step toward tragedy, for Palairet immediately cabled London saying that the Greek premier wanted to know what help he could expect from the British. This was, of course, exactly what Churchill wanted to hear, not the answer he had got from the cautious Wavell, upon whom Churchill looked down.

The British prime minister at once, and under sealed orders, sent his foreign secretary, the sartorially splendid Anthony Eden, and the schoolmasterish Chief of the Imperial General Staff, Sir John Dill (formerly Commandant of the Staff College at Camberley), to Cairo and Athens. When the orders were opened en route, Eden found he had been given a free hand; only remember, wrote Churchill, that you are my heir.

After a long journey from England via Gibraltar and Malta, Eden and Dill's flying-boat finally landed on the Nile. They consulted with Wavell and Longmore in Cairo, then on the 22nd flew out into the Western Desert for short conversations and refueling, before flying on to Athens. After landing at Menidi, they drove straight to the Tatoi Palace in the woods north of the capital.

There, late that night and on into the morning of the 23rd of February, they conferred with the Greek leaders. This was very much a meeting between a great power and a minor one, with the Greeks at an additional disadvantage because not all their experts were present. Eden made it clear that he wanted a military and not a political agreement. So maps of northern Greece were produced and eventually a grease-pencil mark was drawn. This became known as the Aliakmon Line, but it was never anything more than a chimera. Nor, as far as Wavell was concerned (though he kept his own counsel), was it intended to be more than that.

A veteran of the Middle East from the First World War, when he had been chief of staff to the victorious Sir Edmund Allenby in the Palestine campaign, Wavell was familiar with Cairo and had his own intelligence network in the Eastern Mediterranean, long before ULTRA, the deciphered German Enigma messages, became available to him on March 16.

Moreover, Wavell was well aware of the sieve-like nature of Cairo and Alexandria, where many Italians lived amongst the Egyptians in the British protectorate. Thus he plastered the walls of his office with maps of Greece, remarking that this would be his spring campaign. Actually, his objective was to be Tripoli, Libya as his troops had paused at the gateway at El Agheila.

But Wavell lacked intelligence from Tripoli because the British had neglected to set agents in place before the war. Thus he was not aware of, nor was British intelligence prepared for, the arrival in Libya and shortly after in the Western Desert of the charismatic *Feldmarschall* Erwin Rommel. Although he was one of the leading Panzer generals of the campaign in France, London thought Rommel was an obscure German officer being exiled to North Africa. Before the end of February he was pushing the British back toward Egypt.

The Tatoi Palace conference considered the long attempts by the Greeks to create a viable Balkan Alliance of themselves, the Yugoslavs, the Romanians, the Bulgarians, and the Turks. Though a fresh effort had started in 1935, it had been unsuccessful. General Papagos had tried again quite recently, when the German menace began to appear in the Balkans. Greece needed Romania to balance Bulgaria, and Yugoslavia to block the route down through the Monastir Gap. Turkey was friendly, actually sending Greece anti-tank ammunition once war broke out. The basic difficulty was that each country faced several potential enemies and none had strong armed forces; consequently, they were unwilling to make commitments to support their neighbors.

Nevertheless, the conference decided that because the Monastir Gap was crucial to the whole defense of northern Greece, it was vital to know how the Yugoslavs stood. Papagos refused to move his last two divisions, the 19th and 20th, which were in truth only cobbled-together units from Macedonia and Thrace (where the Turks promised to hold the Bulgars in check), until he had assurance that the Yugoslavs would act favorably. So it was agreed that a mission would go to Belgrade, just across the Danube from major German forces, to try and persuade the Etonian-educated Regent, Prince Paul, to play the game or be called a cad. Dill was dispatched to Belgrade, while Eden went back to Cairo and then on to Ankara to try and persuade the Turks. Wavell went back to his headquarters to organize the dispatch of an expeditionary force not of nine divisions now, but only of three-and-a-half. The parties were to meet again in Athens on March 3.

While Dill duly made his way to Belgrade, one of Wavell's very small staff, Major Francis de Guingand, went up country to Larisa and from there flew up about Mount Olympus. He realized at once that this was not a country in which the motorized British Army of the day could operate easily. It was mountainous, had few roads and only a single-track railway from Athens to the north. Under the circumstances he knew evacuations would have to take place, and secretly later helped to prepare the invaluable plan for them.

During his visit to Ankara Eden made little headway with the Turks, in spite of quoting Persian poetry to them. Ankara had already sent a mission to Cairo; it had reported back that the British had nothing to spare, so the Turks kept their own counsel.

Much more important, however, was the fact that Belgrade's answer that the Yugoslavs would not defend the Monastir Gap was delivered to Eden by their ambassador in Ankara. Owing to poor staff work in the British party, this critical response was never forwarded to General Papagos. So he was absolutely correct when, on March 3, he told the reassembled meeting in Athens that he had not moved the 19th and 20th divisions because that action was not to have been taken until the Greeks knew the response from Belgrade. Papagos certainly did not deserve Dill's strictures.

In the course of the meeting in the British Legation, Dill grilled Papagos like a schoolmaster to get him to make up the 19th and 20th divisions to full strength. In the end Papagos said that he would do it, but he had no more men. And the two divisions which were hastily sent out on to the western end of the Aliakmon Line were untrained and far too thin on the ground to resist a German attack. Nor was there time for the Greek commander-in-chief to disengage troops on the Epirus front and march them by the necessarily zigzag routes across the mountains to the new position.

In the meantime, while the conference of March 3-4 was already in progress, Wavell's staff had begun to organize the first sea lifts of troops to Greece. In this they were aided by a certain confusion caused by the passage through Cairo of Prime Minister Robert Menzies of Australia. He had agreed to the use of Australian troops without their commander, General Thomas Blamey, having been, in the latter's view, properly consulted.

Blamey was later unhappy not only over this, but also over his belief that the Australians had been promised there would be fourteen to twenty RAF squadrons in Greece. The ghosts of the Dardanelles in 1915 and of Chanak in 1921 hovered in the background.

Given his needs for shipping to resupply the Western Desert Force, Wavell did not have a surplus of vessels at his disposal. And the German mining of the Suez Canal by air from Rhodes had blocked that vital waterway. Nevertheless, the C-in-C Middle East had decided to send troops to Greece even though, or because, his intelligence told him that as soon as the snows melted in the Bulgarian passes, the Germans would push through them to Athens, where it was expected that they would arrive on March 22. With the twenty to forty ships he had available, Wavell began to transport forces and vehicles to Greece.

Wavell also knew that the German embassy in Athens was open and that any arrival of British troops would be signaled to Berlin. He was quite correct. The German military attaché met the ships at the docks in Piraeus and walked amongst their tents on Mount Hymettus once they had arrived.

In the meantime, London had been appalled to get Eden's account of the agreement that he had made in Athens. But the two chiefs of staff in Whitehall—the First Sea Lord and the Chief of the Air Staff—took the view that Eden must have been advised by Dill. As he was their colleague on the spot, they deferred to his judgement, feeling that he knew things they did not. However, they might have been suspicious when it took them so long to get Wavell's shipping schedule, which showed that three-and-a-half divisions would not be fully in Greece until mid-May. Menzies, the Australian, attended the War Cabinet meetings and was the only one who raised objections to the way in which Churchill, who ruled the War Cabinet and the Chiefs of Staff, pushed through the affair.

In the meantime Wavell had chosen as the commander of Operation Lustre the Military Governor of Cyrenaica, the solid, reliable Sir Henry Maitland "Jumbo" Wilson, who arrived in Athens in mufti as "Mr. Watt." He stayed in the Legation while his headquarters was established at the Hotel Acropole opposite the National Museum. Given his secret plans for Lustre, Wavell wanted a reliable commander who would obey orders, while at the same time he freed the brilliant General Richard O'Connor of Wilson's oppressive hand for the further campaign in the Western Desert. Unfortunately, O'Connor was captured when Rommel sprang his surprise.

So as Eden left the Middle East and went home, British troops sailed for Greece, debarked in Piraeus, and slowly began the road and rail journey north to the Aliakmon Line. There they began to dig in wearing their gasmasks. On March 16, P/O's Silver and Green, cypher officers, arrived from the Code and Cypher School at Bletchley Park in Britain and were logged in at British Air Forces Greece HQ in the Marasleon School.

On March 25-27 there was a coup in Belgrade with the military seizing power. Shortly thereafter, King Peter and his Regent Prince Paul arrived in Athens, were seen by King George, and sent on to the Middle East. Meanwhile, a last minute Yugoslav attempt to co-ordinate plans was hopelessly late. The Germans had built bridges across the Danube and were moving into Bulgaria. On the Albanian Front the Greeks with RAF support were desperately trying to push the Italians further back into Albania and bring about a victorious conclusion to that struggle. But winter weather had been cruel and thick snow still blanketed the area. Snow, too, was still in the Bulgarian passes well after Wavell had believed that the Germans would be in Athens. In the meantime, convoys continued to deliver British troops and weapons to Piraeus and they continued to dribble north.

The suspense was finally broken on Sunday, April 6, 1941 by the Germans breaking through the Ruppel Pass and debauching onto the plains north of Thessalonike. There they made brief contact with forward British armored cars. London had already been alerted by signals from Major Reid's special reconnaissance group fifteen minutes before the German *chargé d'affaires* notified the Greek Foreign Ministry that the Germans were invading.

In the next twenty days the British and Greeks on the eastern side of the Hellenic peninsula withdrew and all who could be evacuated had left Greece by the 26th, leaving behind some 10,000, out of the roughly 63,000 British troops landed, as prisoners of war.

In many respects, as the official histories and other documents show, this was never a serious campaign. The fact is that the records clearly reveal that there were brief clashes between small units. From these the parties involved generally skillfully withdrew over the hill, jumped in their trucks and sped south to the next blocking point. Others marched back from near Florina around through Trikala and thence to the Thermopylae Line, which was only held for a short while, evacuation having already begun. By this time the Greek troops to the northwest were already laying down their arms.

The high Greek and British commanders met at Livadia in the wake of the suicide of the Greek Premier on the morning of April 18th. It was decided that there was no hope of creating a Fortress Greece, as the Greek army could not withdraw in time to pull within the bastion; there were neither the airfields nor the RAF and troop reinforcements to hold it, nor were there the ships to bring in the necessary rations to support both the military and the civilian population. On April 23rd, therefore, the Greek government moved to Crete and General Papagos resigned his command.

The British maintained that they had gone to Greece for the highest of moral reasons (not as originally argued because there was a chance of military success), but King George had supported Papagos' view that for them to remain and for the Greeks to fight would mean the devastation of the country.

Some of those evacuated from Greece went to Crete, most went to Egypt. General Bernard Freyberg, the commander of the New Zealand Division, who had been Blamey's deputy in Greece, was placed in command of Crete. A holder of the Victoria Cross from the First World War, he was a competent professional soldier who would remain in high command throughout the remainder of the war.

Freyberg had several problems. Most of the troops who had been evacuated from Greece had few but their personal weapons. There was a shortage of transport and artillery. The island's defenses had been neglected for the past six months when they might have been put in order. Very little had been done about the airfields, especially in the Mesara valley on the south side of the island, slightly less vulnerable than the three on the north side at Maleme, Heraklion, and Rethymnon, all of which were known to the *Luftwaffe* and liable to attack by fighters from both the mainland and Rhodes. Furthermore, though London had warned that the Germans were planning an airborne attack, the lessons of the campaign in the Low Countries and France had not yet been sent to Cairo by the War Office in London.

Freyberg was faced with inadequate resources, virtually no Cretan military support, few engineer stores, and very little time. ULTRA told him that the attack would be on or about May 20 as, owing to dry weather in Greece and the German ability to operate off of rough surfaces, airfields were easily made available by conscripted labor on the mainland.

While the German seaborne invasion attempt was beaten back by the Royal Navy, the latter suffered such losses in daylight that it soon had to be withdrawn. The burden of the attack was placed upon the German paratroopers and airlifted mountain troops, the burden of the defense upon the New Zealanders.

Lack of knowledge of airborne tactics hampered both the ground defense and the RAF. The latter were quickly forced to withdraw as aircraft on the ground were ruthlessly attacked from low level by strafing fighters, or bombed. The shortage of dispersal pens meant that aircraft quickly became casualties. And Crete was too far from the Western Desert for fighter patrols, even with jerry-rigged long-range fuel tanks, to be effective. Moreover, the Middle East was at this time extremely short of aircraft.

The New Zealand infantry suffered not only from lack of knowledge as to how to site airfield defenses and mopping up parties, but was also short of transport, so that it could not reach vital points in the desperate minutes after the Germans landed. The battle around Maleme especially was critical and might have been won if reinforcements could have arrived promptly on May 20. One reason they did not, of course, was the shortage of reliable signals equipment. At this stage of the war, vacuum tube sets were extremely vulnerable to vibration and jolting and most had collapsed in Greece early on.

The battle of Crete lasted but a few days. By the end of May, thanks to control of the sea, the defenders had been evacuated, leaving behind only the Cretan women and children who had rushed out to kill as many Germans as they could to save their homes.

General Wavell wrote his memoirs, but he died before they could be published and the family will not allow access to them. Thus it was not until my *Diary of a Disaster* in 1986 that the full story could be told from the official British records, which were opened in 1972, and the later Greek *White Paper,* compiled and released thanks to Melina Mercouri, then a Minister in the Greek government.

There are, of course, several elements of confusion in this story, which are covered in more detail in my *Diary of a Disaster,* recently translated into Greek by Major-General Konstantinos Kanakaris and published by the Hellenic Army Directorate of History in 1996. Aside from the confusion of grand strategies on the British side, in general compounded not only by lack of means but also lack of knowledge in London, there had not been a great deal of explanation in English for what happened, until the publication of John S. Koliopoulos' *Greece and the British Connection, 1935-1941* (1977) and his more recent appraisal of Metaxas' foreign policy in *The Metaxas Dictatorship* (1993).

Perhaps the least known side of the story has been that of Wavell's grand deception not of the Greeks nor of the Germans and Italians, but of Churchill. The Commander-in-Chief in the Middle East was a professional who had his own quiet way of not losing the war by following some of the former hussar's madcap wartime proposals for which there were inadequate forces.

Wavell and Metaxas both understood the odds. A number of lesser people did not. There were those in the Middle East forces who started off arguing that there was, as Dill also noted, a reasonable chance of success, when there simply was not. And in only a matter of six weeks the British position had changed from going to Greece's aid being a military gamble to being a moral obligation. In war as in life, however, hard decisions have to be made. Wavell gambled on the Bulgarian passes being open in early March. He lost. He took a chance that he could make a gesture without having to pay the price. He lost.

But Wavell had his eye on the grand strategy, which was to clear the Italians out of North Africa and reopen the Mediterranean, thus not only shortening the shipping routes but also relieving the siege of Malta.

If he had not sent troops to Greece, he might have fortified Crete, or at least made it defensible, and have launched a successful attack on the Dodecanese so as to get the Italians out of that flanking position. And if Wavell, the master of deception and making the most of limited resources, had not had to dispatch forces to Greece, Rommel in the Western Desert would have been a different story.

If only the Italians had remained the enemy and if Wavell had had the shipping, he might have been able to send enough Italian metric arms from the campaigns in East Africa and the desert to help the Greek army in Albania.

But in all of the first half of 1941, time was a vital commodity and shipping was terribly slow. Timing was also vital. Metaxas well understood that, as did Papagos. Koryzis and Palairet did not. Once the Germans invaded, there was not the time nor were there the forces to create a Greek redoubt. So as Metaxas had pointed out—and Papagos later argued—the way to save Greece had to be to capitulate to the Germans.

Crete might have been held if it had had a single-minded commander at least from early December 1940; if the Cretan division could have been retained; if sufficient forces, vehicles, guns, airfields, and fighters could have been established before May 1941, and if the lessons of the campaign in France had been available.

Ultimately British aid to Greece was a case of not matching ends to means, the first duty of a statesman and his military advisers. In the end, it was a series of small Greek tragedies—from the death of Metaxas onwards—which culminated in the loss of Greece and Crete and in the occupation. The elements of confusion were there on both the Greek and the British sides in those long, muddled six months. ✦

Further Reading:

This chapter is based on my book *Diary of a Disaster: British Aid to Greece, 1940-1941*, Lexington KY: University of Kentucky (1986), which contains an essay on sources, and on the chapters in Higham and Thanos Veremis, *The Metaxas Dictatorship: Aspects of Greece, 1936-40*, Athens: ELIAMEP-Vryonis Center (1993), and Hellenic Army General Staff, Army History Directorate, *An Abridged History of the Greek-Italian and Greek-German War, 1940-1941* (Athens: Army History Directorate Editions, 1997).

More recent works on the British generals involved are Harold E. Raugh, Jr., *Wavell in the Middle East, 1939-1941: A Study in Generalship,* London: Brassey's (1991); Paul Freyberg, *Bernard Freyberg, VC: Soldier of Two Nations,* London: Hodder and Stoughton (1991), and Antony Beevor, *Crete: The Battle and the Resistance,* London: John Murray (1991). See also Higham, *The Bases of Air Strategy,* Shrewsbury, UK: Air Life (1998) and "The Ploesti Ploy: British Considerations and the Idea of Bombing the Roumanian Oilfields, 1940-41," in *War & Society V* (September 1987), pp. 57-71.

On Italian tanks and the economy refer to John J.T. Sweet, *Iron Arm: The Mechanization of Mussolini's Army, 1920-1940,* Westport, CT: Greenwood Press (1980).

See also John S. Koliopoulos, *Greece and the British Connection, 1935-1941,* and "Metaxas and Greek Foreign Relations, 1936-1941" in *The Metaxas Dictatorship.*

I have been fortunate that on two of my visits to Greece Major-General Konstantinos Kanakaris showed me all the places where the British had been, as well as aspects of Greek culture, for which I am very grateful to the Hellenic Army Directorate of History. In addition, for another project as well as during official visits in 1991, I have been able to see a great deal of Crete.

In the course of the 1991 congress, I met Colonel C.M. Woodhouse. Monty told us at breakfast one day of how, on the morning of May 20, he had taken a brown envelope with a signal in it to Freyberg, who read it and stuffed it in his pocket, then invited Lt. Woodhouse to breakfast. When at 0900 the first German planes appeared, Freyberg remarked that they were right on time. Woodhouse assumed that he had taken the general ULTRA. However, this could not have been since there was a specially assigned captain who handled such signals and saw that they were burnt after reading. Moreover, the ULTRA records show that Cairo was not forwarding ULTRA to Freyberg once the Germans attacked as they were not sure of his security. (ULTRA in DEF 3/686 set in Hale Library, Kansas State University, Manhattan.)

The Role of the Greek Merchant Marine in World War II

Matheos D. Los

We were left alone *on the ocean, with only the sky and the sea for company. The darkness was still deep and the weather somewhat mild despite the south wind that was blowing....Suddenly, after about an hour, we heard the sound of engines and almost immediately we saw the black mass of the submarine emerging in front of us again. When it neared, a machine gun started firing at us. The bullets fell like hail into the sea and onto our raft. For a moment the shooting stopped and the submarine shone a small spotlight to verify that its heinous crime had been completed. The Germans, apparently realizing that the two of us who had remained on the raft had not been killed, threw hand grenades. One of them exploded on the right side of the raft very close to me, causing several large wounds on my shoulder. In spite of the terrible pains I continued to play dead. At the same time the submarine shone the spotlight on the raft again and because they didn't see any movement, it seems they presumed me dead. Then the sound of the engines started again and I saw the submarine moving away. In a little while, however, I heard its guns again. It had closed in on my unfortunate companions, who were desperately swimming in the water or clinging on to floating wreckage, speechless. At first the firing of the machine gun was continuous, then it became more sporadic. Clearly, having shot all those who were grouped around the wreckage, they were searching for others who were isolated, and shot them too. The massacre lasted all night and when dawn started to break, the shooting stopped. The submarine submerged after making sure it had completed the slaughter.*

This is the eyewitness report of Anthony Liosis, chief mate of the Greek cargo ship *Peleus* which was torpedoed by a German submarine on the night of March 13, 1944 in the Atlantic, six hundred miles from the coast of Africa. After sinking the cargo ship, the captain of the submarine thought it wise to wipe out the survivors of the torpedoing, so that his own position could not be traced.

MATHEOS D. LOS is General Manager of Vrontados S.A. in Piraeus and Secretary General of the Union of Greek Shipowners.

That and innumerable other cases make up the drama of the sacrifice of Greek merchant shipping during the Second World War. A drama with the oceans of the world as its stage, and with two protagonists with entirely different roles and methods as the leading players. On one side was the war machine of Nazi Germany, armed with the most modern lethal weapons of the time. Dominant here were the infamous U-boats, whose mission was to close the sea-lanes used by the Allies for their supplies. On the other side was the Allied merchant fleet, with vessels of five to ten thousand tons, mostly steamships, with speeds rarely exceeding ten knots, entirely unprotected and manned by unarmed seafarers. The fleet's only protection was the alertness and seamanship of its crews, since at least during the early years of the war, the Allied convoy escorts were unable to protect the merchant ships effectively.

The field of action of both protagonists in the drama was mainly the Atlantic Ocean. It was in that arena, throughout the war, that the fight until death known in history as the Battle of the Atlantic was carried out. In the early years of the war, chasing Allied merchant ships seemed a simple task for the Germans, who called the period from the outbreak of war up to March 1941, "happy time." And not without reason. Up to then the total lack of organization and protection of the convoys, as well as information leaks (emanating from the Swiss co-insurers of the cargoes in Zurich) about departures of ships from America, greatly assisted the destructive task of the U-boats.

Later, things changed. The Allies realized that the merchant fleet was the "fourth arm" of their war effort, and they gave top priority to the protection of their convoys. The objective was to keep up the flow of transports to the fronts at all costs—the Western front in Europe with convoys from North America to the British Isles, and the Eastern front with similar convoys headed for the Soviet port of Murmansk on the Arctic Ocean. The North Africa front was served through Gibraltar and Malta and the Southeast Asia front through Suez or round the Cape to India. Finally, the theaters of operations in the Pacific were served from the U.S. West Coast and from Australia.

The vital contribution of escort vessels by the Americans, who had become actively engaged in the war after Pearl Harbor, the development of radar and sonar technologies, and the breaking of the famous Enigma communications code of the German submarines, changed the rules of the game to such an extent that, by the end of the war, of the 820 U-boats that the Third Reich had in its service, only 102 were left; of the 39,000 men who manned them, only 7,000 survived.

At the same time the Americans flooded the oceans with the famous Liberty ships, those homely but wonderful mass-produced 7,200-ton cargo ships that were turned out at a sufficiently rapid rate to counterbalance the losses of ships sunk by the German U-boats. The Liberty ships, 2,742 of them in all, carried 100 million tons of war materiel during the war. And when the war ended, one hundred Liberties were made available through the mediation of the American government to Greek shipowners who had lost their fleets during the war. Those ships, which our shipping community called the "blessed Liberties," together with hundreds of others acquired later in the free market, made up the nucleus of the post-war Greek merchant marine, which today rules the seas of the world with a fleet of 3,200 vessels of all types and a total capacity of 75 million tons.

For the battle of the oceans in World War II, the Greek shipping industry marshaled more than six hundred ships totaling 1.8 million grt[1]—the ninth largest fleet in the world after those of the United Kingdom, the United States, Japan, Norway and other traditional maritime nations.[2] If we add Greek-owned vessels under the flags of the United Kingdom and of Panama, the Greek fleet was certainly close to 750 vessels and 2.4 million tons, manned with 20,000 seafarers.

Almost all of the Greek merchant fleet consisted of elderly cargo ships, with new construction representing just a few exceptions; average cargo capacity was not over 10,000 tons per ship. At this point it should be emphasized that, in the category of oceangoing cargo ships of over 2,500 tons (the most suitable type to participate in the Allied convoys), Greece in 1937 held second place in the world, with over 1.5 million tons, behind the U.K., which had 3.8 million tons.[3] All those ships took part in the Battle of the Atlantic, while some were also found in the theaters of the Pacific and Indian Oceans. The smaller tonnage ships were used exclusively on the coastal transportation routes of North Africa, while those that had the misfortune to be blockaded in Greece by the German invasion were seized and used by the invaders.

The majority of oceangoing ships managed by Greek shipowners in the pre-war period were over-age steamships.[4] Because of their low speed in

1. All vessel capacities in the text and statistics of this book are in grt (gross register tons). The term corresponds to the total capacity of the ship, which includes the volume of all closed spaces (cargo and ballast holds, machinery, crew accommodation, storage spaces, etc.).
2. See table 1, page 80.
3. See table 2, page 81.
4. According to *Lloyd's Register of Shipping* statistics, in June 1939, seventy-eight percent of the Greek merchant fleet consisted of vessels over twenty years old, sixteen percent between ten and twenty years and just six percent of the ships were less than ten years of age. The same statistics reveal that Greece was classed last among the traditional maritime nations in terms of fleet age profile.

comparison with the more modern Allied merchant ships, the Greek vessels were often left alone behind the convoys, easy prey for the wolves of the ocean, which were waiting to strike. It is noteworthy that the speed of the convoys was set at about eight knots, and that convoy ships were forbidden to delay to search for and rescue men of other convoy vessels that were attacked and shipwrecked.

In addition to the danger of being sunk by submarines, there was the danger from air raids, mines, and Axis raider ships camouflaged as innocent cargo ships. Add to all of these the usual dangers of the sea which Greek seamen faced: the natural elements, mechanical failures (the latter were not unusual occurrences for the over-age ships of the fleet), and the poor navigational aids of that time, which were especially dangerous in unfavorable weather conditions.

Undoubtedly the deck was stacked against the Greek ships and their crews; unarmed and in full knowledge of the dangers they faced, they were the prey of heavily armed and usually invisible Nazi hunters. As for those ships that succeeded in carrying out their missions without being hit by enemy torpedoes, there was always the next mission, to be fought under the same conditions and with the same limited means. When their vessels were sunk by the enemy, those seamen who were fortunate were picked up in time by Allied or even enemy ships, assuming they had not gone down with their ship to its gravesite. Those unfortunate enough to be cast adrift faced an endless ocean and certain death from cold, thirst, and starvation.

When war was declared in 1939 Greece remained neutral. Greek shipping, however, had promised in 1938 to stand at the side of the Allies with ships: either time-chartered directly to the British government or chartered on the free market, but always at the service of the Allies or neutral countries, mainly Switzerland. Thus when Greece entered the war in October 1940, its shipping industry was already in the front line of battle and had already lost eighty ships and three hundred Greek seamen through acts of war.

Upon entering the war the Greek government commandeered the entire Greek merchant fleet and chartered it to the British government for the needs of the Allies. The agreement, known as the Anglo-Hellenic Agreement, was signed under most unfavorable wartime terms for the Greek shipowners, with charter rates barely covering the operating costs of the ships and leaving only minuscule, if any, profit. Furthermore, the wholesale time-chartering of the Greek-flag ships to the British resulted in the loss by Greek interests of their corresponding business and administrative functions.

Meanwhile back home, when war broke out on the northern borders of Greece, the Union of Greek Shipowners (UGS) and the Hellenic Chamber of Shipping jointly launched a fundraising drive among the shipowners and seafarers in order to support the war effort. It produced impressive results. Just a few weeks after the declaration of the Greek-Italian war more than $800,000 was collected, a substantial amount for that time. Later, when the Germans invaded in 1941, the UGS burned all relevant documents so as to prevent the invaders from learning the ownership details of Greek ships. During the German occupation the UGS vigorously avoided cooperating with the occupiers, refusing to divulge details about the shipowning interests of its members, whose ships were fighting their own battles at sea all over the world.

In occupied Greece the resistance from Greek seafarers who were forced to man the transports of the Germans in the Greek archipelago swelled. Greek seamen were sending information to the Allies and sabotaging the merchant ships which had been forced into service by the Germans. The number of Greek seafarers who lost their lives during raids by Allied planes on occupied Greece was not insignificant.

While Greece was paying its blood tribute to the Allied war effort, other countries were enjoying the guilty silence of ostensible neutrality, and cooperating with the Axis forces for the sake of their economic interests. Which countries should one point the finger at first? General Franco's Spain, which in addition to ideological support, provided the Nazis with the manganese ore they needed for the manufacture of large and small gun barrels? Portugal, which supplied tungsten for the German aircraft industry? Sweden, which supplied iron ore? Rumania, which supplied oil? Or Brazil, which provided diamonds for the machine tools of Germany's war industry? These were the raw materials that Hitler's war effort depended on. They were purchased through the kind intervention of the Swiss, who aside from their own exports of high quality arms to the Third Reich, facilitated the international financial dealings of the Germans.

Last we should consider the case of Turkey, which in addition to its mass exports of chromium (a raw material for ball bearings and shell cases), violated its neutrality by sending back to the German occupiers—and to certain death—any Greek patriot who, hoping to reach the free Middle East, escaped by boat or even by swimming to Turkey and fell into the hands of Turkish border guards. Toward the end of the war, realizing that the scales of victory had begun to tilt to the side of the Allies, Turkey decided to enter the war on the Allied side. Since then that nation has been elevated to a highly privileged position among the Western allies and enjoyed all the benefits of German friendship and the Nixon-Kissinger policy known as "Tilt to Turkey."

But Greece and its merchant fleet were loyal to the Allied fight from the very beginning to the very end. The price paid for their loyalty to the Allies and to their common values and ideology was high indeed. Two thousand seamen lost their lives, dragged to the depths of the oceans. As many again were wounded and disabled, thus ending their careers at sea.[5] Finally, one hundred and fifty crewmen developed severe psychological problems as a result of the horrors they had witnessed or the deprivations they suffered while shipwrecked in the ocean. In all more than twenty percent of the Greek seafaring labor force was taken out of action, a percentage higher than the fifteen percent of the seamen of the entire British Commonwealth.

As for ship losses, the numbers speak for themselves. At the end of the war, in terms of the number of ships and tonnage, there was just a quarter of the prewar fleet left.[6] The overwhelming majority of ships lost were sunk by torpedoes from submarines and by air raid attacks. Not a few were sunk by mines both during and after the end of the war and by enemy battleships and raiding ships.[7]

There were also normal losses from accidents at sea not directly linked to the conditions of war. Because of the war, the Allied merchant fleet and the neutral countries which were serving it lost a total of 4,770 ships, totaling twenty-one million tons.[8] Greek shipping's share of these losses came to ten percent of the number of ships and almost seven percent of the tonnage. This was an unprecedented financial disaster for Greek shipowners, many of whom saw their fleets wiped out completely during the war. As if this were not enough, Greek shipowners risked losing their meager profits from the war and, most importantly, their insurance compensation for the decimation of their fleet, monies which were tied up in British banks for years after the war ended.

Having commandeered the Greek merchant fleet at the outset of the war, the Greek state considered it wise to continue playing the role of shipowner even after the war ended, and tried to appropriate the owners' compensations. The solution to this problem was finally provided by the British courts, which handed down a decision particularly humbling to the

5. See table 3, page 82.
6. See table 4, page 83.
7. See table 5, pages 84.
8. See table 6, page 86.

German aircraft over Acropolis.

The struggle goes on at the Bulgarian Front, 1941.

(D.A. Harissiades/Photographic Archive of the Benaki Museum)

At the banks of Devolis, 1941.

(D.A. Harissiades/Photographic Archive of the Benaki Museum)

Planes Wrecked on Italo-Greek Front. Greek troops entering Koritza, a big Italian military base in Albania, said they found these wrecked Italian military planes at the airport. Koritza fell to the Greeks in November. January 3, 1941.

(AP/Wide World photos)

Italian Prisoners line up for "chow." Guarded by Greek soldiers, Italian prisoners wait in line for food at their barracks in Athens. Each man in line has his tin dish ready. January 7, 1941.

(AP/Wide World photos)

Greeks play with captured weapons. Greek soldiers amuse themselves with weapons and helmets captured from the Italians on the Albanian fighting front. February 8, 1941. (AP/Wide World photos)

Italians reach Athens as captives. Columns of Italians, captured by the Greek Army on the Albanian fighting front, march through an Athens street. February 8, 1941. (AP/Wide World photos)

German soldiers on the Acropolis in Athens. April 29, 1941.

(AP/Wide World photos)

Victory parade in Athens. Victorious German troops paraded past Field Marshal General List in Athens. The photograph shows the units of armored cars passing Field Marshal General List. May 3, 1941. (AP/Wide World photos)

German Troop Carrier Down in Flames. A German troop-carrying plane that took part in the invasion of the island of Crete falls in flames to the ground near Candia, after being struck by shells from a British anti-aircraft gun. June 23, 1941.

(AP/Wide World photos)

Liberation of Athens. October 12, 1944.

(Voula Papaioannou/Photographic Archive of the Benaki Museum)

210 Jewish children (Greek citizens) whose parents were killed by the Germans were collected throughout Greece and sent to families in Palestine which were going to adopt them. The work was done by UNRRA which provided transport, the Joint Distribution Committee and the Greek Jewish Agency. The photograph was taken in Piraeus, Greece by Voula Papaioannou prior to August 1, 1946.

(Voula Papaioannou/Photographic Archive of the Benaki Museum)

Greek government.[9] The shipowners did not lose their funds, but because of currency restrictions, the monies continued to be tied up for years in British banks, a factor that put a brake on the post-war development of Greek shipping.

In addition to the serious financial problems mentioned previously, shipowners had to deal with problems involving some of their crews. An essentially non-existent Greek state and the exclusion of Greek shipowners by the Anglo-Hellenic Agreement from the management of their own vessels during the war gave an opportunity to a small number of unionists, who were instigated by the communists, to spread anarchy among crews by calling for excessive pay demands.

In brief, the contributions of Greek shipowners and seamen to the Allied cause in the Second World War is not well enough known. As we have seen, their loyalty to the Allies and to their values and ideology was not circumstantial. Greek shipping has proved over and over again that it is always ready to offer its services for the good of the nation and humankind, whenever the need arises. It proved this recently during the Gulf War of 1991, when of the one hundred and twelve merchant vessels chartered for the United Nations intervention in Kuwait by the Americans, more than half were vessels controlled by Greek interests. During the same period Greek shipowners, in solidly respecting the United-Nations-sponsored trade boycott of Iraq, gave the world their own lesson in trade ethics.

In conclusion, what was the fate of Captain Anthony Liosis? He and his two companions, after undergoing the frightful experience of thirty-six days and nights on a raft with the bare minimum of water and food, were finally rescued by a passing ship.

It was God's will that Captain Liosis was saved and was able later to testify at a war crimes trial in Hamburg. Just as it was God's will that in the dock at the same trial was the captain of the submarine U-852, Heinz Wilhelm Eick. Captain Eick was sentenced to death along with two other officers of the submarine because after sinking the Peleus "they deliberately murdered the survivors of the vessel by machine gun and hand grenades, contrary to the law of war." As for the rest of the heroic crew of the *Peleus* and the two thousand other Greek heroes of the seas who were lost during the years of World War II, they remain in the memories of their loved ones; the stars at night shine on their watery graves at sea; no material honors, no medals, only silence—the fate of true heroes. ✦

9. We refer here to the case of shipowner A. Vergotis, where the Greek government not only suffered a major legal defeat, but was also humiliated in court by the British judge.

Appendix: Statistical Tables

TABLE 1:
THE MERCHANT FLEETS OF THE MAJOR MARITIME NATIONS ON THE EVE OF WORLD WAR II (JUNE 1939).

Nation	Number of Ships	%	Total Tonnage (in grt)	%
1. UNITED KINGDOM	6,722	22.6	17,891,134	26.1
2. USA	2,853	9.6	11,361,533	16.6
3. JAPAN	2,337	7.9	5,629,845	8.2
4. NORWAY	1,987	6.7	4,833,813	7.1
5. GERMANY	2,459	8.3	4,482,662	6.6
6. ITALY	1,227	4.1	3,424,804	5.0
7. NETHERLANDS	1,523	5.1	2,969,578	4.3
8. FRANCE	1,231	4.1	2,933,933	4.3
9. GREECE	**607**	**2.0**	**1,780,666**	**2.6**
10. SWEDEN	1,231	4.1	1,577,120	2.3
11. USSR	699	2.3	1,305,959	1.9
12. CANADA	792	2.7	1,223,961	1.8
13. DENMARK	705	2.4	1,174,944	1.7
14. SPAIN	777	2.6	902,251	1.3
15. PANAMA	159	0.5	717,525	1.0
16. FINLAND	402	1.4	590,254	0.9
17. BRAZIL	293	1.0	484,870	0.7
18. BELGIUM	200	0.7	408,418	0.6
19. YUGOSLAVIA	187	0.6	410,486	0.6
20. ARGENTINA	295	1.0	290,602	0.4
21. OTHER NATIONS	3,077	10.3	4,115,074	6.0
WORLD TOTAL	**29,763**	**100.0**	**68,509,432**	**100.0**

Notes:

- Ships of less than 100 grt are not included.
- Sailing ships and non-propelled craft are not included.

Source: Lloyd's Register of Shipping, Statistical Tables.

TABLE 2:
THE MAJOR FLEETS OF OCEAN TRAMP SHIPS OF ABOVE 2,500 GRT IN 1937.

Nation	**Total Ocean Tramp Tonnage (in grt)**	**Percentage of Ocean Tramp Tonnage in Total National Merchant Fleet**
1. U.K.	3,826,000	19%
2. GREECE	**1,583,000**	**86%**
3. JAPAN	1,100,000	25%
4. NORWAY	800,000	19%
5. ITALY	660,000	21%
6. GERMANY	480,000	13%
7. SWEDEN	225,000	16%
8. SPAIN	220,000	23%
9. NETHERLANDS	180,000	7%
10. DENMARK	150,000	14%
11. FRANCE	134,000	4%
12. OTHER NATIONS	474,000	
TOTAL	***9,832,000***	

Notes:

- Ocean or deep-sea tramp: any vessel with a tonnage of 2,500 grt or above which, in the long run, does not have a fixed itinerary and which carries mainly dry cargoes in bulk over relatively long distances and from one or more ports to one or more ports. (Source: B.N. Metaxas, *The Economics of Tramp Shipping*, London: Athlone Press, 1971, p.6).
- The above statistics were compiled by the Tramp Administrative Committee in view of the establishment of the Minimum Freight Rate Scheme of the River Plate. The Scheme was introduced from March 1935 through the day following the eruption of World War II (9/4/1939). Its main objective was to confront the great dry cargo market depression of the 30′s by imposing a minimum freight rate level for grain cargoes out of the River Plate in South America, the main loading area of ocean tramps of those days. The Scheme was conceived and promoted by the Greek Shipping community. It was originally backed by the British and, later on, by the Norwegians, the Dutch, the French and the Italians. Although the figures refer to the year 1937, they are extremely useful in our research, being (as estimated) very close to pre-war figures.

Source: Tramp Shipping Administrative Committee, Epitheorissis Emporikou Naftikou 1938, p.1019.

TABLE 3:
LOSSES OF SEAMEN SERVING ON BOARD MERCHANT SHIPS
DURING WORLD WAR II

Nation	**Seamen Lost**	**%**
1. UNITED KINGDOM and others	31,908	55.6
2. USA	5,662	9.9
3. NORWAY	4,795	8.4
4. GREECE	**2,000**	**3.5**
5. NETHERLANDS	1,914	3.3
6. DENMARK	1,886	3.3
7. CANADA	1,437	2.5
8. BELGIUM	893	1.6
9. SOUTH AFRICA	182	0.3
10. AUSTRALIA	109	0.2
11. NEW ZEALAND	72	0.1
12. NEUTRAL COUNTRIES	6,500	11.3
TOTAL	***57,358***	***100%***

Notes:

- The total number of Greek seamen lost during the Second World War is the lowest estimate. The percentage of those lost in comparison to the total active Greek seafaring work force before the War is at least 15 percent. The same percentage applies for the United Kingdom.
- United Kingdom's seamen include Lascars, Chinese, Arabs and other miscellaneous nationalities, such as those from British colonies and those from Europe serving on British-flag merchant ships.

Sources: "Naftika Chronika," 1/15/1966, p. xvii.
Slader J. The Fourth Service-Merchantmen at War 1939-1945, p.320.

TABLE 4:
THE GREEK MERCHANT FLEET BEFORE AND AFTER WORLD WAR II (1939-1945)

	GREEK MERCHANT FLEET AT THE BEGINNING OF THE WAR		WARTIME LOSSES				REMAINS OF THE GREEK MERCHANT FLEET AT THE END OF THE WAR	
Types of Ships	**Total Ships**	**Total Tonnage (in grt)**	**Total Ships**	**%**	**Total Tonnage (in grt)**	**%**	**Total Ships**	**Total Tonnage (in grt)**
CARGO SHIPS	500	1,766,353	372	74.4	1,300,827	73.6	128	465,526
PASSENGER SHIPS	55	49,995	52	94.5	43,686	87.4	3	6,309
CRUISE LINERS	1	16,990	—	—	—	—	1	16,990
VARIOUS	21	3,977	7	33.3	2,009	50.5	14	1,968
SAILING SHIPS	712	55,160	551	77.4	52,634	95.4	161	2,526
TOTAL	**1,289**	**1,892,475**	**982**	**76.2**	**1,399,156**	**73.9**	**307**	**493,319**

Notes:

- Table 4 includes ships exclusively under Greek flag. Additionally, at the beginning of the war, the Greek-owned fleet comprised 124 cargo ships (454,318 grt) under British and Panamanian registry. Another 22 cargo ships were permanently operating in the coastal trades of China. Finally, an unspecified number and tonnage of riverships and tugboats were employed in the Danube.
- During the War, the Greek government purchased six cargo ships (39,335 grt). Another 15 (107,500 grt), of which 14 were Liberty ships, were ceded to Greece by the U.S. government for the nation's war requirements.

Source: "Naftika Chronika," 1/15/1966, p. iv, xii, xiii.

TABLE 5:
ANALYSIS OF GREEK FLAG MERCHANT SHIP LOSSES DURING WORLD WAR II.

A. Losses classed by cause of loss

Cause of Loss	Total Ships lost	Total lost (in grt)
Torpedoed and/or rammed by submarine	134	545,464
Sunk by aircraft	144	267,151
Sunk by mine	24	76,578
Sunk by raider ship	9	43,425
Sunk due to marine accident of unspecified direct or indirect pertinence to wartime conditions	32	114,836
Sunk by mine or torpedoed	1	7,247
Sunk by surface warship	1	440
Sunk by unspecified shell fire	1	194
Sunk as block-ship during Normandy Invasion	2	7,390
Sunk due to confirmed war cause but of unspecified nature	67	113,498
Sunk after the end of the war by mine or underwater explosion	12	18,450
Sold	25	92,876
Captured by enemy	45	123,062
Total	**497**	**1,410,611**

B. Losses classed by size of ship

Size of Ship	Total ships lost	Total tonnage lost (in grt)
Of 499 grt or less	75	18,435
Above 499 grt	384	1,392,176
Unspecified	38	–
Total	**497**	**1,410,611**

C. Losses classed by type of ship

Type of Ship	Total ships lost	Total tonnage lost (in grt)
Dry Cargo Ships and Tankers	370	1,315,147
Passenger Ships and Yachts	49	35,152
Hospital Ships	6	8,975
Tugs and Salvage Vessels	13	1,729
Unspecified	59	49,608
Total	**497**	**1,410,611**

D. Losses classed by time of loss

Time of Loss	Total ships lost	Total tonnage lost (in grt)
Lost prior to October 28. 1940	96	377,394
October 28, 1940–December 31, 1940	15	42,942
1941	212	454,449
1942	65	246,324
1943	25	99,530
1944	19	44,736
January 1, 1945–August 14, 1945	2	12,064
Lost after August 14, 1945	12	18,450
Lost at unspecified date	51	114,722
Total	**497**	**1,410,611**

Source: Haratsis. S.J. Hellenic Merchant Marine Losses During World War II. Athens: Hellenic Navy. Navy History Service. Naval History Section. 1992.

TABLE 6:
LOSSES OF ALLIED AND NEUTRAL COUNTRY MERCHANT FLEETS (1939–1945)

CAUSE OF LOSS	UNITED KINGDOM SHIPS	UNITED KINGDOM '000 grt	USA SHIPS	USA '000 grt	OTHER ALLIES SHIPS	OTHER ALLIES '000 grt	NEUTRAL COUNTRIES SHIPS	NEUTRAL COUNTRIES '000 grt	TOTAL SHIPS	TOTAL '000 grt
SUBMARINE ATTACK	1,360	7,620	440	2,740	670	3,260	300	930	2,770	14,550
MINE HIT	340	830	15	90	75	210	90	270	520	1,400
RAIDER SHIP ATTACK	210	970	13	90	87	460	20	50	330	1,570
AIRCRAFT ATTACK	440	1,590	58	360	202	770	50	110	750	2,830
OTHER ACTS OF WAR	220	370	12	30	138	330	30	60	400	790
TOTAL	*2,570*	*11,380*	*538*	*3,310*	*1,172*	*5,030*	*490*	*1,420*	*4,770*	*21,140*

Notes:

- In total. Allied and neutral country fleets lost 40 percent of their pre-war capacity by acts of war. The respective percentage of the United Kingdom is 54.19 percent and for the United States almost 35 percent. Nevertheless, those two countries had the capability to renew their war casualties during the war, whereas this was impossible for Greece and the other Allies.
- Vessels captured by or employed in the trades of the Axis are not included. However, Finnish, Hungarian, Italian and Japanese merchant ships lost before these countries entered the War are included. So are French ships before the occupation of France and merchant ships of free France not controlled by the Vichy Government.
- Losses from usual sea perils are not included. These are comprised of 610 British (1,200,000 grt), 251 Allied (710,000 grt) and 490 neutral (680,000 grt) ships.

Sources: "Naftika Chronika," 1/15/1957, p.141.
"Naftika Chronika," 1/15/1966, p. xii.

Bibliography

Antonopoulos, Costas, "And (Shipping) Follows Its Destiny 1939-1945." "Naftika Chronika," 1/15/66 (in Greek).

Babouris, Ep., *The Greek Merchant Marine During the Last War.* Athens: Hellenic Maritime Museum, 1949 (in Greek).

Batis, Efstathios, *The Battle of the Oceans-the Parallel Epic.* Athens: Pitsilos, 1993 (in Greek).

Batis, Efstathios, *Operation Burning Bush: The Unknown War in the Greek Archipelago.* Athens: Pitsilos, 1996 (in Greek).

Bourneuf, Gus Jr., *Workhorse of the Fleet: A History of the Design and Experiences of the Liberty Ships Built by American Shipbuilders During WW II.* Houston: American Bureau of Shipping, 1990.

Botting, Douglas, *The U-boats.* Amsterdam: Time-Life Books, 1981. *The Seafarers* Series.

Dounis, Christos E., *In Memoriam: Seamen and Ships Lost During the Second World War (1939-1945).* Athens: Pitsilos, 1997 (in Greek).

Foustanos, George M., *A 75-Year Voyage: The Chronicle of the Union of Greek Shipowners.* Piraeus: Union of Greek Shipowners, 1991 (in Greek).

Haratsis, S.J., *Hellenic Merchant Marine Losses During World War II.* Athens: Hellenic Navy. Navy History Service, Naval History Section, 1992.

Hellenic Ministry of Reconstruction, *The Sacrifice of Greece in the Second World War.* Athens, 1946.

Lloyd's Register of Shipping. Statistical Tables. London.

Los, Matheos D., *Ages of the Sea: A Brief History of the Greek Merchant Marine.* Athens: Akritas, 1988.

Los, Matheos D., *Post-War Greek Shipping: The Road to the Top.* Piraeus: Akritas, 1991.

"Naftika Chronika," "1931-1956: Twenty-Five Years of Spectacular Achievements," editorial. 1/15/95 (in Greek).

Slader, John, *The Fourth Service: Merchantmen at War 1939-1945.* London: Robert Hale, 1994.

Ziegler, Jean, *La Suisse, l'Or et les Morts.* Paris: Seuil, 1997.

The Costs of Resisting the Axis and America's Responses

The Costs to Greece of World War II and the Post-War American Reconstruction Program: Eight Voices

James C. Warren, Jr.

Just seven weeks before the dark night of Nazi occupation descended on Greece, there appeared one of those extraordinary documents which are destined to become a living part of history. I refer to the "Open Letter to Adolf Hitler," penned by George Vlachos, editor of the Athens newspaper *Kathimerini*. Here is his last paragraph:

What would your army do, Your Excellency, if instead of horses and artillery we sent to receive them on the frontier our twenty thousand wounded in their bloody bandages? But no, that cannot be. Small or great, that part of the Greek Army that can be sent will stand in Thrace as they have stood in Epirus. There they will await the return from Berlin of the Olympic Runner, who came five years ago to light the torch at Olympia. We shall see this torch light as a fire, a fire that will light this little nation, which has taught all other nations how to live, and which will now teach them how to die.

This open letter to Hitler summoned Greek courage for all to see. It was also a warning, to all who would listen, of the fearful costs of war to be paid by the Greek people. Through the voices of actual participants or witnesses, I shall sketch those costs:

1. famine and starvation,
2. the unraveling of the nation's social fabric,
3. reprisal-the Nazi response to the Resistance,
4. the Nazis' scorched earth policy, and
5. the Nazis' willful destruction of the national currency.

JAMES C. WARREN, JR., is Advisor to U.S. firms doing business in Greece.

Famine and Starvation

Here is the voice of the Athenian writer Petros Haris in his book, *Death of a City:*

During the day, starving people roamed the streets with unsteady steps. They were seeking out those who trafficked in bread and olive oil on the black market. And during the night, they had to listen to the fearful footsteps of the enemy patrolmen who-knowing how much they were hated-were always on the alert, finger on the trigger. The city had to listen to the cries of its starving people, to watch their slow death. Every day the city would have more dead to mourn.

Greece had never been self-sufficient in food, even in antiquity. Before the war, the typical pattern of food availability was an average daily per capita diet of 2,500 calories. This was based in large measure on domestic production of about 800,000 tons of wheat per year, and imports of wheat, which averaged 400,000 tons *per annum.* During World War II, Greek production of wheat fell to a low point of 375,000 tons, while imports were cut off for most of two years. The Germans, meanwhile, had expropriated both public and private stocks of food: wheat, olives, olive oil, figs, raisins, potatoes, and rice. Much of Greece literally starved to death; others were saved in the years 1943 and 1944 only by the Red Cross and the partial lifting of the British sea blockade.

The pre-war availability of 2,500 calories per person per day fell during the occupation to a low of 900 and never got above 1,400-and these are only statistical averages. The peacetime normal number of deaths in the city of Athens for the month of December had been 3,300; in December 1941 it was three and a half times that figure, more than 11,000. Four hundred and fifty thousand people perished of starvation in Greece during World War II.

The Unraveling of the Nation's Social Fabric

A by-product of famine and its partner, inflation, was the shredding of the nation's social structure. Under duress, a massive transfer of wealth took place. Here again is the voice of the writer Petros Haris:

It was during the second year of the war that the city began, like a lady of noble birth fallen on hard times, to take its silks and precious valuables out of the family chests and jewel boxes and send them off to the provinces in exchange for olive oil, flour and potatoes. And when there was no more jewelry to sell, then people would start disposing of their furniture and clothing.

The Transport Director for the Red Cross adds his voice to this assessment:

Although it has permitted villainous exploitation and the enrichment of persons of doubtful moral standards, the black market undoubtedly saved from certain death by starvation the greater part of the middle classes in the big urban center.

After the clothing, jewelry, and furniture there remained only apartments and houses to sell in order to buy bread to live. It has been estimated that, during the Nazi Occupation, 350,000 city properties changed hands at less than ten percent of their pre-war value, dumped on the market for food. The author George Theotokas, one of the great figures of twentieth-century Greek letters, observed: *"The new rich are adventurers who act as if in a jungle, and each grabs what he can."*

Reprisal—the Nazi Response to the Resistance

Quoted below is a radio message from a British officer in the Greek mountains, Colonel Arthur Edmonds, to his headquarters in Cairo:

Four April, Andartes ambushed two lorries Huns Kastoria-Amyntaion Road near Kleisoura, killing/wounding twenty-eight. Following day column twenty-seven Hun vehicles burnt all Kleisoura, killed four hundred villagers.

Here is a New Zealand voice, that of John Mulgan, an officer with the British Army who had been parachuted into the Greek mountains in September 1943. It was said of him by his commanding officer: "No one had so much success in persuading the ELAS guerillas to cooperate in his plans." Mulgan was credited with destroying twenty-five German trains. He writes:

As we worked through the summer of forty-four, the bill seemed to run higher. How many hanged hostages balance the enemy's loss of a wrecked locomotive? I remember, many times, the look on the faces of peasant women loading the family donkey with what they thought might be saved from the wrath to come.

What George Vlachos was telling the world in his "Open Letter," Mulgan reduces to its essence in one telling sentence: *The women did not ask us to stop sabotaging the railway line but requested, modestly, that if we did anything, it should be on a scale comparable to the reprisals that would surely follow.*

The Nazi's Scorched Earth Policy

A policy of devastation was carried out even as the Germans were retreating from Greece. Many have seen newsreel photos of the Germans dumping railway cars into the Corinth Canal. But consider the systematic destruction of ports and harbors—not just mining and booby-trapping, but the planned sinking of vessels in, and at the entrance to, every harbor, and the dynamiting of moles, silos, and cranes.

Then there was the fiendish machine of Teutonic invention that, attached to the caboose of a Nazi train fleeing north, systematically chewed bites out of the steel tracks.

War's end left Greece without a transportation and communications infrastructure.

The Nazis' Intentional Destruction of the National Currency

The corruption of the social fabric resulting from the contamination of the drachma, the national currency, had consequences that persisted for more than ten full years after the war's end, long after much of the physical damage had been repaired.

The Nazis simply used the printing press to pay their bills and the bills of the puppet government they installed in Athens. In October 1940 the price of bread was ten drachmas per *oka* (2.82 pounds) and that of olive oil, 50. When the Nazis pulled out in October 1944, the prices were, respectively, 34 million and 400 million drachmas.

One more pair of numbers: an early act of the Greek government, upon returning from exile, was currency reform. A new drachma replaced the old, inflated currency. The ratio between old and new? One new drachma was to be exchanged for 50 billion old drachmas.

Surveying the country in 1945 one would have had to calculate as follows.

Of habitations:

—2,000 villages burned or razed;
—400,000 dwellings, one out of four, destroyed or damaged.

Of livestock resources:

—2 million sheep slaughtered or requisitioned;
—2 million goats, likewise;
—30 percent of the stock of pigs and cattle lost;
—25 percent of the nation's draft animals butchered.

Of transport:

—80 percent of all locomotives destroyed;
—all railway bridges with a span of 10 meters or more destroyed;
—all motor bridges destroyed;
—one half of the motor-road mileage rendered unserviceable.

Greece was free of the Germans in 1945, but the country was crippled by the after-effects of their occupation.

Reconstruction, Civil War and Development

For the first two post-war years an exhausted Greece was kept afloat by British and United Nations subsidies, and by the running down of its own reserves of foreign exchange. However, political terror and personal vendetta had so polarized the nation and its political establishment that virtually nothing was done to repair the terrible damages wrought by the war and Nazi occupation. When the subsidies came to an end and the foreign exchange reserves had touched bottom, Greece was not only broke, it was paralyzed.

Into this crisis, in the early months of 1947, stepped the United States. The American program of reconstruction was launched immediately, and in the teeth of what had by then become a vicious civil war. The following voice is that of the BBC's (British Broadcasting Corporation) correspondent, Kenneth Matthews:

The Gorgopotamos Railway Bridge had been reduced to ruins by the Germans on their retreat. It seemed that so teasing a guerilla target would not be raised again for the duration of the civil war. But the Americans thought otherwise. They had come to restore communications, hadn't they? To put Greece literally as well as figuratively back on the rails, hadn't they? And, Jesus! They were not to be deterred by a few hoodlums!

Over the next seven years the Americans, with their culture of growth, broke forever the old zero-sum game that had hobbled Greece time out of mind. By 1949 most wartime damages had been repaired. By 1952 the Greek economy was actually operating at a level fifty percent greater than before the war. By 1953 the U.S. Currency Stabilization Program had returned to Greece a real national currency, a currency whose integrity had been stolen by the Nazis and whose place had been taken for more than ten years by the British gold sovereign. By 1954 major American aid was no longer needed.

The Greek Economic Miracle

The best part of the story comes at its conclusion, for in the succeeding dozen years the Greek economy—without foreign aid—took off. The country enjoyed a real economic growth rate matched only by Germany and Japan. In the collective voice of historians and economists, this period is described as *"the Greek economic miracle."* ✦

*The Rescue of the Jews of Volos**

Yolanda Avram Willis

Introduction

Not enough is known in the United States about Greece's "NO" to Mussolini's October 28, 1940 ultimatum of surrender. Even less is known about Greece's "NO" to Hitler's Final Solution.

From the moment of negotiating the armistice before her formal surrender in the spring of 1941, Greece's terms included the provision, never honored by the Nazis, that the occupation forces would not single out any Greek citizens on the basis of religion. Until the last German occupier left the country or surrendered to the Allied liberators, the Greek Orthodox Church, the national Resistance and countless private citizens assisted, defended, or hid Jews. The EAM-ELAS Resistance had a formal policy of protection and rescue and is rightfully credited with the survival of thousands of Jews. Several units of the more politically conservative EDES partisans also came to the assistance of hunted Jews.[1]

In addition, the Church of Greece and the intelligentsia openly protested the deportations of Jews. Damaskinos, Archbishop of Athens and All Greece, secretly issued 560 fictitious baptismal certificates and ordered churches and monasteries to shelter any Jew who knocked on their doors. After the war, the state of Israel honored the Organization of Cities' Police Departments, and in particular Athens Chief of Police Angelos Evert, for their clandestine production of thousands of false Christian identity cards, which were indispensable in the rescue of Jews.

YOLANDA AVRAM WILLIS, lecturer and writer. Dr. Willis speaks of righteous Greek rescuers of Jews from personal experience. During the Holocaust, her family was hidden by Greek Orthodox people in Crete and in several places in Athens. Prior to the German invasion, she lived in Larisa, where her father was the President of the Jewish Community.

1. EAM in Greek was an acronym for National Liberation Front, the political branch of the leftist resistance. ELAS (National People's Liberation Army) was the armed branch of EAM. Together they represented the largest and most effective resistance against the occupation forces. EDES is an acronym for National Republican Greek League.

Unlike the similarly high rates of loss in Eastern Europe, the tragic murder of 87 percent of Greece's Jews was neither the result of widespread anti-Semitic attitudes of the Christian population, nor of general collaboration with the Nazis in the capture of Jews.[2] One reason for the appalling losses was the very high concentration of Jews in the first community subject to deportations: German-occupied Thessalonike (Salonika) was home to over 70 percent of the Jews of Greece.[3] Beyond the scope of the present account are other complex factors which contributed to the destruction of 17 of the 25 pre-war, legally constituted Jewish communities, among the oldest Jewish settlements in Europe, dating back at least 2,300 years.[4]

The topic of this paper is the role of the city of Volos, located northeast of Athens in the province of Thessaly, in rescuing over 80 percent of its Jews. Volos is a particularly illuminating case of the seamless confluence of rescue efforts at many levels, including:

1. The excellent relations between the Greek Orthodox and Jewish religious leaders.
2. The quick response of the Jewish lay leadership.
3. The contributions of the civilian authorities.
4. The assistance of private citizens, both in the city and the surrounding villages.
5. The policy of Jewish protection by the EAM-ELAS national Resistance.

This account is written in non-fiction, short-story format, befitting the almost mythic rescue of the great majority of the Jews of Volos. It begins with the story of two Volos heroes, one Greek Orthodox, one Jewish, both men of the cloth. What these clergymen did during the Holocaust is the subject of legend and the substance of history.

Their contributions have been painstakingly gathered in a book by Raphael Frezis, President of the Jewish Community of Volos. My stories,

2. See Mark Mazower, *Inside Hitler's Greece: The Experience of Occupation, 1941-44* (New Haven and London: Yale University Press, 1993), pp. 235-261.
3. Statistics based on Joseph Nehama and Michael Molho, *In Memoriam,* Jewish Community of Thessalonike, 1974 (in Greek). Additional statistical information from Martin Gilbert's *Atlas of the Holocaust,* (William Morrow, 1993).
4. Since 1882 Greek laws have given official status to Jewish communities. In 1922 the requirement for official recognition became a minimum of twenty Jewish families. See Joshua Eli Plaut, *Greek Jewry in the Twentieth Century, 1913-1983* (Teaneck, NJ: Fairleigh Dickinson University Press, 1996), pp. 36-39. According to Greek custom, the names of these legal entities are capitalized, as in "the Jewish Community of Athens."

which follow, are enriched and enlivened by oral histories and less formal interviews with several eyewitnesses, both survivors and rescuers. Most of the details in my narrative, however, are based on the exhaustive and definitive original research presented in Mr. Frezis' book, augmented by documents and private communications, which I hereby gratefully acknowledge.[5]

Conspiracies of Goodness[6]

The city of Volos fans out inland from its extraordinary nearly circular bay. Over its harbor rises Mount Pelion, beautiful, verdant, and studded with tiny, red-tile roofed, whitewashed villages, summer havens famous for their crisp, pure air.[7]

The Germans took full command of Volos on September 12, 1943, four days after the Italians left. Soon after, they arrested and executed on the spot eighteen Christian Voliotes, and thus established a reign of terror.

On Thursday, September 30, 1943, Chief Rabbi of Volos Moses Simon Pesach was summoned by the German *Kommandant,* who had ordered Mayor Nicholas Saratsis to send two men to bring Pesach to the *Kommandatura,* the German headquarters. Pesach told them that he was officiating at High Holy Day services. It was the first day of Rosh Hashana, the Jewish New Year. He said that he was forbidden to conduct secular business. The men had strict orders to escort the rabbi immediately and by force if necessary. The rabbi persuaded the two emissaries to leave. It was not dignified nor commensurate with his position to arrive at headquarters under guard, Pesach argued. He would go to see the *Kommandant* on his own, after he arranged to be replaced at the synagogue.

As soon as the two messengers left, the rabbi headed for City Hall. The mayor was away. The rabbi decided to wait, even though he was late for the *Kommandatura.* Finally, the mayor returned. He did not know the reason for the summons, but advised Pesach to go see the *Kommandant.*

---

5. Raphael Frezis, *The Jewish Community of Volos,* (in Greek) (Volos: Hores Publishers, 1994). Other input from several issues of *Chronika,* published by KIS, the Central Board of Jewish Communities.
6. See Frezis. Interview with Mrs. Geoula Sabethai Frances, Larisa, April 1994. Interview with Dr. Dimitris Tsilividis, Volos, October 1996. Dr. Tsilividis had received a detailed account of this incident in a letter from his wife's uncle, Metropolitan Ioakeim.
7. My family used to spend the summer months in the village of Portaria on Mt. Pelion. I brought my first baby there in 1961, when I returned for the first time since 1940, the last summer of peace.

When Pesach showed up at the *Kommandatura,* he was decked out in his most impressive clerical vestments. In his tall, black velvet clerical hat and silver beard, Pesach was an elder of great presence. On his chest, in addition to the Star of David hanging from its heavy chain, was the coveted award, the Gold Phoenix Cross.

Kommandant Kurt Rickert told Pesach that the Rosenberg Kommando had arrived in Greece and was demanding the list of Volos-area Jews. The rabbi claimed that he was not familiar with administrative matters and had no Jewish archives. He was only the spiritual leader of the Jews of Volos. Angry, the *Kommandant* ordered Pesach to return with the lists. As he was leaving, the rabbi temporized. Choosing not to arouse the Germans' suspicions, he implied that compliance would require time.

Agitated, Chief Rabbi Pesach took off for the *Episkope* (Diocese) to see Metropolitan Ioakeim.[8]

"Who or what is 'The Rosenberg Kommando'?" the rabbi inquired anxiously. *"Kyrie Synadelphe* (Mr. Colleague,) what do you advise me to do?"

Metropolitan Ioakeim looked troubled. He said the question required a careful response. He asked the rabbi to wait while he sent a trusted cleric to get information from an undisclosed source. The metropolitan did not trust the phones. His man crept secretly to the German consul's office.

Consul Helmut Sefel had lived in Volos for several years before the war and had established himself as a successful businessman as well as a diplomat. He had excellent relations with the townsfolk and especially with the metropolitan. His response to Ioakeim was to tell Rabbi Moses and the Jews to run away, before the deadline for "The List" expired.

Without mentioning Sefel, Metropolitan Ioakeim advised his colleague to take his flock and flee. The rabbi was reluctant. Where could he go? How would he and his family get there? The metropolitan promised transport. The rabbi was concerned about the community's ancient, irreplaceable holy scrolls of the five Books of Moses and other ritual objects, and his own extensive library. Ioakeim said there was plenty of room in the Diocese, he would keep safe anything the rabbi entrusted to him until Pesach's return.

Before they parted, Ioakeim pulled out a piece of paper, and pen in hand he wrote:

> *Beloved in the Lord:*
>
> *I warmly commend to you the elder teacher, bearer of this letter, and beg every brother who encounters him, to listen to him atten-*

8. Ioakeim is sometimes transliterated as Joacheim or Joakim.

tively and with good will and to provide him with every assistance, whatever he may need for his survival and that of his flock, so that they will not fall victims of the present difficult situation.

With God's blessings,

Ioakeim of Dimitriada

The letter was stamped with the official metropolitan seal. Handwritten letters were also sent to the Resistance and the regional clergy, requesting that the rabbi and his followers be given every protection, assistance and succor. They were signed and stamped with the metropolitan's distinctive signet ring. Word quickly got around that priests were to accord the rabbi the same respect and bestow on him the same honors as if Ioakeim himself were present.

Immediately after leaving the metropolitan's office, Rabbi Moses Pesach went to the Greek authorities and asked for their help. He requested that they delay compliance with the German orders for at least five days. He then notified the Jewish community lay leaders of the Nazi intentions, and together they set the wheels in motion for the rescue of the Jews of Volos. The Jews were swiftly notified. The majority were persuaded to leave their homes, businesses and possessions. Greek Orthodox families took in some. The Jewish community passed the hat, so that the rich would help poorer members with the costs of escape. Most were assisted in fleeing by the Resistance, which operated an "underground railroad" to nearby villages.

All of the synagogue treasures began their journey to the Greek Orthodox Diocese that very night. The next day two Jewish men appeared at the *Episkope*, bringing a heavy metal box which Ioakeim hid behind some ecclesiastical tomes, in a secret compartment where he always kept his bejeweled mitre.

The next night the rabbi vanished, sending an unmistakable signal to the Jews of Volos. Before he left he had been promised the cooperation of both Mayor Nicholas Saratsis and Nomarch (Province Governor) I. Pandazidis. They kept their promise to delay and obstruct the Nazi orders for the lists of Jews, but they were not the only ones. The conspiracy of goodness begun by the two clerical colleagues was joined by the Head of City Records, Zisis Mandidis and the Chief of Police, Elias Agdiniotis. Agdiniotis accelerated the issuance of countless Christian identification cards, a task which had begun weeks earlier at the instigation of the Resistance.

Under the Nazi peril, the established Jewish leadership had been joined by new and younger faces, people vigorous and enterprising. These Jews had had the foresight to ask the police for fake Christian identity cards, even before the demands for registration began, around the time the

Italians withdrew in early September. Plans were made for EAM-ELAS to help. Several young Jewish men and women were already secretly members of the Resistance. Many more would join the national struggle from their mountain hideouts. Some fought in armed actions against the invaders. Two Jewish Voliotes were killed in action.

A ten-point anti-Jewish order from Athens arrived at the Volos police headquarters on October 4, bearing the signature of Jurgen Stroop, infamous for his burning down of the Warsaw Ghetto in May 1943. The ninth point made the police responsible for the enforcement of all German anti-Semitic edicts. But by then the majority of the Jews of Volos had fled.

The electric company had been the first organization to be asked for "The List," followed by City Hall. However, Joseph Trousmuth, a German and long-time high-level manager at the utility was thwarted in his eagerness to comply. Trousmuth had a fanatical admiration of the Nazis. But a spontaneous conspiracy was quickly formed by Greek electrical workers, thanks to a Jew, Minas Misrahi. Minas' co-workers so liked him that they not only warned him of the danger, but also made sure to stall and confuse compliance with the Nazi orders.

When the list was finally turned over to the Germans by the Greek authorities, it was a wonder of ingenuity. City officials had set out to compile a list of their own invention. Old archives were ransacked for suitable names: dead Jews were included; Jews who had emigrated to Palestine before the war were added; Jews known to have fled to Athens earlier in the war were also listed.[9]

The righteous conspirators were not limited to Greeks. In addition to the lifesaving warning from the German consul, help came from the International Red Cross, through Messieurs H. Heney of Switzerland and G. Oberhenali of Sweden. They were persuaded to continue the Red Cross rations previously earmarked for Jews within Volos, but allow them to be sent instead to the villages where the Jews had scattered.

Within three days of the summons to the Chief Rabbi on September 30, 1943, 65 percent of the Jews had vanished. Only with the extraordinary and widespread cooperation of the officialdom, the Church, the Resistance and the citizenry could such a feat have been achieved. It was pulled off as if all those eager Nazis had been asleep.

9. The author cannot help but chuckle at the fanciful notion of Greek bureaucrats roaming the Jewish cemetery and combing the gravestones for "suitable" names.

The Rabbi on the Bishop's Throne[10]

On Friday, the first of October, at approximately eight in the evening, Moses Pesach and his family were led by two *andartes* (partisans) on mule-back to the village of Kerasia, the regional headquarters of EAM-ELAS. Later, when that hamlet was set on fire by the Germans, they were resettled at Keramidi on Mount Pelion where, in accordance with the metropolitan's letter, they were given the best house in town, right on the village square. On Sunday afternoons, a delegation would appear from the church. Once more, they had overestimated the amount of *prosforo* (offering of liturgical bread) needed and would the rabbi consent to take some of the leftovers?

Shortly after getting settled, the rabbi called in the other Jews who, like him, had taken refuge at Keramidi.

"We have no synagogue here. See this?" said the rabbi pointing to the church. "It is also the house of *Adonai.* On Sundays, we will join the others in church. And when the procession of Christian ritual objects goes by, we will show our respect by bowing our heads."

Every Sunday, many of the Jews hiding in that village followed Pesach's lead and went to church, where the priest invited the rabbi to sit on the bishop's throne. The priest, taking to heart the metropolitan's true message, acted as if the rabbi walked in the hierarch's own shoes.

Barba'lias[11]

Geoula Sabethai was already "organized" in EPON, the youth branch of the EAM national Resistance, when her family received the warning from the synagogue on Rosh Hashana to abandon Volos. Even though twenty-year-old Geoula was her elderly parents' youngest child, she had taken over the arrangements for their escape. Her older brother Raphael, nicknamed Falinos, who was twice her age, was working in Athens and her older sister Eliza, thirty-four, was preoccupied with the care of her small child.

Brimming with spunk and determination, Geoula threw together a small bundle of bare necessities and urged her family to hurry. She then ran out to find a taxi willing to take them to the mountains. But when she returned home, Geoula found that her father had no intention of leaving Volos.

10. Interview with Mrs. Geoula Sabethai Frances, Larisa, April 1994 and telephone conversation, September 1998.
11. See note 10 above. Additional telephone interviews with Geoula Sabethai Frances, October 1998, and Karolina Varon Alhanati, now residing in Florida, September 1998.

Mr. Elias Sabethai, tall and spry at seventy, believed it was quite unnecessary to leave their home. Nothing would happen to them. What had happened six months earlier in Thessalonike was not applicable here in Volos. The Volos Jews were different: they spoke perfect, unaccented Greek. Most did not even know "Spanish" (Ladino).[12] This urgency to go to the mountain wilds was all a misunderstanding.

"If you don't care about yourself, think of the child," argued Eliza, pointing to her three-year-old son. But nothing said by Geoula or her mother or the Alhanatis, friends who were to share their get-away taxi, made any difference to Mr. Sabethai. He was staying.

So they tied a large burlap sack of wheat on the back fender to provide them with sustenance in their hide-out, and then they all squeezed into the large hired taxi without him. Virtually nothing else could be fitted into the overcrowded cab, which wheezed and labored through the slow climb up the mountain. When they got to their destination at Kanalia, they discovered that, somewhere along the way, a thorny branch had ripped a hole in the sack, and all their precious wheat had poured out.

After everybody got out of the cab at the village, Geoula got back in and prepared to return home to persuade her father to join them. The return trip downhill was much quicker. When they reached the outskirts of Volos, however, they encountered a Resistance checkpoint.

"Where do you think you are going?" asked the *andartes.*

"I need to get my father."

"When your father decides to leave, he'll leave. Once you go up the mountain, you are not permitted to return to Volos." Geoula knew she had no choice but to ask the driver to take her back to Kanalia.

Meanwhile, Geoula's brother, Falinos, was making his way from Athens to Volos. Falinos was eager to get home but it took him four days to reach his destination. Transportation was scarce and makeshift. He finally found a *"gazozen,"* a truck that had been converted to a bus burning foul-smelling oil. When he reached Volos, his father told him what had happened to the rest of the family.

---

12. In Volos, Ioannina, and a few other Greek locations, the pre-Sephardic tradition of the Romaniotes prevails. Romaniotes (from the word *Ρωμιος*), or Greek-speaking Jews have lived in Greece since at least the time of Alexander the Great, many bringing their knowledge of Greek from other parts of his empire. Since 1492, however, following the expulsion of the Jews from Spain and later from Portugal, the dominant Jewish tradition in most of Greece has been Sephardic rather than Romaniote. Thus, the "Yiddish" of the majority of Greek Jewry is Ladino, based on medieval Spanish.

"Your sister, the *andartissa* (female partisan), persuaded them all to take flight," complained the older man.

It was the young man's turn to argue with his father, who kept insisting he had a business to run. How could he close down his fabric shop and abandon his inventory? This was the season his customers needed warmer fabrics to sew new winter clothes. Surely Falinos, who sold their merchandise wholesale to shops in Athens, should understand.

Falinos let the matter go, until he met a Gentile friend who asked him:

"What are you doing here in Volos? They are now arresting Christian 'suspects' and executing them at the cemetery. Another German efficiency measure....You must get out of town immediately."

Falinos brought his friend's warning to his father.

"I am going nowhere without you, Papa. During the war, you lost one son. Now, do you want to lose another?"

The two men were suddenly overcome with emotion, remembering Ariel, dead at twenty-seven for lack of medicine for his "bronchitis," which had quickly turned into a virulent case of tuberculosis in the 1940-41 bitter winter of the Italian war. The two brothers had been in business together. After Ariel's death, Falinos had become so despondent and reclusive that the old man feared for him. Elias Sabethai had been forced to intervene with friends in Athens to take Falinos into their business and give him a fresh chance to recover.

Shaken now by Falinos' argument, the father agreed to leave. The two men fled to the safety of the partisan-controlled village of Kanalia, where their womenfolk were anxiously awaiting them. They arrived in time for Yom Kippur.

Within a couple of days the *andartes* sent word that the Jews must go farther up the mountain, to Keramidi, the most remote village on Pelion, where the Germans had yet to set foot. They were given two mules to transport the elderly Mr. and Mrs. Sabethai and their three-year-old grandson, Sammy. The mules also carried a tiny portion of Elias Sabethai's inventory of cloth to be bartered for their immediate needs. But the Sabethais were not alone. With them were the Alhanatis, a family of Jewish refugees from the northern cities of Drama and Kavalla. Elias Sabethai took turns on the mules with the Alhanatis, whom he had taken under his wing when they had arrived in Volos to avoid the pre-invasion relentless bombings. Along with two or three other Jewish families, the younger Sabethais and Alhanatis set out on foot, over goat paths, on the four-hour trek to safety.

At Keramidi they found their rabbi, affectionately called "Moushon" Pesach, and more Jews. The village was among the most primitive in the area, with no running water and no paved road. It took the women twenty minutes to fetch drinking water in earthenware jugs from the nearest spring. Laundry was carried on their backs, over a stony goat path, to running water half an hour away, and dried over low bushes before it would be light enough to carry back to Keramidi. During the rainy season, the villagers gathered rainwater through pipes fitted to their roofs and flowing into shallow cisterns. The water was good for cleaning and bathing but not drinking, because, untreated, it tended to crawl with tiny worms.

Geoula went to work in the fields. Her friend Karolina Varon and another Jewish girl mended army uniforms for the Resistance. Nights, Geoula and Karolina made socks and special waterproof *koukoules* (warm hoods) for the partisans by knitting goat's hair. Falinos was invited to go to a remote sheepfold where one of the villagers, Thanasis Youlas, had 4,000 sheep and goats. There, learning to help with the animals and enjoy nature, Falinos found some peace from the torment of the unanswerable "why" of that war and its losses.

At Keramidi, Elias Sabethai's role changed from reluctant fugitive to valuable leader. He was skillful in finding housing, not only for his family but for the other Jewish newcomers. His positive outlook helped boost the morale of the Jews. Many of the villagers had been his customers for years, loyal to him for his durable fabrics and decent prices. They called him "Barba'lias," "Uncle'lias." Soon the entire village, including the fifty-odd Jews, took to referring to him that way.

Barba'lias found a mule driver who would periodically go to Volos and bring back the specified lengths of fabric from particular bolts packed in the prenumbered five bales entrusted to a Gentile friend. In this way Mr. Sabethai was able to continue to serve some of his customers and support his family. They all did their part, and the villagers responded with help and hospitality. When the Alhanatis, who had become penniless after three years of living as refugees and losing their father and principle breadwinner, could not endure the huge rats in the corn warehouse where they had been housed, the Youlas family offered them a house gratis. The kindness of Thanasis Youlas was to be loyally reciprocated by Barba'lias and his family when the Youlas sheepfold was looted and burned down by anti-communist forces during the civil war following liberation. For two years Thanasis, who was a wanted man as a presumed leftist partisan, lived in safety and comfort with the Sabethais in Volos.

In Keramidi Barba'lias and his entire family, along with many of the refugees, followed the rabbi's example and attended church on Sundays. Afterward, they all had plenty to eat when the rabbi shared with his flock the priest's gift of "leftover" liturgical bread.

Two Widows in Upper Volos[13]

Dimitra Solomou had been friends with Aliki Mourtzoukou and her brother, Anselmos, since they were kids. Their mothers were also friendly. The two girls had graduated from secondary school in 1940, four months before the war broke out. Dimitra had finished the Volos Gymnasium, Aliki the Commercial School. Anselmos was already employed at the fabric factory of his cousin, a prominent industrialist by the same name.[14]

When the warning came that the Jews of Volos were in peril, the Jewish girl, Aliki, approached her Greek Orthodox friend, Dimitra, asking for shelter. Dimitra, who was about twenty and working as a typist for the Volos Port Authority, took Aliki's plea home.

"Mother," she said, "Aliki and her family need a place to hide." She asked her mother, Mrs. Katerini Solomou, to take in the Jewish girl, her brother and their widowed mother, Xanthi Mourtzoukou. Dimitra's mother, herself a widow, made a modest living as a seamstress, supporting two other teen-age daughters and her ten-year-old son. Their two-story house was small. How could they manage to house and feed these people and keep it a secret too? Dimitra's mother did not voice the risk of leaving her four children orphans. Already there were German warnings posted all over town that anyone who hid Jews would be shot without a trial.

"Dimitra," asked her mother, "what about the Germans who now command the Port Authority? How can you go to work there, and then come home to Jewish fugitives? It's just too dangerous."

Mother and daughter talked about this terrible dilemma late into the night. In the end the decision, although terrifying, became inevitable. The next day the household had three more members. The Solomou children doubled up, freeing a room for the Mourtzoukou family.

And then the hiding, while eluding the Nazis and other prying eyes, started for all of them. They all ate as one family, sharing meager provisions. Food was scarce. As hidden people, the Mourtzoukou family had forfeited their ration coupons. But more importantly, it was too dangerous

13. Interviews with Mrs. Dimitra Solomou Katsemi, Volos, September and October 1996, and telephone conversations, August and September 1998.
14. The custom among Greek Jews is to name their children first after the paternal and then the maternal grandparents. In contrast to Ashkenazi (central or eastern European Jewish) tradition, there is no proscription against selecting the name of a living person. It is, therefore, a frequent occurrence that two or more first cousins share the same name. They are distinguished from each other by using their father's given name as a middle name.

for Mrs. Solomou to be noticed buying food for three extra people. She decided to seek customers in the surrounding countryside, where her family configuration was not known and where she could be paid in food, usually in produce, occasionally in flour or olive oil. Once in a while she brought home an egg. There was, of course, no transportation. She had to walk the distance from her village of Anakasia, at the foothills of Mount Pelion, to the village of Ai' Georgi Iolkou and to other villages in the Upper Volos area, where she went to sew in humble country homes.

Every day had its near misses, ingenious solutions, and occasionally some chuckles. Dimitra, after work, bought what staples she could find in Volos. Once in a while the Germans gave the port employees extra bread to bring home. That bread, laced with irony, tasted especially good when Dimitra shared it with her hidden Jews.

Mrs. Mourtzoukou was frightened by the German military convoys of jeeps and trucks passing by the Solomou house, which was located on the main provincial road to Mount Pelion. After some months, as the Nazi noose tightened, the two widows searched out a safer arrangement. It was finally decided that it would be wiser for the Mourtzoukou family to move to a more secluded location, away from military traffic. The new house was carefully selected. Although old and in poor condition, the new hideout had the advantage of being in Aghios Onoufrios, the next village, separated from their own only by a shallow creek. The house was located on a small hill and within view of the Solomou home, which was also built on an elevation.

No sooner were the fugitives gone, than there was a *bloko,* a dreaded roundup, in Mount Pelion, reaching from the high village of Portaria all the way down to Upper Volos. Nearby homes were ransacked by the Germans, dogs sniffing, heavy boots punctuating their terrifying search for fugitives. When the roundup was over, Dimitra, worried that the Mourtzoukou family may have been captured, stepped outside and looked anxiously toward her friends' house in the next village. She caught a glimpse of Anselmos Mourtzoukou standing on the front stoop and, reassured, waved to him. It had been a close call.

Under fire, the two families had developed strong bonds, and it had become important that Dimitra's family stay in touch with their Jewish friends. There were occasional evenings when one of them would sneak out to visit the other home, and Mrs. Solomou never failed to share some of the fresh produce she earned through her dressmaking.

A year passed until liberation ended the hiding. The villagers on Upper Volos and all over Pelion had become aware of the hidden Jews. Although the fugitives tried to keep a low profile, many, like the Mourtzoukou family, went out for food and other necessities. In Resistance-controlled villages most Jews circulated freely, knowing they would be warned by the locals in the event of a German raid. People sheltering Jews in the Pelion foothill hamlets were often known to their neighbors. But none of those neighbors denounced either the Jews or their rescuers.

The two widows and their children survived. On April 26, 1995, Dimitra Solomou's family and other rescuers were honored by the Jewish Community of Volos in a moving ceremony attended by government officials, hierarchs of the Church of Greece, and the Israeli ambassador. Dimitra's plaque said, in part, "...inspired by feelings of love, self-sacrifice, and altruism, with danger to her life...[she and her mother had saved] the Xanthi Mourtzoukou family. This heroic deed...makes us proud to be Greek."[15]

In addition to the Solomóu family, several other Voliotes were honored, including Metropolitan Ioakeim, who was recognized posthumously. Among the honorees were Mayor Saratsis, German Consul Sefel, Police Chief Agdiniotis, the Red Cross, and the Organization of Railroad Workers.

Taking Stock

Upon liberation, the Jewish community's box of valuables was to be returned unopened, as were the synagogue's treasures and the rabbi's entire library. This was, in itself, remarkable, as the Germans systematically confiscated and sent to Germany Jewish libraries and ritual objects and thus looted Greece, and especially Thessalonike, of centuries-old treasures. At the urging of the metropolitan, most private possessions, which had been hastily entrusted to neighbors, were also returned after the war.

Chief Rabbi Pesach had suffered almost unbearable personal losses. Of his seven children, two sons who were serving as teachers in northern Greece were captured, never to return. His daughter Alegra had joined the Resistance, was captured and tortured. She had escaped recognition as a Jew and was released, but she was never the same. He lost a son-in-law, Albert Cohen, at the hands of the Bulgarian occupation forces. Pesach's wife died in 1944 in a deep depression from bereavement and hardships. Their home had been sacked a few days after they fled, when the synagogue and almost every Jewish home and business were looted and vandalized by a mob led by the electric company's Joseph Trousmuth.

Despite it all, Pesach continued to provide able leadership to the community during the return and rehabilitation of the few concentration camp survivors. In 1950-51 he was both a victim of and a provider of relief from

15. Copy of certificate provided by Mrs. Dimitra Solomou Katsemi.

the earthquakes and floods which struck Volos. He is listed in the synagogue as a "Great Benefactor" in the rebuilding of the Jewish community.

In 1957, two years after his death, the Greek and Israeli governments agreed to move Pesach's remains to the Mount of the Wise in Jerusalem. Many of his own treasured books, his vestments and other personal possessions, which had been kept safe by Metropolitan Ioakeim during the persecution, are now in a tiny museum on an Israeli kibbutz.

Not everyone who remained in Volos had been fortunate to find rescuers like the Solomou family who hid Xanthi Mourtzoukou and her children. Some had not believed the warnings and did not take adequate precautions. They, along with some who were forced by economic pressures to return from the mountains too soon, were rounded up in April 1944, six months after the mass exodus. One hundred thirty Jews were deported, of whom 121 were murdered in Nazi concentration camps. In addition to those who did not survive the deportations, 34 others died, either captured and executed by the Germans within Greece, while fighting with the Resistance, or through wartime hardships.

The overall Jewish survival rate in Volos was 82 percent as compared with 13 percent nationwide, with 645 of 872 Jews returning to their hometown. According to the 1947 Jewish census, there was a 74 percent return rate to Volos, versus the national return rate of 13 percent. In addition to the returnees, 72 others survived, including those who stayed on in Athens, where they had gone to hide, and those who escaped the country during the Holocaust.

Thus the Jews of Volos had one of the best survival rates in Greece, over 80 percent, ranking third in the nation behind Zakynthos, Karditsa, and Agrinion, from which no Jew was deported (100 percent survival) and Katerini (over 90 percent), and ahead of Athens (66 percent of the pre-war Jewish community).[16]

These statistics encapsulate the achievement of the people not only of Volos, but also of the outlying villages. Though their decency and courage are not widely known, especially abroad, they wrote one of the finest chapters in modern Greek history. They gave the world a priceless reminder that the age-old Hellenic humanitarian tradition endures.

Postscript

To this day, the people of Volos remember their own two clergymen as they were on that fateful day in 1943, when their combined efforts mobilized so many to cheat the Nazis of hundreds of Jewish deaths. On Sunday,

16. See note 3.

September 27, 1998, the City of Volos and the Jewish Community of Volos hosted the unveiling of an impressive Holocaust monument commemorating the 155 murdered Jews of the city. On a central square, a large throng of local and out-of-town visitors listened to presentations recounting the remarkable rescue of the Jews of Volos. The regional press covered the event and once again described the past awards for heroism bestowed on Chief Rabbi Pesach and Metropolitan Ioakeim.[17]

The rabbi had already received many honors over the years, including decorations by both Greece and the Allies. Before the war, on January 16, 1939, he had been recognized as "A Great Chief Rabbi" by King George II. The king had bestowed on Pesach the prestigious Gold Phoenix Cross for his contributions to Greece in past national struggles. After the war, the British Allied High Command of the Middle East gave Chief Rabbi Moses Pesach an award for his life-saving assistance to Allied men and retreating Greek troops in fleeing Nazi-occupied Greece via the island of Euboea. That same route to Turkey and the Middle East was later used by fleeing Jews aided by the Resistance, which worked closely with both Pesach and Eli Barzilai, the Grand Rabbi of Greece. On July 5, 1952, Greece once again honored Pesach with a different award, the George I medal. In 1993, almost twenty years after his death, the City of Volos had named a road "Chief Rabbi Moses S. Pesach Street."

A few months before the Holocaust monument's unveiling, Yad Vashem, the Israeli Holocaust Heroes and Martyrs Remembrance Authority, had named Metropolitan Ioakeim of Dimitriada, "Righteous among the Nations." On the night of the unveiling, the Israeli ambassador bestowed on him posthumously a commemorative medal and plaque, which were given to the metropolitan's niece, Mrs. Athanasia Avgerou Tsilividis. She in turn dedicated the awards to the nameless village priests and monks who, following Ioakeim's lead, had protected the Jews. Her uncle, she stated, had practiced the Biblical principle of making no distinctions: "*Ουκ ενι Ιουδαιος ουδε Ελλην*" ("Neither Jew nor Greek.")[18] ✦

17. Various newspaper accounts and speeches sent to me from Volos by Mr. Raphael Frezis and Mrs. Dimitra Solomou Katsemi.
18. Galatians 3:28. See also Colossians 3:11.

Operation Blockade: Greek-American Humanitarianism During World War II

Alexandros K. Kyrou

The Greek-American response to the wartime tragedy of the 1940s in Greece reflected the enduring and strong identification of the diaspora with the welfare and plight of the Greek nation. The Greek-American community was not unique insofar as it, like other ethnic groups in the United States, demonstrated an ardent interest in the events which affected its homeland, but the extent to which Greek-Americans turned their concern into public activism and successful lobbying of government was arguably without rival during the Second World War. Indeed, this largely ignored episode in wartime history is rich in potential lessons for today's policy-makers concerned with the formulation and implementation of global humanitarian relief.

The story of diaspora humanitarian intervention offers an example of cooperation among a non-government actor (the Greek War Relief Association), a transnational organization (the International Red Cross), and national actors (the Allies, Axis, and neutral powers). Moreover, the decisive impact of the Greek-American relief campaign points to the importance of diaspora groups in influencing the strategic calculus of Great Powers whose support for humanitarian assistance is interpreted against *realpolitik* considerations. This study will explore Greek-American efforts to intercede in the international environment as a non-political actor on behalf of humanitarian imperatives in Greece during the Axis occupation of that country.[1] The study will conclude with some summary observations regarding the Greek War Relief Association's impact on larger patterns of humanitarian aid and rehabilitation in postwar Europe.

ALEXANDROS K. KYROU is Assistant Professor of History and Director of East European and Russian Studies at Salem State College in Salem, Massachusetts, as well as a Senior Research Fellow in the Kokkalis Program on Southeastern and East Central Europe at the John F. Kennedy School of Government at Harvard University.

1. The few studies heretofore that have examined the famine and subsequent relief effort in occupied Greece have tended to emphasize the state actors involved in the events

The same day that Mussolini launched his abortive invasion of Greece in late October 1940, the Greek-language press in the United States called upon Greek-Americans to rise to the support of the homeland.[2] Responding quickly, Greek communities throughout the United States met to organize local efforts to deliver aid to Greece. It soon became apparent, however, that a national structure would be necessary to coordinate any large-scale relief campaign.[3] Accordingly, and in response to a call by Archbishop Athenagoras, the head of the Greek Orthodox Archdiocese of North and South America, hundreds of representatives from Greek communities and voluntary associations convened in New York on November 7. Guided by Athenagoras' proposals, the representatives agreed to merge their efforts under one pan-Hellenic and pan-American organization to be

---

to such an extent that the nuanced, or subtextual, role of the Greek War Relief Association, as the critical and decisive factor in the course of wartime humanitarian intervention, has been either misunderstood or ignored altogether. A well documented and highly detailed work in this genre—albeit with unsatisfactory citation practices—is found in Georgios A. Kazamias, "Turks, Swedes and Famished Greeks, Some Aspects of Famine Relief in Occupied Greece, 1941-44," *Balkan Studies* 33, no. 2 (1992): pp. 293-307. For an earlier work which breaks with conventional interpretations by placing the Greek War Relief Association at the center of the international relief operation, see Alexandros K. Kyrou, "Ethnicity as Humanitarianism: The Greek American Relief Campaign for Occupied Greece, 1941-1944," in Dan Georgakas and Charles C. Moskos, eds., *New Directions in Greek American Studies* (New York: Pella Publishing Company, Inc., 1991), 111-127.

2. *Atlantis,* October 28, 1940; *Ethnikos Keryx* (National Herald), October 28, 1940.
3. George Papaioannou, *From Mars Hill to Manhattan: The Greek Orthodox in America Under Athenagoras* (Minneapolis, Minnesota: Light and Life Publishing Company, 1976), p. 135. In trying to deal with the problem of coordinating the spontaneous activities of multiple initiatives for humanitarian aid, numerous Greek-American community leaders pointed to the recent example and success of Finnish-American efforts to dispatch assistance to Helsinki during the 1939-1940 Winter War as an effective model for national organization. The many Finnish-American communities and voluntary associations throughout the United States had successfully merged their initial and varied grassroots relief movements into one nationwide confederation known as the Finnish Relief Fund. As a centralized national coordinating organization, the Finnish Relief Fund was able to maximize and make more effective use of the Finnish-American community's diverse resources than only locally based efforts could have, ultimately sending over $3,400,000 in aid to Finland. *Ethnikos Keryx* (National Herald), October 30, 1940. For an informative discussion of wartime humanitarian aid projects pursued by the largest Eastern European ethnic group in the United States, see Donald E. Pienkos, *For Your Freedom Through Ours: Polish American Efforts on Poland's Behalf, 1863-1991* (Boulder, Colorado: East European Monographs. Distributed by Columbia University Press, 1991), pp. 73-104.

known as the Greek War Relief Association, or GWRA. The representatives established the basis for the executive administration of the new organization, elected the influential business leader, Spyros Skouras, as national chairman, and resolved to adopt a policy of political non-partisanship.[4]

Two days following the New York meeting, the newly incorporated GWRA was officially licensed by the United States Department of State to raise funds for the relief of Greece.[5] Immediately, the national organization and communication networks developed earlier by the Greek Orthodox Archdiocese, major voluntary organizations such as the American Hellenic Educational Progressive Association (AHEPA) and the Greek-American Progressive Association (GAPA), as well as other bodies were mobilized to aid the GWRA.[6] To enhance its image, the GWRA included many prominent Americans of diverse ethnic backgrounds on its staff and in its fund-raising campaigns. The association's Greek-American leadership made a deliberate decision to attract respected public person-

---

4. *Ethnikos Keryx* (National Herald), November 19, 1940; Papaioannou, p. 135; George Papaioannou, *The Odyssey of Hellenism in America* (Thessalonike: Patriarchal Institute for Patristic Studies, 1985), pp. 176-177. For biographical information on Spyros Skouras, see *The Ahepan* 15, no. 1 (January-June 1941), pp. 40-42; and Theodore Saloutos, *The Greeks in the United States* (Cambridge, Massachusetts: Harvard University Press, 1964), pp. 278-280. Although there were some personnel changes within the GWRA's executive committee, the organization's national leadership remained basically consistent in its make-up as follows: Harold S. Vanderbilt, Honorary National Chairman; Thomas J. Watson and Howell W. Murray, Honorary National Vice-Chairmen; Mrs. Lytle Hull, Honorary Chairman, Women's Auxiliary; Archbishop Athenagoras, National Chairman; George C. Vournas, National Vice-Chairman; Spyros P. Skouras, National President; William Helis, National Vice-President; Joseph Larkin, National Treasurer; K.P. Tsolainos, National Secretary; Mrs. L.J. Calvocoresse, Chairman, Women's Auxiliary; Oscar Broneer, Executive Vice-President. The National Executive Committee consisted of Winthrop W. Aldrich, Archbishop Athenagoras, William Helis, Charles D. Kotsilibas, Joseph J. Larkin, Thomas A. Pappas, Spyros P. Skouras, Stephen C. Stephano, S. Gregory Taylor, K.P. Tsolainos, Harold S. Vanderbilt, and George C. Vournas. For more information on the most prominent of the GWRA's national officers, see Bobby Malafouris, *Hellenes tes Amerikes* (Greeks of America) (New York: Isaac Goldman, printer, 1948), pp. 218-219.
5. *Ethnikos Keryx* (National Herald), November 11, 1940, January 19, 1941.
6. Saloutos, p. 345. A well documented official chronicle of the largest and most influential Greek American voluntary/fraternal association is found in George J. Leber, *The History of the Order of AHEPA (The American Hellenic Educational Progressive Association), 1922-1972: Including the Greeks in the New World, and Immigration to the United States* (Washington, D.C.: Order of AHEPA, 1972).

alities outside the Greek-American community to its ranks in order to secure greater public recognition and support for the organization. The measure proved productive, bringing notable philanthropists, academics, and popular performers into the GWRA who, in turn, lent their popularity and influence to the furtherance of the organization—thereby giving the relief effort broader American, not exclusively Greek-American, visibility and appeal.

Concurrent with its administrative development, grassroots support for the GWRA rapidly gathered momentum in the Greek communities throughout the United States. Indicative of both the scope and the intensity of the diaspora mobilization, by November 15 over 350 Greek Orthodox parish communities and over 2,000 voluntary associations had joined the GWRA. Within a few months of its founding, the GWRA had organized some 964 local chapters.[7] More importantly, in the five-month period between the Italian attack and the subsequent German invasion of Greece in April 1941, the GWRA dispatched vital aid to Athens. By mid-November the GWRA's executive committee in New York had established a central committee in Athens, led in part by the United States ambassador to Greece, Lincoln MacVeagh, to administer services and distribute aid in

---

7. For more information on the development and expansion of the GWRA, as well as the organization's relief activities in Greece during the period preceding the Axis occupation, see Demetrios J. Constantelos, ed., *Agones kai Agoniai tes en Amerike Hellenikes Orthodoxou Ekklesias, Enkuklioi kai Eggrapha ton Eton 1922-1972/Encyclicals and Documents of the Greek Orthodox Archdiocese of North and South America Relating to its Thought and Activity, The First Fifty Years 1922-1972* (Thessalonike: Patriarchal Institute for Patristic Studies, 1976), pp. 281-297, 303-306, passim; Greek War Relief Association, *$12,000,000,* (New York: Greek War Relief Association, 1946); Malafouris, pp. 218-226; Papaioannou, *The Odyssey of Hellenism in America*, pp. 176-181; and Saloutos, pp. 345-350. In terms of national level organization the GWRA was divided into nine regions, each with its own administrative director and headquarters as follows: Greater New York (Gregory Taylor, New York, New York); Upper New York State (Dean Alfange, New York, New York); New England (Antonios Pappas, Boston, Massachusetts); Midwest (Harry A. Reckas, Chicago, Illinois); East Central (George Vournas, Washington, D.C.); Middle Atlantic (Stephanos Stephanou, Philadelphia, Pennsylvania); Ohio (Vasileios Chibithes, Dayton, Ohio); West (Peter Boudouris, San Francisco, California); and South (William Helis, New Orleans, Louisiana). For more related information, see "Archbishop Athenagoras to Archdiocese's clergy, community councils, and the Philoptochos Sisterhood, December 13, 1940," in Constantelos, pp. 283-285. The GWRA executive national offices were located at 730 Fifth Avenue in the Heckscher Building in New York City; use of the entire premises had been donated to the organization by the City Farmers Bank of New York City. *Ethnikos Keryx* (National Herald), November 20, 1940.

Greece.[8] Prior to the German occupation of Athens, the GWRA had cabled approximately $3,800,000 to its representatives in Greece.[9] These funds were used for a range of philanthropic assistance channeled carefully to civilians; such aid included food, heating fuel, clothing, and medical attention. The GWRA central committee continued to distribute aid until the last possible moments before the occupation of Athens.[10]

Contrary to universal expectations of an easy and rapid Italian victory, Greece's numerically and materially disadvantaged forces thwarted the Italian invasion by mid-November 1940. That same month the Greek army launched a successful counteroffensive that pushed the retreating Italians deep into Albania. Forced by this humiliating military reversal to rescue Mussolini from Rome's widening fiasco in the Balkans, Hitler invaded Greece and Yugoslavia on April 6, 1941. Overwhelmed finally by the sheer numbers and mobility of the combined Axis armies, Greece was overrun and occupied by German, Italian, and Bulgarian forces.[11] In response to the Axis occupation, Britain sealed off all shipping lanes into Greece. The blockade was intended to deny the Axis any channels for supply and movement. However, its implementation would soon lead to famine.[12]

---

8. *Ethnikos Keryx* (National Herald), November 20, 1941.
9. The GWRA central committee in Athens expended approximately $3,336,000 in relief aid prior to the German occupation of the city on April 27, 1941. On April 14, 1941, the central committee returned, by cable, $255,000 to the GWRA headquarters in New York in order to guard the money from potential confiscation by the invading Axis. Likewise, the remainder of the funds originally dispatched to the Athens committee, totalling $175,000, were deposited in a special pharmaceutical reserve account under the protection of the International Red Cross. *Ethnikos Keryx* (National Herald), May 5, 1941.
10. Malafouris, p. 220; Saloutos, p. 349.
11. Detailed studies of the military phases of Greece's involvement in the Second World War during the period preceding the Axis occupation of the country are found in Mario Cervi, *The Hollow Legions: Mussolini's Blunder in Greece, 1940-1941* (Garden City, New York: Doubleday and Company, Inc., 1971); Greek Army General Staff, *Ho Hellenikos Stratos Kata ton Deuteron Pagkosmion Polemon: Hellenoitalikos Polemos, 1940-1941,* Volumes 1-5 [The Greek Army During the Second World War: Greco-Italian War, 1940-1941] (Athens: 1966); and Alexandros Papagos, *The Battle of Greece* (Athens: J. M. Scazikis "Alpha" Editions, 1949). For an examination of the strategic connection of the German campaign in Greece and Yugoslavia to the Axis invasion of the Soviet Union, see Andrew L. Zapantis, *Hitler's Balkan Campaign and the Invasion of the USSR* (Boulder, Colorado: East European Monographs/Distributed by Columbia University Press, 1987).
12. See John Louis Hondros, *Occupation and Resistance. The Greek Agony 1941-44* (New York: Pella Publishing Company, Inc., 1983), pp. 67-70; Saloutos, p. 349.

Greece was a net importer of wheat and relied on foreign markets for more than one-third of its food needs. More precisely, with an average prewar annual wheat crop of approximately 700,000 tons, and a 1,200,000 tons wheat consumption level, Greece was forced to import yearly 500,00 tons of wheat. The Axis occupation and the subsequent British blockade interrupted the normal means of securing foodstuffs vital to Greece's subsistence. The situation was worsened by the anemic grain harvest of 1941, which produced roughly 200,000 tons less than the prewar average. The Axis expropriation of food stocks intensified the crisis, and the division of the country into Bulgarian, German, and Italian occupation zones disrupted the prewar systems of supply and distribution. Finally, the flow of refugees into urban centers, especially the Athens-Piraeus area, strained already acutely diminished resources to the breaking point.[13]

Reports of starvation in Greece began to appear in the Greek-American press in early July.[14] The obstacle of Axis occupation, rather than discouraging Greek-Americans from pursuing efforts to deliver aid to Greece, underscored the need to provide immediate humanitarian relief to the Greek population. In short, the serious deterioration of conditions in Greece motivated Greek-Americans to seek other means to secure their ongoing and now expanded aid goals.[15]

The Greek-language press led the discussion in the Greek-American community on the widening crisis in Axis-occupied Greece. The press was exceedingly active in advancing the position that Britain's blockade should and could be adjusted to allow for the delivery and distribution of food to

---

One of the most detailed studies of the onset of the wartime famine is found in Dimitri Kitsikis, "La Famine en Grèce (1941-42): Les Conséquences Politiques," *Revue d'Histoire de la Deuxième Guerre Mondiale* 74 (1969), pp. 17-41. For a discussion of the famine and the political dimensions of relief during the last stages of occupation, see Angeliki Laiou-Thomadakis, "The Politics of Hunger: Economic Aid to Greece, 1943-1945," *Journal of the Hellenic Diaspora* 7, no. 2 (1980), pp. 27-42.

13. Karl Brandt, Otto Schiller and Franz Ahlgrimm, "Germany's Agricultural and Food Policies in World War II," *Management of Agriculture and Food in the German-Occupied and Other Areas of Fortress Europe, A Study in Military Government, Volume* 2 (Stanford, California: Stanford University Press, 1953), pp. 235-238; Hondros, p. 67. An excellent analysis of economic conditions in Axis-occupied Greece is found in Stavros B. Thomadakis, "Black Markets, Inflation, and Force in the Economy of Occupied Greece," in John O. Iatrides, ed., *Greece in the 1940s: A Nation in Crisis* (Hanover, New Hampshire: University Press of New England, 1981), pp. 61-80.
14. *Atlantis,* July 8, 1941; *Ethnikos Keryx* (National Herald), July 7 and 8, 1941.
15. Ibid., July 1 and 22, 1941. Blocked from dispatching aid directly to Greece, the GWRA temporarily shifted its efforts to respond to the humanitarian needs of Greeks

the hapless Greek population. The dominant figure in this press movement was Basil Vlavianos, the publisher and editor of the influential, liberal Greek-language New York daily newspaper, *Ethnikos Keryx* (National Herald).[16] Through a multitude of fiery public appearances, as well as countless editorials, Vlavianos called for a change in Britain's blockade against Axis-occupied Greece. Reflecting the attitude of the vast majority of Greek-Americans, Vlavianos insisted that Greece's severe food shortage, in combination with the country's staunch resistance against the Axis, demanded that Allied strategists find some means to re-open the vital shipping lanes to Greece. Vlavianos implored Britain not only to alter its total blockade policy, but to lend all available support in dispatching food and other humanitarian aid to Greece.[17]

Encouraged by Vlavianos and other community leaders, Greek-Americans throughout the United States began a grassroots lobbying campaign. Through mass telegraphing and letter-writing to their elected representatives in Washington, the Greek-American community labored to influence the United States government into bringing pressure to bear on Britain to alter its blockade policy against Axis-occupied Greece.[18] Pursuant to that goal, and after outlining a relief strategy with the help of Norman Davis, the executive director of the American Red Cross, Spyros Skouras met with repre-

---

outside Greece. In short, the national executive committee resolved to send aid to Greek refugees who had fled the Axis occupation for safety in Egypt and elsewhere in the Middle East. These refugees also included a significant number of Greek Americans who had repatriated to Greece before the war. With the consent of the U.S. Department of State, the GWRA established a committee of representatives in Cairo with the president of the Greek Red Cross, Constantine Mouratiadin, as its chairman. By the end of July 1941, the GWRA Egyptian Committee had received $10,000 from GWRA headquarters in New York. These funds, and others which followed, were used to aid in the settlement of growing numbers of Greek refugees in the Middle East.

16. The *Ethnikos Keryx* (National Herald), began publication in 1915 and soon achieved prominence in the Greek-American community as the chief rival of the older, conservative New York Greek-language daily newspaper, *Atlantis*. The two most authoritative studies of the Greek press in the United States are found in Andrew T. Kopan, "The Greek Press," in Sally M. Miller, ed., *The Ethnic Press in the United States: A Historical Analysis and Handbook* (New York: Greenwood Press, 1987), pp. 161-176; and Victor S. Papacosma, "The Greek Press in America," *Journal of the Hellenic Diaspora* 5, no. 4 (1979), pp. 45-61. For a cross-cultural examination of the press, see Charles Jaret, "The Greek, Italian and Jewish American Ethnic Press: A Comparative Analysis," *The Journal of Ethnic Studies* 7, no. 2 (1979), pp. 47-70.
17. *Ethnikos Keryx* (National Herald), August 9, 1941.
18. Ibid., August 7, 1941.

sentatives of the Department of State on August 21, 1941.[19] With the backing of Davis and Ambassador MacVeagh, Skouras presented a plan and request to the Department of State's Division of Near Eastern Affairs for a trial shipment of wheat to Greece. Skouras proposed that the GWRA charter a neutral vessel, load it with wheat in the United States or in some other willing country, and dispatch it to Greece. In order to insure proper distribution of the intended cargo, the GWRA would send a representative oversight group to accompany the relief materials. If the proposed pilot shipment proceeded satisfactorily, the GWRA would follow it with others. In addition, Skouras' plan envisioned the assistance of the Department of State in securing from the various belligerent states safe passage for the relief ship.[20]

With the understanding that neither the American Red Cross nor the United States government would directly participate in the operation, the Division of Near Eastern Affairs recommended Skouras' proposal to Assistant Secretary of State Sumner Welles. The GWRA plan was endorsed for both humanitarian and political reasons. The Division's intelligence sources had concluded that the food crisis was more acute in Greece than in any other part of Europe, and that it was commonly viewed that Britain, and secondarily the United States, had a distinct obligation to save a country in the democratic camp from famine. Moreover, the Division of Near Eastern Affairs reported that the failure to send aid to Greece had created a perception in the Turkish government that the Allies had abandoned Greece after Athens had served their purposes to the maximum. Consequently, analysts in the Near East Division feared that Ankara would not render any support to the Allied effort so long as the Greek crisis was met with indifference from Britain.[21]

---

19. U.S. Department of State 868.48/1143, "Memorandum of Conversation," Shipment of Food to Greece by Greek War Relief Association Acting for the Greek Red Cross, August 21, 1941; U.S. Department of State 868.48/1144, "Memorandum," Proposed Shipment of Wheat to Greece by the Greek War Relief Association, August 22, 1941. The GWRA was able to independently confirm the outbreak of the famine and routinely provided Washington with detailed reports as to its severity. This field reporting was accomplished through the services of a Portuguese agent, Antonio Gomes, who operated as an intelligence officer for the GWRA in Athens from 1941 to late 1943. British Archives R 13659/4/19, "Political Memorandum," From Ridley Prentice to the Political Intelligence Department, n.d. (From the British Archives File of the Michael Matsas Collection, RG 500; Center for Holocaust Studies Documentation and Research, Brooklyn, New York).
20. U.S. Department of State 868.48/1144, "Memorandum," Proposed Shipment of Wheat to Greece by the Greek War Relief Association, August 22, 1941.
21. Ibid.

Turkey's interest in Greece's situation created an opportunity for the GWRA. While evaluating the merits of exerting leverage on Britain to lift its strategic blockade, the Department of State assisted the GWRA in implementing a temporary aid measure. In short, the GWRA leadership fashioned a second relief plan that was endorsed by the Department of State, and ultimately accepted tactically by Britain, whereby food purchased in Turkey by the GWRA would be shipped to Greece and distributed under the supervision of the International Red Cross.[22] Meanwhile, the GWRA began transferring funds to the International Red Cross in Geneva and to its own representatives in Turkey. The funds were to be used for the purchase of foodstuffs, vitamin concentrates, medical supplies, and for the materials' transport to Greece.[23] Preparations for cargo shipment and distribution were entrusted to a certain Delegate Brunel of the International Red Cross Committee in Athens. Acting officially under instructions from Geneva, and in concert with GWRA planning, Brunel sought the advice of the occupation authorities in Athens, and, with their consent, appointed an administrative committee of prominent Athenian philanthropists to deal with the logistical needs pertinent to the distribution of the intended cargo.[24] Brunel also formed an executive steering committee consisting of representatives of the German, Greek, and Italian Red Cross organizations.[25] In a meeting held on October 21 the executive committee formulated a management plan for food distribution based on community and institutional needs. Moreover, the committee garnered assurances of cooperation from the occupation authorities.[26]

Shortly after the executive committee outlined its relief agenda, the steamship *Kurtulus* arrived from Istanbul and anchored off Piraeus. The

22. U.S. Department of State 868.48/1163, the London Embassy to the Secretary of State, Food Supplies for German-Occupied Territories, October 18, 1941.
23. U.S. Department of State 868.48/1181, official Greek War Relief Association correspondence from Spyros Skouras to Assistant Secretary of State Breckinridge Long, October 15, 1941.
24. U.S. Department of State 868.48/1187, the Rome Embassy to the Secretary of State, Food Shipments for Greece from Turkey financed by the American "Greek War Relief Association," November 14, 1941; U.S. Department of State 868.48/1187, Second Secretary of the Athens Embassy, Burton Y. Berry, "Memorandum" (enclosure to No. 2510 of November 14, 1941, from the Rome Embassy), Condensed account of the preparation for and distribution of the first food shipment received from Turkey on the *S.S. Kurtulus,* together with an Annex showing in tabular form the quantity of foodstuffs distributed to the various types of organizations, November 14, 1941.
25. Ibid.
26. Ibid.

unloading and distribution of the *Kurtulus'* cargo began on October 29. Three days earlier, the occupation censors had authorized a release to the press in Greece stating that "the generosity of American relief organizations has made it possible to make distribution among the Greek population of large food supplies which have been purchased and transported from abroad."[27] The GWRA was not mentioned in the statement and the Greek public remained unaware of the organization's role in the delivery of the aid shipment.[28] Nevertheless, the occupation authorities honored their pledge to the International Red Cross Committee by aiding them in the transfer of the foodstuffs.

As an unprecedented operation in exceedingly precarious circumstances, the GWRA's shipment was a remarkable success—almost 3,000,000 pounds of food had been sent to, and distributed in, occupied Greece without Axis interference.[29] Once Allied intelligence reports confirmed that none of the shipment had been seized by the occupation forces, the GWRA was permitted to dispatch the *Kurtulus* on a second relief voyage. After taking on another 3,000,000 pounds of food purchased in Turkey, the ship arrived in Piraeus on November 10.[30] Thus began a regular pattern whereby food and medical shipments arrived in Greece during the early winter of 1941-1942. During this period Brunel and his onsite committees were able to keep the public soup kitchens of the Athens-Piraeus area in operation while improving distribution methods in other relief sectors and laying plans for an expansion of aid to other parts of the country.[31]

Brunel's preparations for implementing larger aid operations, however, were soon dashed. As the winter progressed, and as Turkey's own wheat

27. U.S. Department of State 868.48/1171, Special Assistant to the Secretary of State to the Greek War Relief Association, November 25, 1941.
28. Saloutos, p. 349.
29. U.S. Department of State 868.48/1187, Second Secretary of the Athens Embassy, Burton Y. Berry, "Memorandum," November 14, 1941; U.S. Department of State 868.48/1171, Special Assistant to the Secretary of State to the Greek War Relief Association, November 25, 1941.
30. U.S. Department of State 868.48/1171, the Rome Embassy to the Secretary of State, November 15, 1941.
31. Hondros, p. 72; U.S. Department of State 868.48/1187, the Rome Embassy to the Secretary of State, Food Shipments for Greece from Turkey financed by the American "Greek War Relief Association," November 14, 1941; U.S. Department of State 868.48/1187, the Rome Embassy to the Secretary of State, November 15, 1941; U.S. Department of State 868.48/1171, in reply to SD 868.48/1171, November 14, 1941, Confidential Report for the Secretary of State from Joseph C. Green, Special Assistant to the Secretary in charge of the Special Division, November 25, 1941.

reserves declined, Ankara announced that it would cut off its supply of food to Greece in January 1942.[32] Consequently, the GWRA sought the permission of both the British and United States governments to agree to the use of a market source other than Turkey for the purchase of food for Greece. London, however, objected to any shipment of goods to Greece if the relief materials did not originate in Turkey. This insistence was in fact the result of an adroit extension of Britain's strategic blockade policy. London was willing to widen the relatively small scale exception to its general blockade on the basis of larger strategic considerations. In short, London permitted the shipment of relief supplies to Greece from Turkey to take place in order to reduce Ankara's surplus resources. More precisely, the British authorities feared that Turkey's resources might be utilized by the Germans. As a result, London welcomed any arrangements that diverted Turkish foodstocks and goods to Allied nationals who would consume supplies that might otherwise become available to the Axis.[33] Having accomplished this aim, the British were now indifferent to renewed GWRA pleas for direct aid to Greece.

32. Hondros, pp. 68, 72. The likelihood of a winter wheat export shortage in Turkey had been foreseen by the GWRA as early as August 1941. With an anticipated decline in Turkish agricultural production, coupled with Ankara's policy of low price-fixing, which often led to hoarding by farmers, the GWRA had prepared an alternative contingency for maintaining the flow of food supplies that would not depend on Turkish markets. U.S. Department of State 868.48/1143, "Memorandum of Conversation," Shipment of Food to Greece by Greek War Relief Association action for the Greek Red Cross, August 21, 1941; U.S. Department of State 868.48/1144, "Memorandum," Proposed Shipment of Wheat to Greece by the Greek War Relief Association, August 22, 1941. Shortly before the German invasion, the Greek government had purchased approximately 50,000 tons of wheat from Australia to fill the country's needs through the summer of 1941. The ships carrying the wheat did not reach Greece in time to deliver their cargoes, and remained anchored in Egypt following the Axis occupation. Consequently, in concert with the GWRA's new contingency, the Greek government-in-exile planned to transfer the undelivered wheat languishing in Egyptian ports to Turkey, where it would be used to replenish state stores of grain to levels required by Ankara to reopen access to its larger domestic wheat reserves. This proposal was necessarily complicated because it took into account the British demand that all relief supplies originate in Turkey. U.S. Department of State 868.48/1172, Telegram sent by the Department of State to the London Embassy, November 26, 1941; U.S. Department of State 868.48/1172, Wallace Murray from the Division of Near Eastern Affairs to Assistant Secretary of State Welles, December 3, 1941.

33. U.S. Department of State 868.48/1172, report from the Division of Near Eastern Affairs to Berle, and received by Assistant Secretary of State Acheson, December 6, 1941. For an analysis of the importance of Turkish agricultural and mineral markets

Meanwhile, conditions in Greece reached startling levels by mid-winter 1941-1942. In early January 1942, reports began reaching the United States that as many as 1,000 persons were dying from starvation on a daily basis in the Athens area alone.[34] In response, the GWRA intensified the urgency of its demand that food be sent to Greece immediately.[35]

Due in large part to the ongoing and concerted Greek-American lobbying campaign, as well as mounting intelligence reports, the United States government began to show signs of serious concern over the situation in Greece. Moreover, President Roosevelt and the Department of State had serious political misgivings about Britain's blockade policy. Apart from the risk of alienating Turkey from any potentially productive relationship with the Allies, the blockade gave German propaganda an unparalleled opportunity to attack Britain for the mercenary abandonment of a gravely imperiled ally.[36]

Thus motivated to intervene on behalf of Greece, Washington asked London on December 3, 1941, to supply information on its blockade of Greece and to confirm or deny allegations of responsibility for the famine. The British did not reply to the request and were asked again, on January 5, 1942, to provide a response to the United States government. After more than a week had passed, British Foreign Secretary Anthony Eden answered with a message claiming to exonerate Britain from any role in, or responsibility for, the famine. Eden stated, furthermore, that London's actions

---

to both belligerent camps during the Second World War, see Selim Deringil, *Turkish Foreign Policy during the Second World War: An 'Active' Neutrality* (Cambridge: Cambridge University Press, 1989), pp. 21-22, 128-132. The most authoritative treatment of Turkey in international affairs during the Second World War is found in Frank Weber, *The Evasive Neutral: Germany, Britain and the Quest for a Turkish Alliance in the Second World War* (Columbia, Missouri: University of Missouri Press, 1979). An excellent analysis of Turkish foreign policy objectives is found in Alexis Alexandris, "Turkish Policy toward Greece during the Second World War and Its Impact on Greek-Turkish Detente," *Balkan Studies* 23, no. 1 (1982), pp. 157-197. Turkish diplomacy during the latter half of the war is examined in Edward Weisband, *Turkish Foreign Policy 1943-1945: Small State Diplomacy and Great Power Politics* (Princeton, New Jersey: Princeton University Press, 1973).

34. Office of Strategic Services, Foreign Nationalities Branch, 14/GR-178, January 19, 1942. International Red Cross figures counted over 90,000 deaths throughout Greece during the winter famine of 1941-1942, approximately 50,000 of which took place in the greater Athens area. For more details, see Hondros, p. 71.
35. Office of Strategic Services, Foreign Nationalities Branch, 14/GR-178, January 19, 1942; Office of Strategic Services, Foreign Nationalities Branch, 14/GR-178, March 6, 1942.
36. Office of Strategic Services, Foreign Nationalities Branch, 14/GR-178, March 23, 1942.

were also being performed on behalf of the Greek government then in exile. Eden's assertions, however, appeared disingenuous, for the Greek government-in-exile had earlier dispatched a series of desperate pleas to Washington, asking the United States to take direct action to alleviate the famine.[37]

Despite Britain's previous resolve to maintain the blockade against Greece, pressure from the United States government and mounting international opinion finally induced Britain to reassess its policy. Accordingly, on February 22, 1942, London informed Washington that it was willing to lift its blockade to relief convoys.[38] Moving rapidly after securing the consent of both the British and United States governments, the GWRA put into action an interim relief operation.[39] The GWRA successfully solicited significant donations of humanitarian materials from the American Red Cross and the Medical Surgical Relief Committee of America, secured an aid package from Lend Lease measures, and chartered the Swedish vessel *Sicilia* to transport these and other goods to Greece. Loaded with over 2,500,000 pounds of food and nine tons of medicines, the *Sicilia* departed from New York harbor for Piraeus on March 27.[40]

Although the rapid-response *Sicilia* mission helped to alleviate the food crisis in Greece in the short-term, it was insufficient to end the famine. The GWRA leadership understood that the success of any long-term strategic relief program would require the cooperation of the key belligerent governments. Therefore, following considerable investigation and planning, the GWRA drafted a proposal, which it code-named "Operation Blockade," and in which the GWRA proposed the use of a neutral party to convey cargoes of food, medicine, and clothing to Greece, provided that safe passage could be assured from the belligerent nations.

Following deliberations with President Roosevelt, Assistant Secretary of State Welles, and Red Cross Chairman Davis, the GWRA leadership expanded the outline of its proposal by adopting the former individuals' suggestions to employ a neutral international commission within Greece

37. Hondros, p. 73. For the official British position on London's responses to the famine, see W. N. Medlicott, *The Economic Blockade, Volume* 2 (London: Her Majesty's Stationery Office, 1959).
38. Hondros, pp. 74-75.
39. U.S. Department of State 868.48/3028, March 6, 1942; Office of Strategic Services, Foreign Nationalities Branch, 14/GR-178, March 17, 1942.
40. Greek War Relief Association, "A Statement by the Greek War Relief Association, Inc. to its Chapters and Co-Workers" (New York: Greek War Relief Association, Inc., 1943); Malafouris, p. 221.

to insure the efficient distribution of relief supplies.[41] In this regard, the *Kurtulus* relief period had provided the ideal experiential antecedent for such an international arrangement. Hence, the revised GWRA plan posited that the earlier connections developed between Britain and the occupation authorities through the International Red Cross should now be used to coordinate expanded relief measures. While waiting for a response from London to its Operation Blockade proposal, the GWRA wasted no time in reserving funds for the plan's implementation. In addition, the GWRA used this period to solicit donations of wheat and other foodstuffs from various Allied and neutral governments, and began negotiations with the representatives of a fleet of immobilized Swedish vessels for service of their ships as relief cargo carriers.[42]

Britain accepted the outline of Operation Blockade in principle, but concern over the potential embarrassment and political precedent that lifting the blockade under Greek-American pressure might pose led London to insist that neutral Sweden appear as the originator of the relief initiative.[43] The GWRA agreed to defer public recognition to Stockholm.[44] Thus, on March 2 London and Washington formally invited the Swedish government to undertake the relief program. Stockholm accepted the project and on March 19 the Swedish Foreign Minister, Erik Boheman, presented the proposal to the Axis. The Italians responded in favor of the plan on April 7, and Rome's acceptance was followed by an even more positive reply from Berlin on April 27.

Implementation of the program, however, was forestalled by differences over the structure of the intended relief commission. The German and Italian governments assumed that the existing International Red Cross authorities in Athens, who had administered relief operations since the *Kurtulus* period, would continue to direct the distribution of any future delivery of relief goods. The British government, openly resentful of the International Red Cross apparatus, demanded that the original committees in Athens should not participate in any expanded relief operations and that Swedish authorities be given sole responsibility for the execution of the

41. Saloutos, p. 349.
42. For detailed information on the use of the Swedish vessels employed in Operation Blockade, see Malafouris, p. 222.
43. Hondros, p. 74; U.S. Department of State 686.48/3157, "Memorandum," June 13, 1942; U.S. Department of State 868.48/3168, the London Embassy to the Secretary of State, June 30, 1942.
44. At this stage in the planning process the GWRA's "Operation Blockade" proposal became known as the "Swedish Plan;" see Hondros, p. 74.

program. None of the belligerent powers showed any inclination to compromise and the relief deliberations reached an impasse which lasted until the beginning of August. Under pressure from the United States, the British government finally accepted a compromise plan drafted by Foreign Minister Boheman to establish a so-called Action Committee, composed of Greek, Swedish, and Swiss personnel, and to make the new organization solely responsible for relief distribution. The original International Red Cross Committee would continue to operate, but only as a liaison between the Action Committee and the Axis.[45]

The Action Committee began operations in August 1942 under the new official appellation of Joint Relief Commission. The headquarters of the Commission were established in the Marasleion School in the Kolonaki district of Athens, and a Swedish national, Emil Sandstrom, was appointed by Stockholm as organizational president. The relief apparatus was coordinated between two supreme centers: the Athens general administrative headquarters and the Piraeus office, which oversaw the processing and transportation of relief shipments.[46]

The Athens general headquarters included two subordinate divisions responsible for the distribution of relief. One of these divisions directed provincial distribution and maintained representatives and major relief centers in Kalamata, Patras, Thessalonike, and Volos, while the second division served the Athens-Piraeus area. The supervision of distribution on the islands was administered by a Commission field office in Crete and by two mobile representatives assigned to Chios, Lesbos, and Samos. At the local level, a network of committees and subcommittees, numbering some 1,600 by 1943, rising to approximately 3,000 in 1944, and reaching over 5,300 by 1945, was established to manage the apportionment of supplies in towns and villages.[47] In terms of official personnel, as early as the close of 1942, the Commission included twenty-five Swedish and Swiss executive administrators, almost fifty Greek and Swiss physicians, some 1,000

45. Hondros, p. 74-75; U.S. Department of State 868.48/3157, "Memorandum," June 13, 1942; U.S. Department of State 868.48/4892, Board of Economic Warfare, Blockade and Supply Branch, Reoccupation Division Confidential Report, Greece: Relief Food Distribution by the Joint Relief Commission, June 12, 1943.
46. U.S. Department of State 868.48/4892, Board of Economic Warfare, Blockade and Supply Branch, Reoccupation Division Confidential Report, Greece: Relief Food Distribution by the Joint Relief Commission, June 12, 1943.
47. Kazamias, p. 304; U.S. Department of State 868.48/4892, Board of Economic Warfare, Blockade and Supply Branch, Reoccupation Division Confidential Report, Greece: Relief Food Distribution by the Joint Relief Commission, June 12, 1943.

medical volunteers and nurses, approximately 3,000 labor volunteers, and over 1,200 employees.[48]

In order to protect the distribution process from waste and abuse, each of the Joint Relief Commission's divisions included a so-called verification unit entrusted with inspection duties, as well as responsibility for the regulation of services. The work and enforcement powers of the verification units benefited significantly from the fact that these units enjoyed not only oversight, but extraordinary legal authority. In short, the Joint Relief Commission's verification officers were granted legal rights by the occupation authorities to prosecute any infringements of the Commission's regulations.[49] Although any enormous and complex network such as the nationwide relief system in occupied Greece was obviously not without its share of problems, the legal power extended to the verification units was intended to function, and largely succeeded, as a meaningful deterrent to both inefficiency and potential corruption.

As the Joint Relief Commission developed its administrative and operational apparatus, the GWRA and its Commonwealth counterpart, the Greek War Relief Fund of Canada, or GWRF, obtained a substantial relief donation from the Canadian government.[50] Ottawa donated 15,000 tons of wheat to the relief project, while the GWRA and the GWRF jointly pur-

48. Brandt, Schiller and Ahlgrimm, p. 240; U.S. Department of State 868.48/4892, Board of Economic Warfare, Blockade and Supply Branch, Reoccupation Division Confidential Report, Greece: Relief Food Distribution by the Joint Relief Commission, June 12, 1943.

49. U.S. Department of State 868.48/4892, Board of Economic Warfare, Blockade and Supply Branch, Reoccupation Division Confidential Report, Greece: Relief Food Distribution by the Joint Relief Commission, June 12, 1943. For local case examples of the administration and operations of the relief apparatus, see Philip Argenti, *The Occupation of Chios by the Germans and Their Administration of the Island, 1941-1944* (Cambridge: Cambridge University Press, 1966), pp. 170-175, passim; and Greek War Relief Association, *A Letter from Issari* (New York: Greek War Relief Association, Inc., 1943).

50. Malafouris, p. 222. For information on the GWRF, see Florence MacDonald, *For Greece a Tear, The Story of the Greek War Relief Fund of Canada* (Fredericton, New Brunswick: Brunswick Press, 1954). Major studies of the Greek-Canadian community are found in Leonidas C. Bombas, ed., *Ho Hellenismos tou Montreal/Montreal Hellenism: 1843-1985* (Montreal: The Hellenic Psychological and Pedagogical Institute; Greek-Canadian Documentation Series, 1985); Peter D. Chimbos, *The Canadian Odyssey: The Greek Experience in Canada* (Toronto: McClelland and Stewart Ltd.; Canadian Secretary of State Series: *A History of Canada's People*, 1980); and Stephanos Constantinides, *Les Grecs du Québec* (Montreal: Editions Ho Metoikos/Le Metique, 1983).

chased fifty tons of medical supplies from the American Red Cross. These combined materials were loaded onto three Swedish vessels which left Montreal for Greece on August 7, 1942.[51]

Thereafter, aid shipments became regular and systematic. Relief cargoes originating in both Canada and the United States were transported monthly by a fleet of initially eight, later twelve, and ultimately, by the summer of 1944, sixteen Swedish vessels.[52] From August 1942 onward, the relief project delivered a minimum monthly shipment of 15,000 tons of wheat, 3,000 tons of dried vegetables, 100 tons of powdered milk, and other aid materials to Greece.[53]

The costs of the relief supplies and their transportation were assumed by the GWRA and the GWRF. Eventually, helping to sustain their enormous humanitarian initiative, the GWRA and the GWRF secured various financial and material assistance from the American Red Cross, the Canadian government, the United States government, and other charitable governments and organizations.[54] With these resources and support at its disposal, the Joint Relief Commission operated with remarkable success during the remainder of the occupation and through the first months following liberation. By March 7, 1945, the GWRA had dispatched 101 fleet missions/relief convoys to Greece, which delivered approximately 600,000 tons of wheat and other foodstuffs, 3,000 tons of clothing, and 20,000 tons of medicine and related goods.[55] In financial terms, the Greek-

---

51. Malafouris, p. 222. U.S. Department of State 868.48/4892, Board of Economic Warfare, Blockade and Supply Branch, Reoccupation Division Confidential Report, Greece: Relief Food Distribution by the Joint Relief Commission, June 12, 1943; U.S. Office of Strategic Services, Foreign Nationalities Branch, 14/GR-178, April 24, 1942. Instrumental in the success of the GWRA's medical aid projects were the efforts of Chicago physician Speros Demetriou Soterakos (Soter). Soterakos was responsible for organizing the Medical Division of the GWRA and helped raise $340,000 in relief donations from his colleagues. Soterakos and other prominent Chicago Greek-American professionals and intellectuals are discussed in Andrew T. Kopan, "Hellenic Letters in the New World: The Greek Pioneer Intellectual in Chicago," in Fotios K. Litsas, ed., *Hellenika Grammata: Essays in Tribute to Hellenic Letters* (Chicago: Modern Greek Studies Series, University of Illinois at Chicago, 1985), pp. 206-213.
52. Brandt, Schiller and Ahlgrimm, p.240; U.S. Department of State 868.48/4892, Board of Economic Warfare, Blockade and Supply Branch, Reoccupation Division Confidential Report, Greece: Relief Food Distribution by the Joint Relief Commission, June 12, 1943.
53. Ibid. Beginning in the summer of 1944, the minimum monthly delivery of GWRA food aid rose to 35,000 tons.
54. Ibid.; Hondros, p. 75.
55. Malafouris, p. 222.

American relief effort donated to Greece supplies valued at more than $100,000,000.[56] Through this generosity and humanitarian intervention, the GWRA's Operation Blockade prevented, on a larger scale, during the next two winters of occupation and the winter immediately following liberation, a repetition of the catastrophic winter famine of 1941-1942. Indeed, barring the delivery of any relief materials, official estimates in the spring and summer of 1942 anticipated 1,000,000 deaths for the forthcoming winter, with similar losses to follow in the next winter if the occupation were to continue.[57] Thus, the Greek-American community's humanitarian concern for Greece, the political corollary of which was its concerted lobbying for a change in Allied strategic policy, produced the conditions necessary for the very survival of Greece.

In the final analysis, apart from the single-minded commitment of Greek Americans, the GWRA was successful in its effort to end the famine in Greece because it was equipped with enormous structural resources. The GWRA possessed significant organizational advantages in the form of local, regional, and national networks which had developed before the Second World War as major institutions within the Greek-American community. In short, by marshalling the Greek Orthodox Church, voluntary associations, and other organizations, the GWRA was able to combine the diverse diaspora community networks into a formidable and unified national movement with international clout. The structures of the Church and the AHEPA, for example, both of which had fully evolved into impressive institutions by the 1930s, helped prepare the Greek-American community for successful activism in the 1940s. The GWRA propelled that activism by effectively consolidating the various grassroots organizations into an unprecedented diaspora lobby and campaign for the humanitarian relief of an imperiled and powerless Greece.

The energies directed at providing relief to famine-stricken Greece necessarily took into account not only the financial and organizational needs attendant to such intervention, but also the complex political and diplomatic challenges involved in such an effort. Undaunted by seemingly insurmountable international obstacles, the relative sophistication of the GWRA as a lobbying force helped to produce a level of success for itself that no other comparable organization achieved during the war. In other words, the GWRA effectively compelled the belligerent states to alter their policies in the interests of humanitarian imperatives. Thanks to the GWRA,

56. Greek War Relief Association, *$12,000,000,* pp. 8-9; Saloutos, p. 350.

57. Ibid.; Hondros, p. 75; U.S. Department of State 868.48/3136, Assistant Secretary of State to President Roosevelt, April 15, 1942.

Greece became the only state to benefit from a large-scale relief program planned and originating in the Allied camp and implemented in occupied Europe. Moreover, the actions of the GWRA had major implications for much of postwar Europe. Indeed, the highly successful record of relief in wartime Greece served as the functional antecedent to the United Nations Relief and Rehabilitation Administration's massive program for the relief of the postwar European continent. In short, the planning models and operational methods developed and implemented in Greece by the GWRA were subsequently duplicated and applied on an immense scale by the United Nations.[58]

Greek-Americans during the war years could not have imagined the enormous impact that their relief efforts on behalf of their brethren in Greece would have on populations throughout Europe. By the end of the war, however, the Greek-American community could begin to appreciate the significance of its humanitarian triumphs in Greece. Simply put, there remains no greater tangible evidence of the importance of the Greek-American community to Greece than the fact that the former's wartime humanitarian intervention saved almost one-third of the Greek state's population from starvation. This remarkable episode arguably constitutes the most salient accomplishment of the Greek-American community as an activist lobby. Indeed, at no point since the diaspora's central involvement in the reawakening of Greek national identity did Greeks outside Greece play as crucial a role in the life and survival of the Greek nation as did the Greek-American community during the crisis of the Second World War.

Acknowledgements

I would like to express particular gratitude to Professor Elizabeth H. Prodromou of the Department of International Relations and the Institute on Religion and World Affairs at Boston University for her invaluable analytic comments and interpretative suggestions that contributed immeasurably to this study. I am also grateful to Professor Charles C. Moskos of the Department of Sociology at Northwestern University for his support and encouragement of my research in this area of Greek and Greek-American studies. ✦

58. The official history of United Nations postwar relief operations is found in George Woodbridge et al, *UNRRA: The History of the United Nations Relief and Rehabilitation Administration* 1-3 (New York: Columbia University Press, 1950).

Greece's Strategic Importance: Past and Present

The Role of Greece in the Eastern Mediterranean

Gregorios Demestichas

Introduction

The Eastern Mediterranean is a unique geographical area in that it connects three continents: Europe, Asia, and Africa. Beginning in ancient times and continuing today, the Eastern Mediterranean has been an arena of competition not only for its inhabitants and those of neighboring regions, but also for various world economic powers. A safe prediction for the future is that competition in the region is certain to continue.

Historically, the Eastern Mediterranean region has nurtured great imperial and national as well as religious movements; it has been a place where great civilizations arose, developed, and perished. The area continues to attract the attention of powerful nations. Socio-political and economic rearrangements in the countries that comprise the region follow one after the other, and the threat of war is ever present. It should be noted that no country has ever succeeded in winning a war in the Eastern Mediterranean, without having first secured control of the sea and air in its zone of interest.

The sea routes of the Eastern Mediterranean converge on two nodes of world-wide significance: the Dardanelles, which connect the Black Sea with the Mediterranean through the Aegean Sea, and the Suez Canal, which connects the Mediterranean with the Persian Gulf and the Indian Ocean. Relations among the peoples of this area are tightly linked to these nodes. Their strategic value for the economies of the world powers and political relations among them, and for their relations with third countries, is supreme.

Despite the important changes that have taken place in Central and Eastern Europe, the Eastern Mediterranean remains the focus of international trade. It is still the shortest sea route for oil transport from the Middle East to Europe and a uniquely important route from the Black Sea to other destinations.

GREGORIOS DEMESTICHAS, Ret., former Chief of the Hellenic Navy, Chairman of the Hellenic Institute of Stategic Studies.

The new conditions

We already have seen the realization of some aspects of what has been termed the "New World Order." I estimate, however, that some changes in the international environment might influence future developments in the Eastern Mediterranean, resulting in the adoption of alternative, more realistic solutions to certain current problems.

Since the dissolution of the Warsaw Pact, the United States of America remains the only real superpower in the world. The European Union (E.U.) has not developed a common policy on security and defense issues, and no such policy can be seen on the horizon. The E.U., therefore, cannot play a decisive role on the world political stage, although member states that have strong economies can do so individually. These countries act independently and usually support United States policies. Russia, on the other hand, acts within the limits imposed by its present problems and capabilities and appears, for the time being, to have accepted a more restricted role in and reduced influence on the affairs of Eastern Europe.

The end of the Cold War saw the outbreak of small peripheral wars and localized conflicts sparked by nationalistic movements and territorial disputes, religious and economic differences, and unavoidable changes in the internal political, economic, and social structures of the countries that emerged after the disappearance of the Warsaw Pact and the Soviet Union.

The consequences of these changes were intensely felt in the Balkans, where the communist regimes in Albania, (former) Yugoslavia, Bulgaria and Rumania were replaced by new Western-type governments that are attempting to establish a market economy and adopt democratic values.

On the regional level, therefore, the changes created a new geopolitical area north of Greece, which instead of a neighboring state entity called Yugoslavia, now faces Croatia, Slovenia, Federal Yugoslavia (Serbia and Montenegro), Bosnia and the Former Yugoslavian Republic of Macedonia (FYROM). In addition, important changes have taken place in Albania and Bulgaria, and Turkey has found fertile new ground for its expansionist nationalistic policies.

The new conditions in the Balkans contributed to the emergence of the national claims of all states in the area, claims that shape their short-term and long-term strategy. By studying these claims one may also estimate the partial or total threat a particular country represents to the neighborhood, an important factor for the formulation of the neighboring nations' defense policies. The national claims of the various countries are clear and they are either put into effect or suspended, depending on political timing and circumstances. The tactics of individual nations in pursuing their national claims may vary and be adapted to the circumstances, even though the long-term strategy remains unchanged. It must be noted, however, that only Slovenia, among the new countries, seems to live in peace. For all the other new countries crises will appear periodically due to existing problems, and for as long as acceptable solutions cannot be found for those problems.

The revival of the Albanian nationalism and the oppression of the Albanian people living in former Yugoslavia and specially in Kosovo, west FYROM, south Montenegro and south Serbia, lead to future serious crisis and the area will stay unstable with the war pending to expand, threatening the stability of the Balkans and the sovereignty of the existing states.

The existence of oil and gas reserves in the Caucasus and the Caspian Sea area, combined with the issue of who controls the routes for transporting that energy (both on land and by sea through the Dardanelles) has increased the strategic importance of the Caspian Sea-Caucasus-Black Sea-Dardanelles-Aegean Sea area. It can now be viewed as of equal importance with the Middle East and the Persian Gulf.

Control by Turkey of the routes for transporting the energy reserves of the Caucasus area and the Caspian Sea, combined with its control of oil reserves in the northern part of Iraq will transform Turkey into the gatekeeper for energy supply, with the added danger of Ankara being in a position to hold major energy-consuming countries (i.e., the industrially developed countries) hostage.

A detailed examination of the area in question must deal with alternative transport routes for Caucasian and Caspian energy resources, so as to choose the safest routes or, alternatively, to create the circumstances that will make these routes secure. It is not possible to deal with the selection of the routes without examining the broader political and economic interests of the countries involved and of their neighbors, as well as their relations with the U.S. and Russia.

Briefly, routes that have been proposed for pipelines to carry energy from the Caucasus area and the Caspian Sea would pass through:

- Russia and the new countries that belonged to the former Soviet Union, with their terminals on the Black Sea;
- Eastern Turkey, with a terminus on the Mediterranean;
- Central Asia to the south;
- or a combination of the above.

The solution through Central Asia toward the south entails high risk because of the proximity of Iran and the political instability in all the countries of the region.

Placing a major pipeline in Turkey would bring strong reactions from

Russia. At the same time, Ankara's continuing failure to solve the problem of the Kurdish insurgency renders Turkey's eastern and southern regions exceptionally unstable and unsafe. Furthermore, what would be the effect on the global economy if the entire industrialized world depended on energy reserves entirely controlled by Islamic countries (Turkey, Iran, Iraq, and Libya) that are not all friendly to the West and its values? Although Turkey is a member of NATO and a secular republic, it faces a growing Islamic fundamentalist movement that could further destabilize the country, even if an acceptable solution to the Kurdish problem were found.

The transportation of oil from ports on the Black Sea through the Dardanelles as well as through a pipeline from Bulgaria to northern Greece (Burgaz to Alexandroupolis) and through the Aegean Sea are the most secure routes and therefore the most feasible, as they serve the interests of all the parties involved. This solution is compatible with the interests of the U.S. and the European Union, as well as those of Russia and the other republics of the former Soviet Union, as long as they are on good terms with the West. The routes leading to the Black Sea and to Bulgaria-northern Greece are an acceptable compromise that will satisfy the legitimate interests of all countries.

When the broader regional geostrategic and political environment is examined and seen in the context of the dogmatic Western tilt toward Turkey, it becomes clear that Greek-Turkish problems cannot be constrained within narrow NATO confines. At the present time those problems are entering an intensely critical phase. Turkey, encouraged by numerous factors, has entered a new era of aggressively pursuing and realizing its foreign policy goals in the Aegean Sea, which is both a competitor and a complement of the Dardanelles.

The clouds in the Middle East have not cleared and problems still arise as the prolonged crisis between Israelis and Palestinians cannot be settled as long as violent incidents take place overturning political discussions and agreements. The flare-up of Islamism in the North African countries, however, especially in Egypt and Algeria, may call for dynamic intervention for the protection of peace. In that case Greece, due to the strategic importance of Crete, and the Republic of Cyprus will become strong factors for the enforcement of stability in the region.

The position and role of Greece regarding matters of security and defense in the Eastern Mediterranean

The importance of Greece during the Second World War can be summarized in Churchill's words when he addressed the House of Commons in June 1941, a few weeks after the German invasion and conquest of Greece and Crete:

> *...There are some, I see, who say we should never fight without superior or at least ample air support, and ask when this lesson will be learned. But suppose you cannot have it. The questions which have to be settled are not always questions between what is good and bad; very often it is a choice between two very terrible alternatives. Must you, if you cannot have this essential and desirable air support, yield important key points one after another?*
>
> *The further question arises as to what would happen if you allowed the enemy to advance or overrun without cost to himself the most precious and valuable strategic points? Suppose we had never gone to Greece and never attempted to defend Crete? Where would the Germans be now? Might they not at this early stage of the campaign in 1941 already be masters of Syria and Iraq and preparing themselves for an advance into Persia?*[1]

The position of Greece in the Eastern Mediterranean and the Balkans remains equally strong today—perhaps even stronger—than it was in the past, when there were two blocs, the Eastern and Western. Until the establishment of prerequisites that will bind the interests of all states in the area to the preservation of stability and peace, the so-called New World Order will provide only short-term security.

Greece occupies the most southern part of Europe. The Aegean Sea constitutes the natural extension of the Dardanelles and is the unique route of transport for oil coming either through the Dardanelles or through pipelines terminating in northern Greece (Thrace). Securing stability in the Aegean Sea should be a strategic target of all parties interested in the safe transportation of oil. The Aegean is full of scattered islands, islets and clusters of rocky islets belonging to Greece and inhabited by Greeks. The need for stability in the Aegean, which is a confined sea, dictates that it should be controlled by one country only (in this instance, Greece)—as is the case for the majority of straits or confined sea areas all over the world. Any attempt at division of control over the Aegean Sea will certainly bring severe disputes and destabilization to the region.

Crete, the largest island of Greece, lies at the center of the Eastern Mediterranean. It is equidistant from Sicily, Suez, Lebanon, northeastern Africa and the coasts of the northern Aegean (Macedonia and Thrace). Its

---

1. Anthony Heckstall-Smith and Harold T. Baillie-Grohman, (*Greek Tragedy* London, A. Blond [©1961].

geographical position and its air and naval bases provide effective control of and protection for the sea lines of communication; it connects the Dardanelles and the Black Sea with Suez through the Aegean Sea. Crete also connects the ports of the Eastern Mediterranean with the Adriatic Sea and the Western Mediterranean. Because of its position, Crete is of great strategic value. Whoever controls Crete also controls almost the entire Eastern Mediterranean. Paired with Cyprus, Crete is in a position effectively to control all sea lines of communication in the area.

After World War II, Greece made the right choices. It actively participated in all the important international organizations and is a member of the United Nations, the European Union, NATO and the Western European Union. It has, therefore, the right to play a specific role and demand of its allies the application of all international agreements pertaining to it and to its interests in the region, and to safeguard its rights.

Because of its Eastern Orthodox faith, the religion followed by the vast majority of the Greek people, and its historic ties with the Arab world, Greece has the potential to be the link connecting the West with Russia and other countries that belonged to the Warsaw Pact, as well as with Middle Eastern and African countries. As Greece is a small country, it cannot follow a fully independent policy. It could, however, play the important role of mediator for the protection of the West's as well as the Eastern Mediterranean region's interests, provided that Greece's rights are safeguarded. In other words Greece, being faithful to its alliances and its obligations toward the international organizations of which it is a member, must safeguard its national interests, which in turn should be pursued within the framework of international law and Greece's historic traditions.

The role of Greece will prove important for the international community as well as for its allies, as long as Greece is relieved from the pressures exerted against it by its neighbors, and if its neighbors comply with the obligations they have undertaken toward various international organizations.

Greece is more advanced than its neighbors in various sectors. Its geographical position projects it as a key factor for stability in the Eastern Mediterranean and, as Greece is a node connecting North with South and East with West, for the establishment of honest and sincere communications among the various peoples of the region.

In the event of new disturbances in the wider area, Greece will be able to participate actively in the reestablishment of order, provided it has been relieved of claims against it by its neighbors.

The role of Greece in the Gulf War has not been highlighted enough as an example of Greece's capabilities for participating in solving crises in the wider area. Additionally, an axis comprised of Greece, the Republic of Cyprus, and Israel could emerge as an alternative partnership in the event that Turkey could not or would not participate in a future conflict in the region.

The role of the U.S. NATO, and the E.U.

Having given my estimation of the present role of Greece in the Eastern Mediterranean, I would like to close with my estimation of the role of the United States of America, NATO and the European Union, so that the area will serve their interests in the long term.

One of the principal aims of the U.S. as well as the E.U. should be the prevalence of long-term stability, so that goods, especially Caucasus and Caspian oil, can be transported without obstructions, at least until other oil-rich areas are identified and secured.

While the U.S. has chosen to reduce its expenditure on armaments, it has not encouraged other members of NATO to do the same, in order that the battle-effectiveness of the alliance will be maintained. The relatively strong countries in the Eastern Mediterranean, i.e., Turkey, Greece, and Israel maintain their military forces at a satisfactory level and are in the position to complement effectively the forces of the U.S. and the other members of NATO in the event of a hostile outbreak. At the same time, however, inherent in the existing levels of armaments and the arms race between Turkey and Greece is the danger of an armed conflict, as long as the problems put forth by Turkey from time to time remain unsolved.

Many have praised the Dayton agreement that ended the Bosnian conflict, and some see it as a model to be applied in similar cases. I don't share this optimism. The agreement is fragile, and the various claims put forth by the new states created by the dissolution of Yugoslavia threaten the peace.

At the same time, dangers from religion-based outbreaks, already visible in Turkey and northeastern Africa, combined with the problems discussed above, present the United States and the European Union with difficult roles and choices.

Regarding the Balkans, more specifically the region of former Yugoslavia, a plan is needed that would provide for closer economic cooperation among all the new countries, thereby defusing the passions accumulated by the war and, through economic development, preventing new outbreaks. The obvious solution for a peaceful future for these countries is to create some form of economic union.

Political solutions, such as having recourse to the International Court at The Hague in order to circumvent existing treaties, will not serve any purpose as they will not be accepted by the losing side and may establish destabilizing precedents.

Limits on armament levels for each country would ensure a balance of power for security reasons while not adversely affecting the military power of NATO. At the same time, and given the future expansion of NATO, Article 5 of the NATO Treaty must be reviewed so as to ensure peace among all member states by the inclusion of provisions for the inviolability of the borders of all member states and for the safeguarding of good neighborly relations.

To summarize briefly, Greece can play an important role in safeguarding the interests in the Eastern Mediterranean of allied and friendly countries, provided that Greece receives the support it needs to solve the problems that its neighbors, especially Turkey, are creating.

The Aegean Sea, confined and dotted with Greek islands, must be controlled by Greece. Greece has a long history of always being faithful to its allies and honoring its obligations; it has the right to expect that those allies will support Greece's territorial integrity.

In conclusion, as shown in the preceding analysis of the political and economic realities of Greece's geostrategic position, supporting the role of Greece in the Eastern Mediterranean is an excellent investment in world peace and economic prosperity. ✦

Greek-American Relations From the Early Cold War to the Present: An Overview

Athanasios Platias

This paper, as its title suggests, will attempt to provide an overview of the evolution of relations between Greece and the United States, starting from the early period of the Cold War. The analysis takes as a starting point the promulgation of the Truman Doctrine in 1947. Three periods in Greek-American relations are distinguished:

a) From the Greek civil war until 1974.

b) From 1974 until the end of the Cold War.

c) Greek-American relations in the post-Cold War international system.

From the Greek Civil War until 1974

At the beginning of World War II Ioannis Metaxas, then Greek Prime Minister, summarized Greece's position as follows:

If the Germans prevail, we shall become their slaves. If the British prevail, we shall become their slaves. If none [prevails], Europe will collapse. Anyhow, it [Greece] will collapse.[1]

Indeed, Greece did collapse during World War II.[2] Nor did the end of the war bring peace to Greece. While other nations devoted themselves to recovery, Greece became the battleground of a savage civil war. At the end of the war the royalist government in exile and the communist-led National

---

ATHANASSIOS G. PLATIAS is Associate Professor of Strategic Studies at Panteion University of Social and Political Sciences in Athens.

1. Ioannis Metaxas, *His Personal Diary, 1933-1941*, 4 volumes, Faidon Branas, ed. (Athens: Ikaros, 1960), Vol. 4, p. 484.
2. The war accounted for nearly 550,000 dead. Seventy thousand Greeks were executed by the Germans; 1,770 villages and one-fourth of all buildings were destroyed; two-thirds of the Merchant Marine was lost; communications and transportation broke down; one-third of the forest area was burned; arable land was reduced by one-third; industry was brought to a standstill and inflation was astronomical. See Constantine Tsoukalas, *The Greek Tragedy* (Harmondsworth: Penguin Books, 1969), pp. 91-92.

Liberation Force (EAM) and its People's Army of Liberation (ELAS) started a bloody struggle for primacy in post-war Greece. Without going into an account of the civil war,[3] suffice it to say that the fighting ended in 1949 with the dominance of the royalist forces, which were massively supported by the British and the Americans. The civil war added greatly to the already vast material destruction caused by the Second World War. As a result, Greece emerged from its civil war totally destroyed as well as totally dependent upon American support. As Geoffrey Chandler aptly observed in the 1950s: "Greece is being carried on the wave of American aid."[4]

Under the auspices of the Truman Doctrine and the Marshall Plan, Greece entered the post-World War II international order linked firmly with the dominant Western power, the United States of America. This was the natural result of the fact that the United States had by then become the dominant power in the Eastern Mediterranean, assuming the position hitherto held by Great Britain. Consequently, Greece fell within the American sphere of influence precisely in the same way as it had fallen within the British sphere of influence more than a century ago. Thus, a "patron-client relationship" was established between Greece and the United States.[5]

The Greek-American relationship turned out to be a mutually beneficial one. To start with, the very first benefit accruing to the United States was a political one. The very fact that the communist forces were defeated and Greece joined the Western bloc was an ample demonstration that the Truman Doctrine was working and that the spread of communism could be effectively thwarted.

---

3. The literature on the civil war is voluminous: Edgar o' Ballance, *The Greek Civil War: 1944-1949* (London: Faber and Faber, 1966); Evangelos Averoff-Tossizza, *By Fire and Axe: The Communist Party and the Civil War of Greece, 1944-1949* (New Rochelle, New York: Caratzas Brothers, Publishers, 1978); Tsoukalas, *The Greek Tragedy*, pp. 85-126; John O. Iatrides, "Civil War, 1945-1949: National and International Aspects" in John O. Iatrides, ed. *Greece in the 1940's: A Nation in Crisis* (Hanover, New Hampshire: University Press of New England, 1981), pp. 195-219; Dominique Eudes, *The Kapetanios: Partisans and Civil War in Greece* (New York: Monthly Review, 1978).
4. Geoffrey Chandler, "Greece: Relapse or Recovery," *International Affairs* 28 (April 1950), p. 191.
5. This was admitted publicly by Robert Keeley, American Ambassador to Greece from 1985 until 1990, during his confirmation hearings before Congress (July 25, 1985) and again a year later during an interview with a Greek daily newspaper. See *Eleftherotypia*, July 14 and 15, 1986, pp. 14-15, 18-19 and 44.

Second, Greece was an important link in the American chain of containment. Not only did Greece bar communist access to the Aegean and the Mediterranean, but also, by ensuring contiguity, made it possible for NATO forces to defend Turkey. Simply put, had Greece fallen under communist rule, Turkey would have been strategically indefensible.

Third, Greece assured Western control of the Aegean Sea. The Aegean constitutes an important sea lane of communication (SLOC) that ships have to go through in order to gain access to the Mediterranean. The numerous Greek islands in the Aegean provide an ideal means of preventing a hostile fleet from reaching the Mediterranean.

Finally, the United States obtained a number of forward military bases on Greek territory. The principal American bases established during the 1952-63 period include: the Hellenikon Air Base (1953), the Suda Bay complex in Crete (1959), the Heraklion Air Base (1954), and the Nea Makri naval communications complex (1963). In addition to the military bases, in 1959 the Greek government accepted American nuclear weapons on Greek soil in several Special Ammunition Storage Sites (SAS) all over the country.[6]

Greece also stood to gain from this relationship. American aid to Greece, both economic and military, was massive and was instrumental in the reconstruction of the country after the disasters of the period 1941-49. In addition, the American connection neutralized the threat Greece was facing from the north. Not only was the active communist attempt to seize power in Greece defeated, but the inclusion of Greece in the Western camp effectively thwarted any revisionist dreams entertained by Greece's northern neighbors.

Finally, Greece gained access to a variety of Western institutions, chiefly NATO. In fact, Greece was not among the founding members of the alliance. The opposition of Britain, combined with the strong reluctance of the Scandinavian and Benelux countries resulted in the exclusion of Greece and Turkey. The British insisted that Greece and Turkey were to be central states in an envisaged Middle East defense organization. The Scandinavian and Benelux countries expressed their unwillingness to assume responsibility for the defense of a region geographically distant from Western Europe. They also feared that their obligations under the NATO treaty

6. For a comprehensive discussion of the nuclear weapons agreements, see Christos Sazanides, *Foreigners, Bases and Nuclear Weapons in Greece* (Thessalonike: Published by the Author, 1985), pp. 412-24 (text in Greek).

might force them to interfere in the Greek civil war.[7] As the international situation deteriorated, however, with the outbreak of the Korean war and political turmoil in the Middle East, the United States applied intense pressure on the smaller European states and persuaded them to withdraw their objections to Greek and Turkish accession. Consequently, a unanimous decision was made at the NATO council in Ottawa (September 15-20, 1951) to "extend invitations" to Greece and Turkey to join the Atlantic Alliance. On February 18, 1952 at the NATO meeting in Lisbon both countries were formally admitted to the organization.

On the negative side, Greece incurred some substantial costs for its close relationship with the United States. To start with, Washington frequently intervened in Greek domestic politics. In 1952 Greece, ruled by a coalition consisting of members of the two major centrist parties, was about to hold elections. Then a difference arose over the electoral system. The right-wing party was in favor of the "majority electoral system," while the coalition of centrist parties was seeking to preserve the "simple proportional system." This dispute triggered American interference. While the debate was at its peak, the U.S. Ambassador, John Peurifoy, made a public statement in favor of the "majority system," threatening to halt U.S. aid if it was not accepted. Given that Greece in 1952 was still "breathing with American lungs," it is easy to understand why the government complied with the American request.[8]

The so-called "Peurifoy incident" was by no means an isolated case of interference. Until 1974 the United States had heavy input on decisions dealing with the armed forces, the economy, and foreign policy.[9] In some cases the capacity for interference rested on threats of negative sanctions (viz. threats of withholding military and economic aid provided by the

---

7. See, for example, the Danish views on this issue in Joe R. Wilkinson, "Denmark and NATO: The Problem of a Small State in a Collective Security System," *International Organization* 10 (August 1956), pp. 395-396. For the attitude of Norway and the Netherlands, see *Foreign Relations of the United States 1950,* 3, p. 327.
8. For a detailed account of the Peurifoy incident, see Theodore Couloumbis, "Greek Political Reaction to American and NATO Influences," pp. 53-60, Maurice Goldbloom, "United States Policy in Post-War Greece," in Richard Clogg and George Yannopoulos, eds. *Greece Under Military Rule* (London: Secker & Warburg, 1972). For the views of Peurifoy on the issue of the Greek elections, see his report to the State Department in *Foreign Relations of the United States, 1952-1954,* pp. 270-272.
9. Theodore Couloumbis, John A. Petropoulos, and Harry J. Psomiades, *Foreign Interference in Greek Politics: A Historical Perspective* (New York: Pella Publishing Co., Inc., 1971), pp. 113-128.

Marshall Plan). In other cases, the U.S. intervened directly in the nation's political process.

Another penalty Greece had to pay for its relationship with the United States was to sacrifice the interests of the Greek majority on Cyprus, since the U.S. consistently supported first Britain and then Turkey on the Cyprus problem. Without going into a historical account of this problem,[10] suffice it to say that it stems from the desire on the one hand of an overwhelming majority of Greek-Cypriots (eighty percent of the island's population) for unification *(enosis)* with Greece, and on the other hand the opposition of Britain and later Turkey. During the 1950s Cyprus became an international dispute involving three NATO members: Britain (the colonial power), Greece, and Turkey (due to the Turkish-Cypriot minority, comprising eighteen percent of the island's population).

The Cyprus crisis created a serious problem for NATO due to American insistence on mediating and settling the crisis quietly within the NATO framework. However, if a settlement had been reached within NATO, it would probably have been based on the relative importance of Greece and Turkey, and thus would have favored Turkey. A political compromise within NATO was precisely what the Greeks and the Greek-Cypriot community did not want. They thought that if external powers had to be involved it was better to place the dispute in the broader context of the United Nations, where newly emerged countries were sensitive to demands for self-determination. Britain predictably encouraged U.S./NATO mediation since it would not have been able, in the U.N., to muster support for its imperial policies, especially among members that were former colonies. The issue of internationalization versus mediation brought Greece's relations with NATO and the U.S. to a crisis point.[11]

The London-Zurich agreements of 1959, which resulted from strong U.S. and NATO pressure on Greece,[12] proved that Greek fears regarding the partiality of NATO were justified. Cyprus was proclaimed an independent

10. See Doros Alastos, *Cyprus in History* (London: Zeno Publishers, 1955); Nancy Crawshaw, *The Cyprus Revolt: An Account of the Struggle for Union with Greece* (London: George Allen & Unwin, 1978); Polivios Poliviou, *Cyprus: The Tragedy and the Challenge* (London: John Swain & Son, 1975); Stephen G. Xydis, *Cyprus: Conflict and Conciliation, 1954-1958* (Columbus: Ohio State University Press, 1967).
11. See Evangelos Coufoudakis-Petroussis, "International Organizations and Small State Conflicts: The Greek Experience" (Ph.D. diss., University of Michigan, 1972), pp. 245-329.
12. See, for example, President Eisenhower's message to Prime Minister Karamanlis in 1958. *Presidential Handling,* Verbatim Text, Department of State, June 6, 1958, Dwight D. Eisenhower Library.

state; Britain achieved its primary concern, the maintenance of its military bases in Cyprus; the Turkish and Turkish-Cypriot sides were pleased because the Cypriot constitution gave the Turkish minority disproportionate political power by granting its leaders veto power on important domestic and foreign legislation. The constitution was also designed to preclude *enosis,* the primary concern of the Turks. In addition, the guarantor powers (Great Britain, Greece, and Turkey) were authorized to intervene in the event that the provisions of the constitution were not adhered to (this is the provision under which Turkey would repeatedly threaten to intervene in the years that followed).

The parties least satisfied with the London-Zurich agreements were Greece and the Greek majority in Cyprus. Greece was disappointed in its several attempts to get the U.S. and NATO to support its position in Cyprus. The Greek-Cypriots, instead of *enosis,* for which they had fought for years, received independence. Moreover, the constitution gave the Turkish-Cypriot community exceptional minority rights that were seen as, in effect, denying equality to the Greek-Cypriot majority. In short, there was widespread feeling in Greece that the U.S. and NATO had played Britain's and Turkey's cards rather than Greek ones at this stage of the Cyprus problem. Also, there was widespread resentment among Greek-Cypriots that an unsatisfactory solution had been imposed by outside powers with no participation from the Greek-Cypriots themselves. Against this background, cooperation between the two communities in implementing the provisions of the constitution was essentially non-existent, and disputes arose in almost every sphere of the government. These precipitated a series of crises (1963-65, 1967, and 1974). The 1974 crisis proved decisive. In the summer of that year the Greek military dictatorship overthrew Makarios, the Greek-Cypriot president of Cyprus, and Turkey used this opportunity as a pretext to invade the island.

The response of the U.S. and NATO was to do nothing, which the Greeks viewed as favoritism toward Turkey.[13] Greek politicians of all party affiliations argued that the U.S. and NATO could have taken several actions, both before and after the invasion, which might have prevented the situation from escalating.

First, the U.S. could have discouraged Demetrios Ioannides (the leader of the Greek junta in 1974) from staging the *coup d' état* against Makarios. It is well established that the U.S. knew that a coup was in the works.

13. See Nikolaos A. Stavrou, "Kissinger's Tilt on Cyprus: The New Style of Crisis Diplomacy," in *U.S. Foreign Policy Toward Greece and Cyprus: The Clash of Principle and Pragmatism,* in Theodore Couloumbis and Sally Hicks, eds. (Washington: Center for Mediterranean Studies, 1975), pp. 98-105.

The Pike Committee, which investigated the performance of U.S. intelligence in the 1974 Cyprus crisis, cites several strategic and tactical warning indicators in this respect. Yet the U.S. failed to discourage Ioannides.[14] Some politicians and scholars, including Ioannides himself, argue that the U.S. did exactly the opposite, encouraging him to go ahead with the coup. This would explain his surprise and outrage when he was informed of the Turkish landing; he was immediately enraged at what he considered outright American betrayal.[15]

Second, joint pressure on Turkey by the U.S. and Britain might have stopped or limited the extent of Turkey's intervention. No such pressure was applied.[16]

Third, the U.S. could have pressured Turkey to continue the Geneva talks in 1974. Instead, the Turks mounted a second campaign to secure their territorial objectives and to accomplish the long-desired partition of the island republic, apparently without U.S. objections.[17]

Another cloud over Greek-American relations during this period was the uncritical acceptance by the U.S. of the Greek military dictatorship of 1967-1974. In April 1967 a group of colonels led by George Papadopoulos overthrew the civilian government. Leaving aside the controversial question of

---

14. House Select Committee on Intelligence (1976), quoted in Christopher Hitchens, *Cyprus,* (London, Melbourne, New York: Quartet Books, 1984) p. 76.
15. According to Laurence Stern, Ioannides told colleagues months after the coup that "if you knew what I knew and had the reassurances that I had before the coup, you would have done exactly as I did," complaining that the U.S. had misled him on the possibility of a Turkish invasion. See "Bitter Lessons," *Foreign Policy* 19 (Summer 1975), p. 51.
16. See U.S. House of Representatives Select Committee on Intelligence, *U.S. Intelligence Agencies and Activities: Committee Proceedings,* 94th Cong., 1st sess., 1975, pp. 1302-1303. See also Couloumbis, *The U.S., Greece and Turkey* (New York: Braeger, 1983), pp. 88-93; Hitchens, *Cyprus,* pp. 87-90; Laurence Stern, *The Wrong Horse: The Politics of Intervention and Failure of American Diplomacy* (New York: Times Books, 1977), pp. 110-124.
17. See U.S. House of Representatives Select Committee on Intelligence, *U.S. Intelligence Agencies and Activities: Committee Proceedings,* 94th Cong., 1st sess., 1975, p. 1295. See also Stern, *The Wrong Horse,* pp. 125-133; Stavrou, "Kissinger's Tilt on Cyprus", p. 103.
18. It is well established that the State Department knew that a "Rightist Greek Military Conspiratorial Group" was ready to stage a coup. See Stern, *The Wrong Horse,* pp. 41-46. See also "Greece in Political Crisis," *Administrative History: The Department of State During the Administration of President Lyndon B. Johnson,* November 1963-January 1969, ch. 4, sec. J, LBJ Library. It does not follow, however, that the U.S. engineered the *coup d'état.* In fact, this conspiratorial explanation is superficial and unconvincing.

whether American officials had knowledge of or even were implicated in the military takeover,[18] some of the ensuing events can be briefly analyzed.

The colonels' regime evoked an immediate response in most of Europe, and the NATO alliance divided into two camps over the issue. One, consisting mostly of smaller European members (Norway, Denmark, etc.), argued that Greece should be ousted from the alliance and arms supplies should be halted immediately. The other, led by the bigger NATO countries, such as the U.S. and Britain, argued that Greece's strategic location and importance made it necessary to tolerate the regime. They argued that there was no real choice and that the alternative was worse: movement by the colonels toward neutrality.[19] As a result, the regime of the colonels—who had used a NATO contingency plan to take over and claimed to have done so for security reasons—was accepted as a functioning member of NATO.

Throughout the junta's rule, the U.S. supported it in every respect. Although in theory shipments of heavy weapons were cut off between 1967 and 1970, the U.S. remained the major supplier of military equipment to the dictatorship. The colonels reciprocated for the support they enjoyed. For example, the American bases in Greece remained open and available during the June 1967 war and the Yom Kippur war (1973).

Furthermore, new arrangements for continued use of the bases were negotiated, the most important being the "home port" agreement, which provided permanent port facilities for the Sixth Fleet in Greece.[20] By sending Sixth Fleet families to Greece, the American Navy was able to reduce the length of time that sailors and their families were separated and thus reduce the time and expense of rotating ships across the Atlantic to the Mediterranean. However, the massive arrival of thousands of Americans in Greece further reinforced the belief of Greeks of all political affiliations that the U.S. had somehow been involved in the 1967 coup.

As a further mark of American support for the military dictatorship, Vice-President Spiro Agnew visited Greece in 1971, as did other influential Americans, such as General Andrew Goodpaster, Secretary of Defense Melvin Laird, and Commerce Secretary Maurice Stans. The visitors smil-

---

19. See, for example, the position taken by Assistant Secretary of State for European Affairs Martin J. Hillebrand, in the *International Herald Tribune,* May 15, 1971. See also U.S. Subcommittee on the Near East, *The Decision to Homeport in Greece: Report, December 31, 1972* (Washington, D.C.: GPO, 1972).
20. For an analysis of the home-porting decision, see Thomas Keagy and Yannis Roubatis, "Homeporting with the Greek Junta: Something New and More of the Same in U.S. Foreign Policy", in *U.S. Foreign Policy Toward Greece and Cyprus,* pp. 49-65.

ingly posed next to Papadopoulos, further identifying the U.S. with the military regime.[21]

Finally, Greece faced another negative aspect of its relationship with the U.S., namely the reduction of Greek military capabilities vis-à-vis Turkey as a result of the different roles each country was assigned within NATO. Turkey was supposed to be the primary Soviet target in the area and, therefore, required a robust defense designed to "make a maximum contribution to an allied war effort."[22] The Greek posture, on the other hand, was designed to "insure internal security and to perform limited military missions consistent with U.S. plans."[23]

Given this unequal allocation of defense roles between Greece and Turkey, it is not difficult to evaluate the implications, for Greece's security, of their joint entrance into NATO. The military implications of such role prescriptions within NATO were that Greece was not capable of fighting against any possible Turkish attack. The material preconditions for adequate defense (viz. strong naval and air components) were lacking.[24] Furthermore, when it became apparent during the years 1963-1965 that the continuing deterioration of Greek-Turkish relations over Cyprus might lead to war, the U.S. adopted a policy that emphasized reducing the capabilities of the Greek armed forces to fight such a war.[25] This proved to be a source of frustration and disillusionment for Greece in 1964 and especially in 1974. During the Cyprus crisis of 1963-64, U.S. officials told Greek authorities that in the event of a Greek-Turkish war, Turkish armed forces would not only win the war but, in the words of Robert McNamara, "would literally burn up the Greek countryside."[26] Ten years later, during

21. A total of thirty-eight American generals and admirals visited Greece within the first eighteen months of the dictatorship. See U.S. Senate Committee on Foreign Relations, *United States Security and Agreements Abroad* pt. 7 (Washington, D.C.: GPO, 1970), pp. 1839-1840. See also Phyllis Craig, "The United States and the Greek Dictatorship: A Summary of Support," *Journal of the Hellenic Diaspora* (Winter 1976), pp. 13-14.
22. Kenneth Condit, *The History of the Joint Chiefs of Staff* (Wilmington: Michael Clazier, 1979), pp. 425-426. See also NSC 42/1 in *Foreign Relations of the United States, 1948,* 6, p. 452.
23. Ibid. See also NSC 103, *Foreign Relations of the United States, 1951,* 5, p. 452.
24. See Yannis Roubatis, "The United States and the Operational Responsibilities of the Greek Armed Forces, 1947-1967," *Journal of the Hellenic Diaspora* 6 (Spring 1973), p. 52.
25. Ibid., pp. 49-52.
26. Quoted in Andreas Papandreou, *Democracy at Gunpoint: The Greek Front* (New York: Doubleday, 1970), p. 135; idem., *Journal of Parliamentary Debates,* 17 April 1976, p. 4501.

the Turkish invasion, when Prime Minister Constantine Karamanlis ordered a division sent to Cyprus, he was informed by the General Staff that this was impossible due to lack of adequate air cover.[27]

Thus, the relationship between Greece and the United States during the period ranging from the promulgation of the Truman Doctrine in 1949 until the fall of the Greek junta and the Turkish invasion of Cyprus in 1974 was a mutually beneficial one. At the same time, however, Greece, as the weaker party in the relationship, had to bear some costs. As the Turkish invasion of Cyprus showed, by the end of that period the costs had come to be particularly high. Suddenly Greece realized that it had the worst of the bargain, i.e., it was dependent on the United States and insecure with regard to its chief security concern: the threat from Turkey. It is against this background that Greek-American relations entered the period from 1974 until the end of the Cold War.

From 1974 to the End of the Cold War

The 1974 Cyprus crisis precipitated the fall of the dictatorship. The post-junta Greek governments, both conservative and socialist, tried to minimize their dependence on the U.S. and the Atlantic community. By restricting U.S. freedom of action in Greece, substantially increasing relations with Western European countries, and directing the country's defense effort (e.g., expenditures, organization, deployment, and procurement) to the fulfillment of Greece's national strategic interests, they tried to limit the costs associated with Greece's Atlantic orientation.

The first issue that demonstrated Greece's attempt to increase her independence was the country's withdrawal from the military wing of NATO, as a result of Turkey's second and unprovoked aggression against Cyprus on August 14, 1974, and the second failure of the U.S. and NATO to react. The Greek government believed that Greece's withdrawal from NATO's military wing would draw attention to the Cyprus drama and induce Greece's Western allies to work for a just solution by pressuring Turkey to make concessions. At the same time, the Karamanlis government wanted to defuse the explosive state of public emotions (the public blamed the U.S. and NATO for not preventing the Turkish invasion of Cyprus and for tilting in favor of Turkey).[28]

---

27. See C. M. Woodhouse, *Karamanlis: The Restorer of Greek Democracy,* (Oxford: Clarendon Press, 1982), p. 217.
28. For an analysis of the domestic determinants of Karamanlis' choice, see the account of Minister of Foreign Affairs Demetrios Bitsios in *Beyond the Borders, 1974-1977* (Athens: Kollaros, 1983), pp. 204-206 (text in Greek). See also Woodhouse, *Karamanlis,* p. 219.

It did not take long, however, for the Karamanlis government to reconsider its position. In September 1975, a NATO exercise in the Aegean took place under the command of a Turkish admiral, and operational control of the Aegean was assigned to Turkey. This meant that Turkey had the opportunity to advance its claims in the Aegean from within the alliance, further weakening Greece's position.

In light of this threat, the Greek government changed its position and sought to re-enter the alliance's military branch. As a first step, the concept of a "special relationship" (viz. national control in peacetime and integration in wartime) was developed. This arrangement meant that Greece would not be a member of the Defense Planning Committee (DPC) and would not assign troops to NATO commanders; it would, however, have representatives in all NATO commands-except the one in Smyrna-and would be involved in certain infrastructure projects.[29] In reality, Greece returned to NATO for most purposes within a year after its withdrawal, despite the fact that no progress had been made toward a Cyprus settlement.

At the same time, deliberations on official Greek re-entry moved extremely slowly due to the Greek-Turkish dispute over operational control of the Aegean. NATO established an open-ended committee to resolve the problem, and after four years of negotiations under the auspices of Allied Supreme Commanders Alexander Haig and Bernard Rogers, an agreement was reached on October 22, 1980 (just over one month after a military junta seized power in Turkey). The reintegration agreement, known as the Rogers Agreement, was ambiguous enough for both governments to save face.[30]

In the actions of the Greek government toward NATO after 1974, one can clearly see the tradeoff between reducing Greece's reliance on NATO on the one hand, and on the other, avoiding the total isolation that would simply strengthen Turkey's hand.[31]

The Greek government faced the same dilemma in its policy toward the United States.[32] On the one hand, it tried to reduce Greek dependence on the U.S. by:

---

29. See U.S. Senate Committee on Foreign Relations, *Turkey, Greece and NATO: The Strained Alliance,* 96th Cong., 2d Sess. (Washington, D.C.: GPO, March 1980), p. 59.
30. Some of the ambiguities were exposed in the Greek parliament. See *Journal of Parliamentary Debates,* 22 October 1980, pp. 704-721.
31. Ibid., p. 705.
32. John O. Iatrides, "Greece and the United States: The Strained Partnership", in *Greece in the 1980s,* Richard Clogg, ed. (London: Macmillan, 1983), pp. 168-169.

- diversifying Greece's sources of military support;
- shifting emphasis in Greece's foreign orientation from the U.S. to Western Europe (membership in the European Economic Ccommunity [EEC]);
- reducing the number of the principal U.S. bases in Greece (e.g. termination of the home-port agreement);
- restricting the degree of freedom of the remaining American bases in Greece (i.e., the bases were placed under Greek control);
- initiating a process of re-evaluation of the future of American bases;
- and, at a symbolic level, substantially improving relations with Greece's northern communist neighbors and the Soviet Union itself.

On the other hand, the Greek government tried to mobilize U.S. support for dealing with Greece's primary security threat, Turkey. In particular, Greece:

- pressed the U.S. to maintain the arms embargo imposed upon Turkey;
- requested American guarantees in the form of an official declaration of assistance in the event of a Turkish attack;
- and requested American guarantees in the form of a 7:10 ratio in the military assistance granted to Greece and Turkey.

All these factors taken together show that the post-junta conservative governments made every effort to change the traditional patron-client relationship that had prevailed in Greek-American relations since the announcement of the Truman Doctrine. They followed a clearly pro-Western policy, but refused to make unilateral sacrifices (as they had in the 1950s) to Turkey in the name of safeguarding Western interests.

After 1981, the socialist Greek government tried to show its independence from the United States by a number of symbolic actions. For instance, Greece refused to go along with sanctions against the Soviet Union after the imposition of martial law in Poland, and to condemn Moscow for shooting down a Korean air liner. The so-called "Initiative of the Six" was another such instance.[33] Although these were largely symbolic actions that

33. For highly critical accounts of the foreign policy of the Greek socialist government, see John C. Loulis, "Papandreou's Foreign Policy," *Foreign Affairs,* 63 (Winter 1984/85), pp. 375-381; idem., *Greece Under Papandreou: NATO's Ambivalent Partner* (London: Institute for European Defense and Strategic Studies, 1985); Panagiote E. Dimitras, "Greece: A New Danger," *Foreign Policy,* 58 (Spring 1985), pp. 134-150. For more balanced accounts, see Theodore A. Couloumbis and Maria E Conalis, "Greek Foreign Policy in a European Setting," paper presented at the conference of the Modern Greek Studies Association, New York, October 27-30, 1983; L.S. Stavrianos, "'Greece First' Provokes a Showdown," *International Herald Tribune,* March 26, 1985.

did not harm any vital U.S. interests, they still created enormous problems in bilateral relations.

Greece also made it clear that it would not sacrifice sovereign Greek interests in the Aegean for the sake of allied solidarity. As a result, the Rogers Agreement, which called for the establishment of a new allied air force command in Larissa (SEVENATAF), remained in suspension because of disagreements regarding operational responsibilities in the Aegean archipelago. The Greek government has also refused to participate in NATO exercises in protest of NATO's failure to include the island of Lemnos in allied planning and exercises.

Although the socialist Greek government often employed strong anti-American rhetoric and was critical of the U.S. on both bilateral and global issues, it actually adopted a moderate policy on the continued operation of American bases in Greece, an issue vital for the U.S. Thus, a Defense and Economic Cooperation Agreement (DECA) was concluded in 1983, extending the presence of the American bases for a five-year period.

In return for permission for the continued presence of American facilities, Greece received a generally worded commitment to maintain a ratio of 7:10 in the distribution of American military aid to Greece and Turkey.[34] Furthermore, according to DECA, Greece obtained the right to prohibit the use of the facilities against "friendly countries" in the region. Additionally, Greece would control the bases' activities and could limit or temporarily suspend their operation when national interests dictated such a move. Finally, the extraterritorial privileges of American personnel were modified on Greece's behalf.[35] DECA, when compared to the original 1953 agreement, clearly underscores the degree of change in Greek-American relations.

This was a difficult period for Greek-American relations, marred by Greek resentment over issues such as Cyprus, U.S. support for the military regime, and the subsequent failure of the U.S. and NATO to restrain Turkey and guarantee Greek security in the Aegean. This period was also characterized by the reorientation of Greek foreign policy toward Europe, culminating in Greece's accession to the EEC. It must be noted, however, that no vital U.S. interests were injured by the new, more independent Greek stance. Moreover, Greece continued to seek U.S. support on Cyprus and on dealing with Turkey.

34. In particular, Article VIII of DECA stated: "Such United States assistance shall also be guided by the principle set forth in the U.S. law that calls for preserving the balance of military strength in the region." See *Journal of Parliamentary Debates*, 7 November 1983, p. 1113.

35. For details, see *Journal of Parliamentary Debates*, 31 October 1983, pp. 814ff.

Greek-American Relations in the Post-Cold-War International System

Every discussion of the relations between Greece and the U.S. in the period after the end of the Cold War must be placed in the context of American interests in the Eastern Mediterranean as the post-Cold-War international system emerges. Since the end of the Cold War there has been a steady increase in the importance of this area for the U.S. From the Gulf War onward there has been a continued U.S. presence in the area. Washington has also played a central role in developments in the former Yugoslavia, while the American role in Central Asia and the Caucasus region has also increased. In fact, U.S. foreign policy in the region takes the form of selective and limited engagement, i.e., involvement only in the event that the U.S. needs to advance and defend its interests.

The importance of the Eastern Mediterranean traditionally stems from the fact that it is an extension of both Europe and the Middle East, two of the most important regions in the world.[36] There are, consequently, two good reasons for increased U.S. concern with the broader area of the Eastern Mediterranean.

The first reason is that immediately after the end of the Cold War the U.S. endeavored to increase its influence in those regions traditionally belonging to the Russian/Soviet sphere of influence. This is evident from the NATO expansion in Central and Eastern Europe, from continuous efforts to incorporate the Balkan countries into Western economic and political institutions, and from similar efforts in Central Asia, the Caucasus and the Middle East.

The second reason for the increase in the importance of the region is the strategy of double containment that the U.S. follows in the Middle East with regard to Iran and Iraq. Immediately after the Gulf War the U.S. tried to contain the power of these two states, so as to prevent them from playing a leading role in the Middle East. For this strategy to succeed, it is extremely important for the U.S. to control, as effectively as possible, the Eastern Mediterranean, including Turkey, Israel, and pro-Western Arab states such as Egypt and Saudi Arabia.

Apart from these reasons, which chiefly reflect developments in Eastern Europe and the Middle East, there is a third reason for increased U.S. concern with the Eastern Mediterranean. This is the crucial geoeconomic issue of control of the routes by which the oil of Central Asia and the Cau-

36. Van Coufoudakis, "U.S. Perspectives of Security and Regional Cooperation in the Eastern Mediterranean," Cyprus Research Centre-KYKEM, mimeo.

casus will reach the West.[37] There are three possible routes: through Iran to the Gulf; through Russian territory (to Novorossyisk on the Black Sea) and thence to the Aegean, either through the Turkish straits or via the Bourgas-Alexandroupolis pipeline);[38] through Turkey to the Turkish Eastern Mediterranean port of Ceyhan. With the first option excluded for the time being, both the Russian and the Turkish routes highlight the importance of the Eastern Mediterranean and the Aegean.

Thus, it is obvious that the strategic value of the Eastern Mediterranean region is increasing. As to specific U.S. interests in the area, the first and foremost is the maintenance of stability. This quest for stability has many facets. It covers the Balkans and the containment of nationalism there. It also refers to the continuation of the peace process in the Middle East, the containment of Islamic fundamentalism, the attempt to prevent the proliferation of weapons of mass destruction, and the fight against terrorism. A very important aspect of the pursuit of stability in the region is that every effort must be exerted to avoid a war between Greece and Turkey. Accordingly, Washington tries consistently to avert a Greek-Turkish war both in Cyprus and in the Aegean (viz. the role of the U.S. during the Imia Crisis in 1996).

Another vital interest of the United States is the maintenance and/or use of military bases and facilities in the region, chiefly for power projection in the Middle East. The bases in Greece and Turkey are typical examples and the same applies to the British bases on Cyprus.[39]

Finally, the U.S. considers it in its interest that Turkey be admitted to Western institutions such as the European Union (EU), in an attempt to strengthen Turkey's pro-Western orientation, especially in light of the rise of Islamic fundamentalism.[40]

---

37. See Zbigniew Brzezinski, *The Grand Chessboard* (New York: Basic Books, 1997), pp. 134-150. Also, Stephen J. Blank, *Energy and Security in Transcaucasia* (Carlisle, PA: US Army College, 1994).
38. For an extensive analysis of the Bourgas-Alexandroupolis pipeline see Michael Myrianthis, "Oleaginous Geopolitics in SW Asia and the Burgas-Alexandroupolis Oil Pipeline," Occasional Research Paper 10 (Athens: Institute of International Relations, 1996).
39. For an analysis of the post-Cold-War strategic significance of Greece and Turkey see Van Coufoudakis, "The Relative Strategic Significance of Greece and Turkey Before and After the Cold War," paper presented at the Conference on the USA, Greece and Turkey in the Emerging International System, Athens, June 19, 1993, mimeo.
40. See Ian O. Lesser, *Turkey and the West: Bridge or Barrier?* (Santa Monica, CA: RAND, 1992).

Turning now to Greek-American relations *per se,* one can see that there is an amazing degree of coincidence between Greek and American interests in the Eastern Mediterranean region.[41] Regarding the issue of military bases and facilities, bilateral cooperation has been exemplary. From the Gulf War until the present crisis in Kosovo, Greece has been willing to assist U.S. and NATO forces.

Greece also is in favor of stability in the Eastern Mediterranean region. To start with, it has been very active in pursuing security and cooperation in the Balkans. Regarding this troubled area, the aims that Greece and the U.S. pursue are identical. Thus, both countries are making efforts to promote stability, the spread of democracy, and the establishment of free-market economies in the former communist Balkan countries. In addition, both Greece and the U.S. would like to see those countries entering Western institutions.[42]

Greece supports the peace process in the Middle East and maintains friendly relations with both the Arab countries and Israel. Moreover, as the massacre of Greek tourists in Egypt in 1996 testifies, Greece is perfectly aware of both the dangers inherent in the spread of Islamic fundamentalism and the need to combat terrorism. Once again, Greek-U.S. cooperation in this area is excellent.

The convergence of Greek and U.S. interests also extends to the geo-economic sphere. Thus, even if, at the end of the day, Caucasus oil were to be tranferred to the West via the Russian route, the Bourgas-Alexandroupolis pipeline would secure Western control over the route, thus curbing Russian influence in the area.

Regarding Greek-Turkish rapprochement, Greece and the U.S. have, partially at least, similar views. For such a rapprochement to take place, four preconditions must obtain:

First, the major powers must favor such a rapprochement. Thus, taking into account that the U.S. not only desires but is actively working toward such a development, there is a coincidence between Greek and American views on the subject.

Second, there must be mutual confidence that any Greek-Turkish agreement will be respected by the other party. There is, however, a bad

---

41. See John O. Iatrides, "The New Europe and U.S.-Greek Relations," *Journal of Modern Hellenism* 9, Winter 1992, pp. 51-62.
42. For the Greek policy in the Balkans in the post-Cold-War era, see Haralambos Papasotiriou, *The Balkans after the End of the Cold War* (Athens: Papazisis, 1993) (in Greek); idem., "Greek Strategic Choices in the Balkans," pp. 155-176 in *Institute of International Relations Yearbook,* 1997 (Athens: Sideris, 1997) (in Greek).

precedent in this respect. Although in 1988 Greece and Turkey reached an agreement, the so-called Papoulias-Yilmaz Memorandum, Turkey did not observe the terms of the agreement. This ruined any trust on the part of Greece in Turkey's professed willingness to cooperate. It is precisely at this point that the U.S. can play the most important role of honest broker. Actually, Washington seems willing to play such a role and Greece has asked it to do so. It was in this direction that [then] Greek Foreign Minister Pangalos moved during his visit to the U.S., when he linked the installation of Russian S-300 missiles in Cyprus with U.S. guarantees regarding the overflights of Turkish military aircraft.

For a Greek-Turkish rapprochement to take place, there must be an expectation of mutual benefit. This is indeed what both Greece and the U.S. believe to be the case, i.e., enhanced stability in the region.

Finally, the last, but not least, precondition for a rapprochement between Greece and Turkey is that both countries accept the status quo. This is where the problems lie, with Turkey clearly not accepting the status quo. This is also an issue of Greek grievances toward the U.S., since Athens feels that Washington could have done much more to pressure its Turkish ally to accept the status quo between Greece and Turkey. Remarks such as the one made by U.S. Deputy Secretary of State Strobe Talbott in a recent speech, in which he urged Turkey to "build bridges" in its relationship with Greece are helpful, but not sufficient.[43]

We have seen the high degree of convergence between the interests of Greece and the U.S in the post-Cold-War era. It is only when Turkey enters the scene that friction arises between Washington and Athens.

The first source of friction has to do with the issue of Confidence and Security-Building Measures (CSBMs) between Greece and Turkey.[44] Such measures can theoretically contribute to the elimination of an incentive to launch a war of choice by arranging the forces of the competitors in such a way that neither side thinks that it can initiate war with a reasonable probability of success. CSBMs may also help establish mutually agreed rules of behavior and reduce some uncertainty which can, at times, lead Turkey to miscalculate.

Both Greece and the U.S. believe that CSBMs can contribute to stability in the region. However, there is a difference in outlook, which often

43. See Strobe Talbott, "U.S.-Turkish Relations in an Age of Interdependence," Turgut Ozal Memorial Lecture, Washington Institute on Near East Policy, October 14, 1998.

44. For a more detailed discussion of Greek views on this matter, see Athanassios G. Platias, "Greek Deterrence Strategy," *Hellenic Studies* Vol. 4, No. 2 (Autumn 1996), Centre for Hellenic Studies and Research, Canada, pp. 33-54.

creates difficulties. While the U.S. gives priority to the stability of the region, Greece is chiefly concerned about its sovereignty, with regional stability coming next. Thus, in developing a policy on CSBMs, Greek defense analysts and policy-makers identify at least three requirements:[45]

a) CSBMs be inextricably linked to Turkey's willingness to respect the existing status quo and adhere to existing treaties. CSBMs should not be used to erode Greek sovereignty in the Aegean but only to improve stability;

b) as long as the threat of Turkey exists, the potential benefits of CSBMs will be balanced against the potential weakening of Greek deterrence; and

c) CSBMs or other agreements must be structured in such a way that if Turkey were to suddenly abrogate the terms, such actions would not endanger Greek security.

Another issue on which Greece and the U.S. do not necessarily see eye to eye is Turkey's role in Europe. It has already been pointed out that the U.S. would like to see Turkey enter the EU. Greece's position is not necessarily different. In fact, Foreign Minister Pangalos himself acknowledged that Turkey has a place in Europe. Greece, however, insists that Turkey has to fulfill certain conditions before it is considered ready for accession to the EU. Respect for human rights is one condition that Turkey clearly does not fulfill at present. The same applies to respecting the sovereignty and territorial integrity of EU member states, and accepting that disputes be settled solely on the basis of international law, without threat or use of force.

Since Turkey is manifestly not ready to enter the EU, Greece considers it unfair to be accused of being the party that blocks Turkey's entry. Actually, judging from the previously mentioned speech of Strobe Talbott it would seem that the U.S. has come to share the Greek view. Talbott stated that "many of the obstacles blocking Turkey's path to EU membership today are of Turkey's own making" and, as a means of prodding Turkey to "make the right decisions about its future," asked the EU "to say clearly and unequivocally that it is holding a place for Turkey when it is ready."[46]

There are some other issues that might result in friction between Greece and the U.S. Greece would like to see the United States support the Greek position in cases such as the crisis of the Imia islets. In that instance, it was obvious that the Imia islets are Greek, a fact that all American officials privately acknowledged. Consequently, Greece expected that the U.S. would confirm what was already evident, as they did with regard to Gav-

45. Interviews with policy-makers at the Greek Ministry of Defense, February 1996.
46. See note 43.

dos island and other similar cases.[47] That the U.S. did not do so provoked Greece's displeasure.

Another potential source of friction stems from some recent theories regarding the general approach to the resolution of the Greek-Turkish dispute. According to these theories, if Turkey is to make a positive move on Cyprus, it needs to be given some compensation in the Aegean. Thus, the Cyprus issue is not viewed as an issue with its own special aspects, but as part of a general bargain in which Greece must make concessions in the Aegean so that Turkey might be conciliatory in Cyprus. As far as the U.S. adopts or seems to go along with such views for a "package deal," friction is bound to occur in Greek-American relations.

In general, the prospects for Greek-American relations in the international system that is emerging at the end of the Cold War seem particularly good. The interests of the two countries coincide to a very high degree, while potential points of friction are neither as numerous nor as difficult as was the case in previous periods. Moreover, the climate in bilateral relations has changed for the better. An example of the new situation is that U.S. Ambassador to Greece Nicholas Burns and Presidential Emissary Richard Holbrooke publicly admitted, in November 1997, that it was a mistake for the U.S. to have intervened in the domestic affairs of Greece and to have supported the 1967-1974 military regime.

These symbolic statements were welcomed in Greece. What now remains for the two countries is to show the necessary good will and make conscious efforts to achieve the maximum bilateral cooperation possible. As things stand now, the U.S. and Greece comprise two important stabilizing forces in the Eastern Mediterranean. If they succeed in cooperating as harmoniously and effectively as the convergence of their interests would suggest, it would be most beneficial for the stability of the entire region. ✦

47. For instance, see the statements of American officials in April 1998, affirming Greek sovereignty over the Kalogiri islets.

The Military and Geostrategic Dimensions of the Truman Doctrine

Lt. Gen. Photios Metallinos (Ret.)

On behalf of the Hellenic Institute of Strategic Studies, I thank you for the honor to call me to this stage. I will focus my remarks on the military and geostrategic dimensions of the Truman Doctrine and the Marshall Plan, as seen from Greece's standpoint. In this respect, I do not believe it would be enough just to give you moral satisfaction by referring to the precious contribution of the Marshal Plan to my country.

It is equally important to mention the right use of the American aid by Greece during the civil war, the Greek role in NATO and the West's defense system, and the congruity of Greek policy with common goals in the modern Euro-Atlantic system of collective security.

I will try to relate to you the kind of policy and concerns to which Greece, as a basic strategic factor in the East Mediterranean and a European colleague, remains dedicated in its long-range political orientations, and its loyal support of Euro-American policy on stability and security issues in the area. It is a loyal policy that will survive any dramatic changes that could happen in the wider area.

The political surprise of the disbanding of the Warsaw Pact was welcomed as a happy end of a forty-five-year long European bipolarism. At the same time you are aware that major political surprises are not happy. The postwar history of the U.S. consists of a series of political reorientations and changes in American policy, especially in the Middle East area.

What characterizes the American presence in modern European history is a sincerity in its efforts to promote and secure collective interests within the framework of respect for international justice. It is the kind of morality proclaimed first by President Wilson at the Paris Peace Conference, after WWI.

The Truman Doctrine was a long-range policy that had a decisive effect on the historical evolution of Euro-American relations in the last five decades, resulting in an integrated political and security entity.

LT. GEN. PHOTIOS METALINOS (Ret.), is a Special Analyst in International Relations, Hellenic Institute of Strategic Studies.

The Truman Doctrine is simple and practical in character, transparent in its political goals. Also bold and risky in the extent of its international implications. Generous to both war partners and former enemies, it was a clear political conception elaborated in the light of democratic institutions.

The basic political goal of the Truman Doctrine, as stated by President Truman himself, was "to support free peoples, who are resisting attempted subjugation by armed minorities or by outside pressures."

Greece and Turkey were seen as key countries for the security of the Middle East, as well as of the European and American continents. Thus both Greece and Turkey were able to receive immediate aid to resist Soviet expansionism.

Greece had suffered a communist insurrection, while Turkey was under Soviet political pressure to relinquish control of the Straits to the Soviets.

At the end of WWII, Greece was at the most critical point of its modern history. While the rest of the European countries were trying to recover from the wounds of the war, Greece, although adjudged to be in the Western sphere of influence by the Yalta Conference, suffered a communist insurrection, an effort to force the country into the communist camp. To the ruins of the war were added those of a civil war.

After a heroic resistance against Italian and German attack, Greece had suffered a four-year occupation by Italian, German, Bulgarian, and Albanian forces that caused full devastation of the country. Greece lost eight percent of its population, about 800,000 people, the most of all the belligerent countries. We had 360,000 starvation deaths. Fifty percent of the population were protubercular. 3,700 towns and villages were completely or partly damaged. 1,200,000 people were left homeless and 88,000 rural families lived in ruins. Despite this situation, people's participation in the resistance was whole-hearted.

By September 1946, the countryside was under communist control. The country was divided into two parts, with two different governments. 700,000 refugees from the countryside fled to the large towns to escape the terror of civil war. The country was in complete chaos; the legitimate government was not in control.

In the most critical phase of the civil war, on February 28, 1947 the British government informed the United States about its decision to stop financial and economic support to Greece after March 31, and to retire its troops. Greece turned for help to the American administration.

The Truman administration, and in particular Undersecretary of State Dean Acheson, the person who received the British note, understood the new international role assigned to the U.S.

The Marshall Plan, which was elaborated by the State Department's Policy Planning Group headed by George Kennan, was aiming for the economic, political and moral recovery of Europe. Greece received economic, technical and military aid to nourish its starving population and to resist its communist threat. Thus Greece was spared the communist socialistic misery of the Balkan countries.

America, under the Truman Doctrine, allotted to Greece $300 million and $100 to Turkey in urgent financial aid, for the period until June 30, when the Marshall Plan started.

Within the framework of the Truman Doctrine's military aid, the U.S. took the responsibility of organizing and maintaining the Greek armed forces, starting April 4, 1947. On November 1st, 1947 the military materiel inflow to Greece started.

On July 15th, Dwight Greeswald, the chief of American Mission for Assistance to Greece (AMAG), arrived in Greece. He was accompanied by 206 technical and military consultants. That number grew to 1,216 by next year.

On December 31, 1947 the JUSMAPG was established in Athens to run the Joint U.S. Military Assistance Program for Greece. General James Van Fleet, who arrived in Athens on February 21, 1948, was assigned to JUSMAPG command in parallel to the duties of the American Mission chief.

He was a distinguished and capable officer, a field commander of WWII with an excellent military record that helped him to rapid promotion in the military hierarchy. He was selected for the position by Secretary of State General George Marshall. General Van Fleet was a strong personality and an active officer devoted passionately to the duty of organizing and promoting the Greek Army. General Eisenhower described him as a "non-intellectual character, also straight and decisive."

Greek General Petzopoulos characterizes him as "a great friend of Greece." Tireless in following military operations, ignoring battle danger and field hardships, sharing the agony and pain of the Greek soldier, General Van Fleet was the friendly American figure carrying about everywhere the symbolic flag of the American presence and partnership.

Among the responsibilities of the chief of the American Mission was supervising the flow and utilization of military aid: supplies, materiel, weaponry, ammunition, etc. As an official military advisor he attended closely to and rather shared the monitoring of military operations.

With regard to exceptional responsibilities, the first were officially assigned to British General Scoby, who was appointed the High Military Commander of the troops stationed in Greece, by the Gazera Accords on

September 26, 1944. The chiefs of military missions to Greece, first General Scoby and then General Van Fleet were engaged in high-level military decision-making. Due to the political instability of this era and loose political authority, with the Cabinet changing almost every two months, foreign military involvement in the Greek offices administration was inevitable.

By the end of 1947, Greece had received 174,000 tons of American military materiel, comprised of combat and training aircraft, cruisers, minesweepers, etc., valued at $40 million.

The American engineering unit under AMAG supervision carried out a full program of road and bridge construction, railway repair, airfield and harbor installations, irrigation projects, etc.

By the end of 1949, based on the American ambassador's report to Congress, Greece had received a total of $2 billion in aid, seventy-five percent of which was American aid.

Despite the reorganization of the Greek armed forces, it was common knowledge that the only missing thing was the spark of military leadership.

In October 1948 General Papagos was assigned the Greek armed forces command with field marshall authority. Military personnel were increased to 265,000. Under Papagos leadership successful operations against the communist guerrillas put an end to the civil war at the end of October 1949.

***

Coming to the geostrategic role of Greece in the Eastern Mediterranean, I will stress that the Truman Doctrine came about because Greece and Turkey were seen as the key countries for security in the Middle East and the protection of United States' interests there. Greek and Turkish territory is a unified geostrategic area, with both of the countries functioning as supplementary security factors. The immediate consequence of this strategic fact was the contemporaneous integration of both countries in NATO.

The control of the Straits was a corollary to the main Russian objective of unrestricted access to the Mediterranean. In 1945 during the Potsdam Summit meeting, Russia claimed the right to establish military bases in Thessalonike or Alexandroupolis harbor, as an alternative that would bypass the Straits.

At the same time, the Soviets exerted political pressure on Turkey, aiming at the revision of the Montreux Convention and seeking common control of the Straits with Turkey. (Proposals of June 22, 1946.)

The Truman Doctrine put the policy of containment and resistance against communist expansionism into effect, and was the basis of a long-lasting American policy with global dimensions. NATO, the American Joint Task Forces in the Mediterranean, Atlantic and Pacific communication and surveillance installations and facility bases, are the pylons of American global policy, as it is reflected in the Truman Doctrine and Marshall Plan. The American engagement in WWII had a total cost of $341 billion and 460,000 personnel losses. It was the greatest investment in peace and security the U.S had ever made in its history, and needed a long-lasting guarantee. The Containment Doctrine was the answer to contemporary security concerns, far distant from the American continent. Greece's and Turkey's roles in the Marshall Plan and later in NATO would be key factors in the Balance of Power system, along with European countries reinforced by the American military presence in Europe.

With American military aid, Greece and Turkey upgraded their armed forces. A full network of military bases and facilities was organized within the framework of bilateral accords with the U.S., to support an integrated security system in the Eastern Mediterranean.

The early NATO era for Greece and Turkey was characterized by collaboration and mutual confidence. Our NATO roles were quite clear. Greece had its armed forces oriented to the north thus covering the main Soviet axis of attack flanking the Straits, together with Turkey covering the axis against East Thrace and the Straits.

The strong points of the Greek contribution against the Soviet threat was the Aegean islands area and Crete, affording the necessary depth to defend the Straits and the sea passage to the Mediterranean. The Aegean islands area, being part of Greek sovereignty, was under Greek operational responsibility as part of COMEDEAST. Additional major Greek contributions were American bases and installations on the Greek mainland and the island of Crete, in support of the American fleet in the Mediterranean. Crete represents a strategic point of a major importance in the control of North Africa and the sea lines of communications from and to the Black Sea, to the Middle East, the Suez Canal and the Indian Ocean.

Turkey, besides controlling the Straits, had to cover a wide front with the Soviet Union on Turkey's eastern borders as well as covering the southeastern front, bordering the Middle Eastern countries.

The first problems in the functioning of the NATO defense system arose from an antagonistic stance by Turkey and Turkish claims to exercise operational control upon Greek Thrace and the Aegean area. It was an early indication of Turkey's claims against Greek sovereign territory.

Relations of the two countries in NATO became gradually problematic. The NATO defense system in the area suffered. Turkey vetoed the integration of the Aegean islands into the NATO defense system. There was a dispute initiated by Turkey on the legal status of the islands, questioning signed treaties and Greece's sovereign rights that are based on international law.

Since 1973 Turkey has concentrated its efforts to force upon the Greek islands a regime of condominium, aiming at the exploitation of undersea oil deposits in the Aegean. The crisis in our relations reached its peak with the Turkish invasion of Cyprus in 1974 and the Greek withdrawal from the NATO military branch.

The U.S. position of maintaining an equal distance between Greece and Turkey impaired indirectly Greek sovereign rights in the area and encouraged Turkish claims, which sought an unacceptable negotiation of Greek sovereignty. The Imia issue is a case in point.

Today Turkey's position is in direct dispute of the Lausanne Treaty of 1923, the Italy-Turkish Convention of January 4, 1923, the Italy-Turkish Protocol of December 28, 1932 and the 1947 Paris Peace Treaty concerning the legal status of the Aegean islands. Prime Minister Ozal during his visit to Athens on June 14, 1988, following the Greek-Turkish crisis of 1987 and the Davos talks, was quite clear in his attitude. He put relations with Greece on a new basis, departing from the signed treaties, which he characterized as "unsatisfactory."

The continued Turkish occupation of northern Cyprus impairs relations with Turkey. Greece considers Turkey to be the number one threat against its national sovereignty. Cyprus is the key for the normalization of Greek-Turkey relations. Cyprus is an island of major strategic importance for the control of the Middle East area and the normal oil flow vital to the Western economies.

***

I shall make a brief reference to important changes characterizing the post-Cold-War era and the roles assigned respectively to Greece and Turkey in it.

The most important change is the new conception of collective Euro-Atlantic security, and the multipolarity of the threats, in the place of a bipolar East-West security system based on balance of power.

The new threats in today's security system are foci of instability in the Balkans, the Caucasus, and the Middle East, due to local independence conflicts, terrorism, and Islamic fundamentalism. The uncontrolled proliferation of nuclear weapons and guided missile systems are also threats to European security.

The perspective of a NATO expanding to the Eastern European area, widening its security institutions and its operational area outside its traditional borders is another innovation, with NATO now functioning in the framework of a Security Council mandate. The Gulf, Bosnian and Kosovo wars, where NATO was engaged (directly or not) were a new operational model supporting European security and peace. Today's NATO comprises a unique, organized multinational force, responsible for pan-European security.

The identification of new oil deposits in the Caspian Sea, deposits potentionally equal in volume to those in the Middle East is the new element upgrading the geostrategic importance of the wider area. At the same time, it enhances competition for oil exploitation and control of the maritime and terrestrial lines of oil and gas transportation.

In the light of these new realities, we have to reconsider the roles of countries in the Eastern Mediterranean area.

Balkan conflicts originating in Yugoslavia have been the focus of European and American efforts. The possibility of an uncontrolled instability in the Balkan region is a reality, testing the political and military peacemaking mechanisms. The Dayton peace accords remain only partially carried out.

You are aware of recent Albanian turmoil. There are more potential instability foci in the Balkan region, namely Kosovo, Bulgaria, FYROM, and always Bosnia. A new Marshall Plan type of initiative in the area is deemed necessary.

In the middle of a dangerous instability in the Balkans, Greece remains a unique oasis of stability and economic strength. Greece's efforts to mediate problems in the Balkan area are a function of its temperate and peaceful foreign policy. Greece has offered good services as a political mediator in the Bosnian and new Yugoslavian crises, and today also in the Albanian one, enjoying as it does the confidence of the Balkan countries. Greece is a model for the Balkans, with its stable democratic institutions, healthy economy, advanced technology, and military forces strong enough to support peace in the area.

It is equally important to recognize the beneficial role of Orthodox Christianity, as a supranational element for cohesion among the various nationalities in the Balkans.

Turkey sees its role in the new era as an autonomous power among Islamic countries of the Caucasus, Central Asia and the Middle East. The Islamic area of Central Asia is a priority target for Turkish political and economic influence. Turkey's political engagement in Caucasian conflicts, acting within the framework of a Panturkist ideal, caused an angry Russian reaction. Turkey's parallel effort to interfere in the Balkans, as a protecting power of Islamic minorities, was not fruitful.

The establishment of Black Sea economic cooperation, and the effort to attract oil transportation through Turkish territory is part of Turkish policy to upgrade its economic and political role in the area. As part of this effort, the application of excessive "environmental" constraints in the Straits had blocked Russian oil transportation and is thus a violation of IMO regulations.

Concerning the unstable Middle East area, Turkey seeks a role as a military deputy and supporter of American interests. Sharing a double identity as a West-oriented secular state and an Islamic country, it would like to be a political link between the Western and Islamic worlds, and a buffer zone bordering an unstable area.

The creation of the CFE Exempted Zone in southeast Turkey is positioned in the framework of American interests in the Middle East.

The political and military manipulation of the Kurdish issue by Turkey, parallel to the exploitation of the issue by neighboring countries, contributes to the high tension in the area. Iraqi animosity and its mutual economic interests with Turkey, Turkey's territorial differences with Syria in conjunction with excessive use of Tigris and Euphrates water by Turkey, Iranian economic and cultural rivalry in Central Asia, further complicate Turkish policy in the region.

American policy makers tend to exaggerate the Turkish strategic factor.[1] Political and economic instability, the growing political and social role of the Islamic party, and the Kurdish issue represent some of the major Turkish problems. Demographic alterations in the coming twenty-five years, mainly in the Kurdish and Iranian populations will further complicate the Middle East problem.

War against the Kurds and the partial occupation of Cyprus are exhausting the Turkish economy. The long-lasting Cyprus occupation is a hard test of United Nations credibility and its ability to enforce its resolutions.

Despite American political efforts, Turkey's future in the European Union is quite uncertain. It is not Greece that blocks Turkey's integration. It is Turkey's bad economy, its violation of human rights and liberties, its arbitrary political methods and culture, its expansionist attitude. All of the above, together with Turkey's membership in OSCE and other European organizations create contradictory political swings between the Islamic and European worlds.

1. In accordance with a Langley Foundation study, Turkey is among the sixteen "high treat" countries in the world, threatened with immediate collapse due to its major problems. ("Pontiki" 9-2-96)

We prefer a more European and more collaborative Turkey, instead of an aggressive neighbor swinging between her domestic problems and imperial ambitions. A possible gradual transfer of the economic and political center of gravity of Turkey from West to East, would mean the definite solution of the "Eastern Issue" and endanger the European borders with Greece. Normalization of Greek-Turkish relations to the detriment of Greece's sovereignty rights would be a violation of the tenets of the Truman Doctrine and of international law.

Concerning Greece and Cyprus, the main problem is the political containment of Turkish expansionism through the enforcement of U.N. resolutions on Cyprus. Any attempt to force a political solution of the Cyprus question based on a political compromise in favor of Turkish demands in the area would be a Pyrrhic victory for peace and American credibility, and a drastic break with Truman Doctrine principles.

Greece in the twentieth century offered much and lost too many in the battles for freedom and democracy. In no other period of its long history has Hellenism suffered such a great uprooting. Today's Turkey is built on Hellenic ruins: in Asia Minor, in Pontos, East Thrace and Constantinople, in Imbros and Tenedos islands, and now in the northern part of Cyprus.

Although history teaches us that the most convincing argument in international relations is that of power the greatest achievement of the political human being is the building of universal peace based on mutual confidence and the consolidation of human rights and liberties. Thus was the wall of European bipolarity demolished and all Europe set on the peace. It is not only national power that has made the United States a global force, it is the trust of the people and human expectations for freedom and prosperity.

And now that the wars have come to end, I wish you be happy in peace. Would all mortals from now on, live as one population, in conciliation, for a common prosperity. Consider the universe as your own country, with common laws, where the excellent will govern, independently of their race. I don't characterize people, as the narrow-minded do, as Greeks and barbarians. I am not interested in the descent of the people, nor about the race they are born to. I apportion them with only one criterion, virtue.

For me any good foreigner is a Greek any bad Greek is worse than a barbarian...Alexander the Great, town of Opi, 324 B.C.

Hellenism has honored President Truman by erecting his statue in Athens. As a free person I would like to express my gratitude for what the U.S has offered to my country.

Thank you happy citizens of the free and democratic American states. God blesses your country. ✦

Bibliography

Ambassador Economou-Gouras: *The Truman Doctrine and Greece's Agony,* Athens, 1957.

M. Gen. D. Zaphiropoulos: *Anti-Guerrilla Struggle,* Athens, 1956

L. Gen. Alex. Tsigounis: *Athens's Post-War Division and Guerrilla War, 1945-1949,* Athens, 1966

L. Gen. Th. Petzopoulos: *1941-1950 Tragic March.*

Society for the Study of the Greek History (EMEIÓ): *The Sacrifices of Greece in the War, 1940 - 45.*

Charles M. Mee, Jr.: *The Marshall Plan,* New York, 1984.

Emanuel Wexter: *The Marshall Plan Revised,* London, 1983.

Lawrence Whitner: *American Intervention In Greece 1943-1949* (translation), Salonica, 1991. Columbia University Press, 1982.

Ambassador Mac Veagh Reports: Greece, 1933-1947.

Henry Kissinger: *Diplomacy,* 1994.

The Importance of Greece to the U.S.—Past and Present

Eugene T. Rossides

Throughout the twentieth century, Great Britain, France, Canada and Greece have been the United States' most loyal and trusted allies who have fought as America's allies in four major wars. The role of Greece, as an American ally, however, has been little noted and not fully understood. Nevertheless, Greece has played an exceptional role in world history in this century, a role which has been of particular importance to American national security interests. Unfortunately, career officials in the State and Defense Departments and on the National Security Council staff have failed for a number of reasons to understand and to fully utilize Greece's importance to the United States.

In World War I Greece sided with the allies and played an important role in the Balkans, while Turkey, as an ally of Germany, fought against the U.S. Greece's actions benefited the allies in numerous ways, not the least of which was preventing Turkish troops from reaching the Western Front, thus saving many American and allied lives.

Greece's pivotal role in World War II has not been given the attention it deserves. With Europe under the heel of Nazi Germany and with Britain fighting the Axis powers alone, Greece's courageous OXI (No!) of October 28, 1940, in answer to Mussolini's surrender ultimatum, echoed throughout the world, giving moral support to Britain and the forces of freedom. The defeat of Mussolini's army by Greek forces, who actually pushed the Italians back into Albania, gave to the allies the first taste of victory against fascism. The action in northern Greece and Albania was one of the most important battles of World War II, yet few historians have written about it and few people know about it outside Greece.

Greece's success against Mussolini forced Hitler to change his plans for the Soviet Union and go to the aid of his Italian ally, diverting valuable troops, arms, and equipment to invade Greece. Hitler's action against Greece delayed his planned invasion of the Soviet Union by several weeks, from April to June 1941. The delay has been credited by some military experts

---

EUGENE T. ROSSIDES, ESQ., is Senior Counsel in the international law firm of Clifford Chance Rogers and Wells. He served as Assistant Secretary of the U.S. Treasury Department (1969-1973).

and historians as one of the key factors that prevented Nazi Germany from defeating the Soviet Union. Karl E. Meyer, in a *New York Times* editorial footnote, stated that Hitler himself believed that the several weeks-long campaign required to subdue Greece was responsible for Germany's losing the war against the Soviet Union.[1] For that reason, Greece's courageous fight against the Axis can be characterized as a turning point in World War II.

But the importance of Greece's actions in the war did not end with its defeat by Germany. During the harsh Nazi occupation, Greek resistance activities forced the Germans to retain a large number of troops in Greece, troops which otherwise could have been deployed to the Eastern Front and North Africa, where they could have tipped the balance in both of those campaigns. Greece's resistance efforts equaled, if not exceeded, those of other occupied countries: 600,000 Greeks, eight percent of the population, died fighting or as a result of Nazi Germany's starvation policy.

In contrast with Greece, Turkey failed to honor its treaty with Britain and France to enter the war, preferring to remain neutral and profit from both sides. In fact, Turkey supplied Hitler with chromium, a vital resource for Nazi Germany's armaments industry and war effort. Albert Speer, Hitler's armaments chief, wrote in November 1943, that the loss of chromium supplies from Turkey would end the war in about ten months.[2]

While the rest of Europe was rebuilding following the Second World War, Greece was involved in a civil war against communist forces supported by Stalin and Yugoslavia's Tito, and supplied by them from the Skopje area of Yugoslavia and Bulgaria. Greece's defeat of the communists, with Greek blood and American military aid provided under the Truman Doctrine, but without American combat troops, was an historic turning point in the immediate post-World War II Cold War period and in world history. Stopping the communist takeover of Greece, including Crete, prevented the Soviet Union from dominating the Aegean Sea and Eastern Mediterranean, and most importantly prevented the strategic encirclement by the Soviets of the Middle East's oil resources, including the Persian Gulf area.

Historians have little noted Greece's role in this crucial and turning point period in the Cold War.

The Persian Gulf War

The Persian Gulf War demonstrated Greece's crucial importance to American national security interests in the regions of the Eastern Mediterranean

1. April 16, 1994, A20, col. 1.
2. See Frank G. Weber, *The Evasive Neutral*, p. 44 (Columbia & London: University of Missouri Press, 1979) and Albert Speer, *Inside the Third Reich*, pp. 316-17, 550, n.10, (New York: Macmillan, 1970).

and Persian Gulf; it demonstrated that Greece, not Turkey, is the strategic key to the projection of U.S. power in those regions. The NATO naval base in Suda Bay, Crete, is the key facility for projecting United States power, via the Sixth Fleet, in the Eastern Mediterranean and the Persian Gulf; Suda Bay is far more important to U.S. strategic interests than bases in Turkey. President George Bush recognized the importance of the Suda Bay base when he made his historic visit there in July 1991.

Turkey sat on the sidelines throughout Desert Shield, refusing to send any forces to the U.S.-led coalition, refusing to authorize a second land front from Turkey,[3] and refusing to allow the use of the NATO air base at Incirlik.

Desert Storm began on January 16, 1991. It was not until over 48 hours after the air war had begun, and only after the Iraqi air force and air defenses had been neutralized and the U.S. had achieved air superiority, that Turkey allowed a limited number of sorties out of the Incirlik NATO air base. Only one out of twenty coalition sorties originated in Turkey, and these were clearly unnecessary. The Turkish military and Turkish public opinion opposed the use of the Incirlik NATO air base.

As for the two oil pipelines from Iraq through Turkey to the Mediterranean coast, Iraq—not Turkey—closed the first oil pipeline and reduced the flow of oil through the second by seventy-five percent for lack of customers. Turkey refused to act to shut off the second pipeline until after the United Nations Security Council passed Resolution 661 on August 6, 1990.[4] Other countries acted right away. Furthermore, we did not need Turkey to halt the remaining 25 percent of the second pipeline since a naval blockade would have prevented any movement of Iraqi oil from Turkey's Mediterranean port—if there had been any customers for it. Turkey's President Turgut Ozal admitted this in a news conference on June 7, 1991 in Istanbul when he stated: "If Turkey had not imposed an embargo and shut the pipeline it would have led to a blockade."[5] Once the Security Council acted, Turkey had no choice but to close the remaining pipeline, otherwise she would have been in violation of Security Council Resolution 661 and Article 25 of the United Nations Charter, which requires member states to comply with Security Council resolutions. By failing to implement S.C. Res. 661, Turkey would have jeopardized her relations with the nations that supported the resolution, including the U.S., and its trade with and aid from the U.S. and other countries, as well as aid it receives from international organizations.

Turkey's advocates assert that Turkish troops closed its 206-mile-long border with Iraq. In reality, the border was never fully closed. There was

3. See the *Washington Post,* January 16, 1991, at A6, col.5.

4. *Washington Post*, August 8, 1990, at A12, col. 4.

5. Associated Press, June 7, 1991.

large-scale, open, organized smuggling along the Turkey-Iraq border.[6] Turkey's proponents also assert that Turkish troops "tied down" 100,000 Iraqi forces. Again, the reality is otherwise. The Iraqi troops were stationed along the Syrian and Turkish borders in northern Iraq before the invasion of Kuwait, and Iraq had no plans to move them south. Those troops had to be kept there in order to control the Kurds and check the Syrians.

While Turkey sat on the sidelines throughout Desert Shield (August 2, 1990—January 16, 1991), delayed support for the U.S.-initiated freeze on commercial dealings with Iraq and negotiated for compensation, the Mitsotakis government of Greece gave full support to Desert Shield/Desert Storm. Greece did the following:

1. immediately condemned Iraq's aggression;
2. authorized from the first day of the crisis the use of the Suda Bay naval base to provide operational, logistical, and command support for the U.S. Sixth Fleet twenty-four hours a day;
3. authorized the use of the U.S. air base at Suda Bay to provide similar support to the U.S. Air Force in the buildup of U.S. air power in Saudi Arabia and other Persian Gulf countries;
4. authorized military overflights and base access generally for the buildup in the Persian Gulf (the extraordinary number of over 32,000 military and civilian overflights of Greece occurred during Desert Shield/Desert Storm); and
5. joined the coalition forces and sent two naval frigates to the Persian Gulf, and offered air combat patrols and medical facilities.

The Greek merchant marine played a substantial role in the movement of cargo to the Persian Gulf for the U.S. and allied forces. The Greek merchant marine is an important asset to U.S. and NATO interests that is often overlooked in considering the relative strategic and military values of Greece and Turkey.

Operation Desert Shield/Desert Storm demonstrated that Turkey is not needed to protect the oil resources in the Persian Gulf, and of limited value for U.S. national security interests in the present post-Cold War, post-Persian Gulf era. While it would be helpful to have a cooperative Turkey as an ally, it is not essential for the protection or advancement of U.S. interests.

The war proved that the following are necessary to protect oil resources in the Persian Gulf:

1. the cooperation of the Gulf states with the U.S. by authorizing U.S.

6. See the *Wall Street Journal*, October 30, 1990, at 1, col.1, and Turkish newspapers, *Sabah*, September 3, 1990, and *Cumhuriyet*, September 22, 1990 and the weekly magazine, *Yuzil*, September 9, 1990.

air and land bases in those countries, not in Turkey;
2. the use of the naval base at Suda Bay, Crete;
3. the use of the British bases in Cyprus; and
4. the use of the U.S. naval base and facilities in Diego Garcia in the Indian Ocean.

I have been espousing Greece's importance to U.S. interests for years. Following are the comments of several outstanding Americans regarding Greece and the U.S., namely General Andrew J. Goodpaster, USA (Ret.), U.S. Ambassador to Greece Nicholas Burns, Admiral Henry C. Mustin, USN (Ret.), the Honorable Lawrence J. Korb, Ph.D., former Assistant Secretary of Defense and now Director of Studies at the Council on Foreign Relations, and Monteagle Stearns, U.S. Ambassador to Greece from 1981 to 1985:

General Andrew J. Goodpaster

General Goodpaster, the former Supreme Commander of NATO, in the introduction to this volume wrote: "in one special moment in history Greece at heavy cost and sacrifice and with great courage and determination played a pivotal role in World War II in defying the forces of tyranny and Axis aggression that were arrayed against not only Greece but the whole of Western civilization. It is an inspiring story." At AHI's conference on The Truman Doctrine of Aid to Greece: A Fifty-Year Retrospective, the general titled his remarks, "The Truman Doctrine: A Turning Point in World History." He stated:

> "The fifty-year retrospective of the Truman Doctrine enables us to recall the danger to Greece in 1947 and the beginnings of the Marshall Plan. I think it is important to keep memories of those events alive. This was a turning point in world history, not just the history of the twentieth century, but a turning point in American history and particularly in the history of America's relationship with Europe. I am going to comment from the standpoint of the organizations which I was serving, regarding the threat, at that time, to Greek independence and democracy and the response that was made to that threat. This was an issue that broadens into the response to the challenge of all of post-war Europe."

Ambassador Nicholas Burns

During his confirmation hearing on September 23, 1997 before the Senate Foreign Relations Committee, Ambassador Burns said the following:

> "Greece is a dynamic and increasingly important ally with which the U.S. should have the closest possible relations. For nearly two centuries now the American and Greek people have

shared ties of kinship, commerce, culture, alliance. The democratic principles of ancient Greece inspired our founding fathers, and in this century we sealed our bond in World Wars I and II, Korea, during the long decades of the Cold War, and just recently against the dictator in the Gulf.

I believe we are now entering at a particularly important and exciting moment in the history of U.S.-Greek relations. Tensions and disagreements that marred our relations with Greece from time to time in the past are receding.

If confirmed, I will work to take advantage of this opportunity and to help construct what I think should be one of our central strategic aims: a new era of trust and cooperation, economic growth, and friendship between our countries. Indeed, I think it is fair time for us as Americans to remind ourselves of the importance of Greece to the American people as a valued NATO ally, as an increasingly prosperous member of the E.U. [European Union], a leader in the Balkans, and as a force of stability and peace in the Eastern Mediterranean."

Ambassador Burns also stated—and it is the first time that a U.S. Ambassador to Greece has so stated—that the strongest link between the U.S. and Greece is the Greek American community.

In his remarks during his swearing-in ceremony on October 17, 1997, Mr. Burns said:

"When you think about it, the U.S. has few relationships in the world that are united more closely by ties of history, political philosophy, alliance, and blood than is our relationship with Greece. We are democracies; we had our freedom against tyranny in the American Revolution followed by Greece's forty years later. We are countries that prize freedom and peace above all else, and our countries fought in four wars together in this century."

Mr. Burns also said "the U.S. supports active Greek efforts to promote stability, peace, and prosperity in the Balkans, where Greece has the potential to be uniquely influential."

Admiral Henry C. Mustin

Admiral Mustin, a defense consultant, serves as a trustee of the U.S. Naval Academy Foundation and vice-chairman of the Amphibious Warfare Committee of the National Security Industrial Association. His remarks at AHI's conference on The Truman Doctrine of Aid to Greece were titled, "The Strategic Importance of Greece from the Truman Doctrine to the Present." In them, Admiral Mustin stressed the importance of the Eastern Mediterranean Sea to the security interests of the U.S. He pointed out that in 1989-90, the "collapse of the Soviet Union changed everything," that with the end of the Soviet threat the U.S. had to recognize the new realities in Europe, and that "an essential part of that new reality is the role of Greece." He set forth the following "three key elements of present-day U.S. and NATO security policy toward Greece:"

> "First, the southern region of NATO, not the central European region, is where the military action is....Bosnia and the Balkans dominate American newspapers and Greece is at center stage. Greece's historical ties to Serbia and the other Balkan nations, as well as its geographical location, make it a key player in U.S. and NATO security policy in the southern region.
>
> Second, the Eastern Mediterranean will remain strategically important to the West because of economic realities. Much of Europe's oil comes through the Mediterranean via the Suez Canal, and the Caspian Sea is an emerging source as well....From a strictly maritime viewpoint, the United States has a three-pronged role in securing sea trade in the Mediterranean, and Greece, still the 'unsinkable aircraft carrier,' is a key player in each prong.
>
> - All hands have to perceive that U.S./NATO naval strengths are adequate to ensure continuity of sea trade with the U.S. and among its friends and allies...
> - U.S./NATO has to be visibly capable of maintaining the security of the sea-lanes in peace and war, and this includes the safety of both ships and port facilities.
> - U.S/NATO has to be prepared to support maritime trading partners in periods of crisis to ensure continuing economic and political viability.
>
> Third, even more so now than in 1947, the U.S./Greek security relationships must be viewed from the perspective of the entire region. The Middle East peace process, the Muslim fundamentalist movement, current developments in Turkey, and the ever-present need for oil, raise the tensions—and our security interests—in the region to new heights.
>
> Greece has traditionally pursued a policy of friendship with the Arab states of the Middle East....Greece's strong ties with the Arab world enabled other Western nations, including the U.S., to use Greece as an interlocutor. Greece's important role has continued through the Middle East peace process....As we look to the year 2000 and beyond, Greece will remain a unique bridge between the West and this strategically critical area.

In recent years, a number of countries, including the U.S., have watched the spread of radical Islam with alarm. Western countries have pursued a policy of outreach to the moderate Arab states and none has done so more effectively than Greece....

Finally....Greece sits astride the critical sea-lanes that link the Middle East with the industrialized world. Now the discovery of Caspian Sea oil and the talk of pipelines to bring it to Mediterranean ports only validates what strategic planners have known for years: Greece is critical to the free flow of oil from the Middle East."

Lawrence J. Korb

Dr. Korb, former Assistant Secretary of Defense and now Vice President and Director of Studies at the Council on Foreign Relations titled his remarks at AHI's conference, "The Strategic Importance of Greece to the Balance of Power in the Mediterranean and Europe." He spoke about Truman Doctrine aid to Greece and "why it was important and why we did what we did and how important it was, both for the future of that part of the world and for the winning of the Cold War." He said:

"It is obvious when someone asks about the strategic importance of Greece to the balance of power in Europe, in the Mediterranean, and in Southeastern Europe, that the answer is the same one that any good realtor gives you when you are buying a house: location, location, and location. If you take a look at a map, you will discover that Greece protects what the navy calls a line of communication through the Mediterranean to the Middle East and to North Africa.

It is no accident that the Russians have always tried to exercise their influence in that area. It is no accident that the British resisted a hostile power taking control of that particular area, and it is no accident that when the U.S., back in the '70s, was looking for strategic home ports outside the United States, the navy settled on Athens as the place. Given the shrinkage in the military budget and given the fact that Francis Fukiyama (author of "The End of History") was not right, and the end of the Cold War was not the end of history, it would be good for the U.S., for the young men and women on the ships, to have a strategic home port and I could think of no better place to put it in than Greece. It was also important for us to project our power in that area. Sometimes, because of the end of the Cold War in the late '80s and early '90s, we forget some of the things that occurred in the Middle East in the '70s; for example: the Jordanian crisis and the Yom Kippur War. It was very important that we had bases there and we had somebody to allow us to use those bases and to use those forces to deal with these crises. In 1952, Greece joined NATO, thus insuring the southern flank would be intact to deal with Soviet communist expansionism. And of course, the 1953 military facilities agreement with Greece would not have been possible without the Truman Doctrine.

When you ask what were the motivations for the Soviet Union in this area, the answer is that it was not only the strategic location, but also the fact that Russians have always wanted warm-water ports, especially in the Mediterranean. By taking control of Greece, this would have fulfilled not only something strategically important to the Soviet empire but also the Russian dream to have warm-water ports. It would also have enabled the Soviets to circle the Middle East oil resources and the Western European democracies. Many people have written that had we lost Greece, we probably would have lost all of Europe.

So Greece was very critical not only for its location but also for its symbolism. And even today, even with the end of the Cold War, there still are a number of problems in the international system. The focus has shifted from Central Europe down to Southeastern Europe and the Balkans, and our relations with Greece and Greece's relationship to that area continue to be important. If we are ever going to solve the situation in the Balkans, Greece has to play a big role.

In addition to its strategic location, Greece is an important symbol. If Greece were not the birthplace of Western civilization and democracy, I doubt that President Truman would have been able to convince the Congress, dominated by the Taft wing of the Republican Party, to make that commitment and appropriate the funds.

If one had to pick a country to begin the stand against the Soviet Empire, to begin the process of the policy that we now call containment, I cannot think of a better place than Greece. In fact, in the speech that Truman gave to Congress in which he proposed what would later become known as the Truman Doctrine, he only got three applause lines. And one of his applause lines had to do with his statement that each dollar spent would count toward making Greece self-sustaining.

If you put yourself in Congress in 1947, less than two years after the end of World War II, with a president coming before you and asking for a momentous change in American foreign policy, you would not exactly be enthusiastic but, in fact, stunned. I think it was significant that, in that atmosphere, the Congress did applaud when Greece was mentioned.

It was also important that we were able to achieve our objectives in Greece without sending American ground troops. So Greece has been important because of its location, because of what it is, and because of the U.S. being able to achieve its objectives."

Ambassador Monteagle Stearns

Ambassador Stearns titled his remarks at AHI's conference on The Truman Doctrine of Aid to Greece, "The U.S.-Greek Strategic Relationship During the Cold War and Beyond." He pointed out that during the Cold War the U.S. did not develop a Greek policy or a Turkish policy, but rather attempted to fit Greece and Turkey into the West's Soviet policy. He stated:

"We in the U.S. and in Western Europe discounted the importance of regional problems. After the promulgation of the Truman Doctrine, the U.S. did not really develop a Greek policy or a Turkish policy. We simply tried to fit Greece and Turkey into our Soviet policy and the fit was never a comfortable one. But, this had another effect that was even more uncomfortable. It meant that we discounted the importance of regional problems—the problem of Cyprus, the problem of the Aegean, and the problem of Greek-Turkish relations generally—because we believed, incorrectly, that when Greece and Turkey were admitted into NATO in 1952, their ultimate security aspirations had been achieved. Everything else was of lesser concern. And this was, of course, far from the truth. Particularly, as the Cold War turned into a frozen war, Greek preoccupations, and to some extent Turkish preoccupations, with regional issues became much more important in the two capitals.

Not so in Washington. The mistake that the United States government made in this period, the post-Truman Doctrine period, was a peculiar American mistake. It was to regard Greece and Turkey as components of a strategic equation, rather than as products of their own historical experience. With the Cold War behind us, we must dismiss from our minds blocs and strategic equations and begin to approach regional problems on their merits."

Ambassador Stearns' remarks are a devastating indictment of U.S. foreign policy toward Greece and Turkey during and after the Cold War. That policy was driven, then and now, by career officials in the State and Defense departments and on the staff of the National Security Council.

This tragic mistake of U.S. foreign policy was compounded by the career officials during this period when they failed to deal even-handedly, as an honest broker or mediator, with Greece and Turkey and opted instead to favor Turkey over Greece to the severe detriment of U.S. national interests.

There are many examples, from the 1950s to date, of the appeasement of Turkey and the failure to apply the rule of law to Turkey by the executive branch of our government, to the detriment of U.S. interests and Greece. The two most striking examples are the Cyprus problem and the Aegean Sea issue.

Cyprus

The most glaring and obvious example is the failure of the State Department, on July 20, 1974 when Turkey invaded Cyprus, to halt immediately all military arms and equipment to Turkey as required by U.S. law, which prohibits the use of U.S. military aid for aggression. Henry Kissinger was Secretary of State at that time and bears the primary responsibility for this violation of American law. He is also responsible for encouraging the criminal coup against President Makarios of Cyprus on July 15, 1974, and for encouraging the illegal Turkish invasion five days later, on July 20, 1974.

It is important to bear in mind that he had the full support of key career officials, from Under Secretary Joseph Sisco and Assistant Secretary of State Arthur Hartman on down except for one lone voice, that of the Cyprus Desk officer, Tom Boyatt. Kissinger transferred Boyatt to Chile in 1974 and replaced him with Ledsky Nelson, who worked to subvert the application of the rule of law to Turkey. Since then the career officials in State and Defense have covered up the U.S. involvement on Turkey's side. As Laurence Stern, the late diplomatic correspondent and foreign news editor of the *Washington Post* stated in his book, *The Wrong Horse:*[7]

> "One of the most important keys to an understanding of the Cyprus muddle is the realization that the United States, far from being a disinterested broker to the disputes of the past, was a deeply involved participant."

The Aegean

The Aegean Sea issue is another example of the executive branch's policy of "tilt toward Turkey." During the islet of Imia crisis in the Aegean on January 28-31, 1996, the U.S. played a helpful role in preventing an armed clash between Greece and Turkey. However, the failure of the Clinton administration, with Assistant Secretary of State Richard Holbrooke in the lead, to recognize and state that under the treaties involved and international law the islet of Imia is sovereign Greek territory, is a stark example of the appeasement of Turkey, the tilt toward Turkey, and the reckless dis-

7. Laurence Stern, *The Wrong Horse* (New York: Times Books, 1977).

regard of the rule of law in international affairs.

The appeasement of and double standard on applying the rule of law to Turkey in the Aegean by the executive branch created the Aegean issue for Turkey, put Greece's sovereignty in the Aegean at risk, and is the cause of Turkey's continuing claims on Greek islands in the Aegean and indeed, for Turkey's claim to one-half of the Aegean Sea.

The disgrace of U.S. policy in its pro-Turkish tilt on issues concerning Greek-Turkish relations is further compounded when one considers that:

1. Greece has been and is more important strategically to U.S. interests than Turkey, as demonstrated by World Wars I and II and most recently in the Persian Gulf War; and
2. Turkey has been an unreliable ally that actively aided the Soviet Union militarily during the Cold War, going back to at least the 1973 Middle East War.

The Development of a Special Relationship Between the United States and Greece

The United States should heed Ambassador Stearn's remarks and develop a Greek policy and a Turkish policy. The U.S. should develop a special relationship with Greece because of that country's key strategic value for U.S. interests in the region, Greece's history, its reliability and because the U.S. is able to achieve its objectives with such a relationship based on mutual interests and benefits.

Fundamental to a special relationship is the support of democracy, the rule of law, majority rule with protection of minority rights, and the basic human rights and values set forth in our Constitution and Bill of Rights that Americans and Greeks fought for in World War II.

Unfortunately, the State and Defense Departments have not changed their policy toward Turkey despite the end of the Cold War in 1990. They continue to apply a double standard on the rule of law for Turkey and excuse Turkey's numerous violations of law and horrendous violations of human rights. And they continue to fuel an irresponsible arms race between Turkey and Greece.

Greece today is still the key for U.S. interests in the region in protecting the sea-lanes in the Eastern Mediterranean and Aegean Seas for the transportation of oil, natural gas and trade goods generally, and in promoting democracy, economic progress and stability in the Balkans. The U.S. has an important opportunity today to further American interests in the region by developing a special relationship with Greece, with mutual benefits to both countries. We should do everything possible to seize the opportunity. ✦

Contributors' Biographies

GREGORIOS DEMESTICHAS, RET., former Chief of the Hellenic Navy, Chairman of the Hellenic Institute of Strategic Studies. He graduated from the Naval Academy in 1960 and received his commission as Ensign. He served on various units and staffs, as Commanding Officer on various types of warships, as Head of Staff Departments, as Commander of squadrons (Fast Patrol Boat Squadron, Destroyer Squadron), Commander Destroyers Commander of large navy units (Comedeast WHQ Comcent, Salamis Cockyard, Naval Training Command) and as Deputy Chief Hellenic Navy General Staff. On February 1992 he was promoted to Vice Admiral and was appointed Chief of the Hellenic Fleet. He participated in the May 1973 movement of the Navy against the dictatorship of April 21, 1967 and as a result was imprisoned and subsequently discharged and deprived of rank. After the restoration of democracy in Greece, he was reinstated to active service. He is a graduate of the General Naval Training School, Hellenic Navy War College and the Naval Tactical School and Communications School in Great Britain. He also received a degree in economics at the Athens University and a degree in Shipping Law at the London University. He has received numerous awards including the Commander's Badge of the Order of Honor, the Knight Gold Cross of the Order of Phoenix and the medal of Military Merit 1st Class and the Medal for Resistance against the 1967-1974 dictatorship.

ANDRE GEROLYMATOS, Associate Professor, Department of History, Simon Fraser University, (SFU) Vancouver, B.C. He received his B.S. with Honors in Classics at Concordia University (1978), M.A from McGill University (1982) and Ph.D. from McGill University (1991). He served as Director of the Hellenic Studies Center at Dawson College in Montreal (1987-96); in 1996 received the Hellenic Studies Chair, SFU and in 1997 was appointed Director of the Research Institute on Southeastern Europe, SFU. He serves on the International Advisory Board of the Journal of the Hellenic Diaspora since 1990, is editor of the Journal of Modern Hellenism since 1992 and secretary of the Hellenic Congress of Quebec (1990-93) and the Hellenic Canadian Congress (1989-1993). Dr. Gerolymatos has published several publications including two books *Espi-*

onage and Treason: A Study of the Proxenia in Political and Military Intelligence Gathering in Classical Greece (1986) and *Guerrilla Warfare and Espionage in Greece (1940-1944)* (1992).

GENERAL ANDREW J. GOODPASTER, USA (RET.) Former Supreme Commander of NATO, Gen. Goodpaster graduated from the U.S. Military Academy (1939) and received a M.S. in engineering and M.A. and Ph.D. in international relations from Princeton University (1947-50). During WWII he commanded the 48th Engineer Combat Battalion in North Africa and Italy, receiving the U.S. Distinguished Service Cross. From mid-1944 to mid-1947 he was assigned to the Operations Division, of the War Department and on the Joint War Plans Committee of the Joint Chiefs of Staff. During his military service, General Goodpaster was Staff Secretary and Defense Liaison Officer to President Eisenhower (1954-1961); commander of the 8th U.S. Infantry Division in Germany; assistant to the chairman, Joint Chiefs of Staff; Director, Joint Staff; Commandant of the National War College; Deputy Commander of U.S. Forces in Vietnam; Commander-in-Chief, U.S. European Command and Supreme Allied Commander, Europe. He assisted President Nixon in organizing his administration for the conduct of foreign policy and international security affairs. After retiring in 1974, General Goodpaster was a senior fellow at the Woodrow Wilson International Center for Scholars, Smithsonian Institution, and assistant to Vice President Rockefeller on the Commission of the Organization of the Government for the Conduct of Foreign Policy. He was recalled to active duty as the 50th Superintendent of the Military Academy in 1977 serving until 1981. He was awarded the U.S. Medal of Freedom as well as military decorations, including the Defense Service Medal with Oak Leaf Cluster; the Army Distinguished Service Medal with three Oak Leaf Clusters; the Navy and Air Force Distinguished Service Medals; the Silver Star; the Purple Heart with Oak Leaf Cluster, the Presidential Unit Citation and the Department of Defense's (1977). He is chairman Emeritus of the George C. Marshall Foundation and serves as Senior Fellow at the Eisenhower Institute.

JOHN O. IATRIDES, Ph.D., Professor of International Politics at Southern Connecticut State University. He received his education in Greece, Netherlands and the United States. He served with the Hellenic National Defense General Staff (1955-56) and the Office of the Prime Minister of Greece (1956-58). He has taught courses on contemporary Greece at Harvard, Yale, Princeton and New York universities. His publications include: Balkan *Triangle: Birth and Decline of an Alliance Across Ideological Boundaries* (1968), *Revolt in Athens* (1972), Ambassador *MacVeagh Reports: Greece 1933-47* (1980), *Greece in the 1940s: A Nation in Crisis* (1980) and *Greece at the Crossroads: The Civil War and Its Legacy* (1995).

ROBIN HIGHAM, Professor at Kansas State University. He received his Ph.D. from Harvard in 1957 and the Samuel Eliot Morison Prize of the American Military Institute for his contributions to the field of military history. For twenty-one years he has served as the editor of *Military Affairs*, for eighteen years of *Aerospace Historian*, and since 1976 of the *Journal of the West*. He is also President of Sunflower University Press. Among his numerous books and articles are *The Diary of a Disaster* (1986) a study of the British aid to Greece in 1940-1941 (1986 and in 1996 published in translation by the Hellenic Army Directorate of History), edited with Thanos Veremis *The Metaxas Dictatorship: Aspects of Greece, 1936-1940* (1993), and as-yet published study of prehistoric Crete.

ALEXANDROS K. KYROU, Assistant Professor of History and Director of East European and Russian Studies at Salem State College in Salem, Massachusetts. Professor Kyrou completed his Ph.D. in Eastern European History at Indiana University in 1993. He has taught as a Visiting Lecturer and Visiting Professor in the Departments of History and Political Science, respectively, at Indiana University–Purdue University Fort Wayne. Professor Kyrou's teaching and curriculum development experience is quite extensive and includes courses on Byzantine history and civilization, the Ottoman Empire, Balkan history, Eastern European history and politics, Yugoslavia, and the Greek-American experience. Professor Kyrou is a former Hannah Seeger Davis Visiting Research Fellow in the Program in Hellenic Studies at Princeton University, as well as a Research Scholar at the Balch Institute for Ethnic Studies in Philadelphia. His diverse publications include several articles on the Greek diaspora, Albanian history, Bulgaria and the Bulgarian-American community, and United States foreign policy in southeastern Europe.

MATHEOS D. LOS, Secretary General, Union of Greek Shipowners. He received his B.A. in Economics and Business Administration with honors and Ph.D. both at the University of Lausanne, Switzerland. In 1974, Dr. Los entered his family's shipping business and since 1981 is the General Manager of Vrontados S.A. in Piraeus. He is a member of the Board of Directors of the Union of Greek Shipowners (UGS) since 1980. He is President of the UGS Nautical Education and Public Relations Committees and a member of the Foreign Affairs, Finance and Labor Issues Committees. Dr. Los is an alternate member of the Board of Directors of the European Community Shipowners Associations (ECSA). He is a member of the Shipping Policy Committee of the Hellenic Chamber of Shipping and one of the founder members and honorary Vice-Chairman of the Hellenic Marine Environment Protection Association (HELMEPA). He is also a full member of the Hellenic Maritime Museum in Piraeus, and the American Bureau of Shipping (ABS). Dr. Los has written numerous articles and books on shipping regarding economic policy, government relations, labor issues, seamen's education, environmental issues and historical and cultural topics.

LT. GEN. PHOTIOS METALLINOS, RET., Special Analyst in International Relations, Hellenic Institute of Strategic Studies. He graduated from the Military Academy of Greece (1957) and the Armor School of Greece (1958) and obtained additional training at the U.S. Armor Maintenance School, West Germany (1960); Special Forces Training and Parachute Fighters School (1963-64), War College (1974-75) and the U.S. Command and General Staff (1983). After thirty-three years of service in the Greek army, serving in Greece and Cyprus, he retired with the rank of lieutenant general. Currently he a member of numerous organizations and institutions, including the Coordination Center of Hellenism, the Hellenic Institute of Strategic Studies, the National Defense School Graduates; Association and the Hellenic Association for Atlantic and European Collaboration. His recent paper on the current history of Greece received the First Prize of the Panhellenic Union of Literature, and his articles on Greek defense issues have been published in several magazines, including the *Parliamentary Inspection, Modern Army* and *Research*.

JAMES E. MILLER, Professor at the Department of History, John Hopkins University, Washington, DC. He is Chair of Italy and Greece-Cyprus Area Studies courses at the Foreign Service Institute. Dr. Miller is the specialist in Southern European Affairs at the Historian's Office, U.S. Department of State, and Adjunct Professor of European Studies at the John Hopkins School for Advanced International Studies. He previously served as country analyst for Italy at the State Department's Bureau of Intelligence and Research. Dr. Miller has taught at a number of U.S. and European universities including the University of Florence and the University of Naples. He is the author of three prize-winning books and has received awards from the American Historical Association, the Organization of American Historians and the Society for the History of American Foreign Relations. Dr. Miller is a member of the Modern Greek Studies Association and the Society for Times Historical Studies.

S. VICTOR PAPACOSMA, Professor of History at Kent State University and Director of the Lemnitzer Center for NATO and European Community Studies. He received his Ph.D. and M.A. from Indiana University and his A.B. from Bowdoin College. His area of specialization is Balkan history and he has published extensively on modern Greek issues. Among his publications are *The Military in Greek Politics: The 1909 Coup d' État* (1977) (also in Greek translation, 1981) and *Politics and Culture in Greece* (1988). He has co-edited *Europe's Neutral and Nonaligned States: Between NATO and the Warsaw Pack* (1989), *NATO after Forty Years* (1990), and *NATO in the Post Cold War Era: Does It Have a Future?* (1995).

ATHANASSIOS G. PLATIAS, Associate Professor of Strategic Studies at Panteion University of Social and Political Sciences in Athens. He is also Head of Research at the Institute of International Relations, Athens. Dr. Platias received a degree (with excellence) in Public Law and Political Science from the University of Athens, and an M.A. and Ph.D. from Cornell University. He was a Ford Foundation Fellow at the Center for Science and International Affairs, Harvard University (1979-80), a Research Fellow at the Peace Studies Program, Cornell University (1980-83 and 1985-86) and SSRC-MacArthur Fellow in International Peace and Security, MIT (1987-1989) and at the Center for International Affairs, Harvard University (1988-89). Dr. Platias is the author of numerous books and articles in five principle areas: (a) Military Politics and Strategy; (b) Greek Foreign and Defense Policy; (c) Nuclear Proliferation; (d) Nuclear Arms Race and Arms Control; and (e) Theory of International Relations.

EUGENE T. ROSSIDES, Retired Senior Partner, in the international law firm of Clifford Chance Rogers and Wells (now Clifford Chance Rogers and Wells). Served as Assistant Secretary of the U.S. Treasury Department (1969-1973) where he supervised the U.S. Customs Service, Secret Service, Bureaus of Alcohol, Tobacco and Firearms, the Mint, and Engraving and Printing, and the Federal Law Enforcement Training Center. He is the founder of the American Hellenic Institute, the AHI Foundation and a member of the board of directors of the Eisenhower Institute. He is the editor of the Handbook on United States Relations with Greece and Cyprus, the American Hellenic Who's Who 1994-1995 (5th ed.) and author of "Cyprus and the Rule of Law," 17 *Syracuse J. of Int'l L. and Com.* (1991) 21-90. He is the co-author of the *United States Import Trade Law* (1992), chief import editor since 1979 of BNA's International Trade Reporter and author of its Reference File. He received his B.A. degree from Columbia College (1949) and J.D. degree from Columbia University Law School (1952). Mr. Rossides served as U.S. Representative to Interpol (1969-73). In 1982-84, he served as a member of the Executive Committee of the President's Private Sector Survey on Cost Control in the Federal Government—The Grace Commission.

CONSTANTINE SVOLOPOULOS, Department of History, University of Athens. He studied history at the University of Athens (B.A. 1964) and Political Science at the University of Strasbourg and Paris (M.A. 1973). He obtained his Ph.D. in History in Strasbourg (1967) and Athens (1974). He was elected Professor of the Law School at the University of Thessaloniki in 1981, and of the Department of History (1995-97). Between 1981 and 1990 he was Director of the Institute for Balkan Studies in Thessaloniki; since then, has been Director of the "Constantine G. Karamanlis Foundation." Mr. Svolopoulos has published several Publications including the *Venizelos and the Political Crisis in Crete, 1901-1906* (1979); *Greek Policy in the Balkans*, 1974-1981 (1987); *Greek Foreign Policy, 1900-1945* (1992); *Constantinople, 1056-1908. Hellenism at its Height*" (1995). He also published "Greek Diplomatic Documents, 1940-41" (1988) and recently, of the twelve volumes "Constantine Karamanlis: Archives."

JAMES C. WARREN, JR., Advisor to U.S. firms doing business in Greece. He received his A.B. *magna cum laude* from the Woodrow Wilson School at Princeton University in 1949 and served in the U.S. Army Air Corps. He served as Chief, Import Program Office, of the Marshall Plan Mission to Greece for over four years. He later made a career in the international petroleum business in Southeast Asia, Japan and New York City bringing him back to Athens, where he became General Manager of Exxon's marketing interests in Greece for eight years. Mr. Warren has served as a Trustee of Anatolia College, Thessalonika, Greece, president of the Board of American Community Schools, Athens, Assistant to the President, Bates College, Maine; Vice President of the American Farm School of Greece and member of the Modern Greek Studies Association. He also served as chairman of the Greece and Cyprus Advance Area Studies for the Foreign Service Institute (1991-94). Currently he is working on a book on the Marshall Plan adventure in Greece and is conducting research at the Truman Library in Independence, Missouri, the National Archives and the Library of Congress.

YOLANDA AVRAM WILLIS, lecturer and writer. Dr. Willis speaks of righteous Greek rescuers of Jews from personal experience. Her family lived in Larisa, where her father was the President of the Jewish community until the war started in 1940. During the Holocaust, her family was hidden by Greek Orthodox people in Crete and in several places in Athens. After the war she attended the American College in Athens, then came to the U.S. to study on a Fulbright Scholarship, was elected to Phi Beta Kappa and graduated with honors. She earned an M.A. degree in Chemistry and a Ph.D. in Sociology. Dr. Willis worked in industry as a manager, educator and management consultant for twenty-two years. In 1992 she embarked on an oral history project, interviewing rescuers and survivors of the little known Holocaust in Greece. Dr. Willis lectures nationally and is an active member of the Holocaust Commission, the board of the Holocaust Center of Pittsburgh. She teaches Holocaust courses at Carnegie Mellon University's Academy for Lifelong Learning, and has served as a volunteer interviewer for Steven Spielberg's Survivors of the Shoah Visual History Foundation. In 1996 Dr. Willis facilitated the production of a documentary film on rescue in Greece, titled *It Was Nothing, It Was Everything.* In 1997 she was privileged to accompany His All Holiness Patriarch Bartholomew on his first visit to the U.S. Holocaust Memorial Museum, where she made a short presentation. She is writing a book, *A Hidden Child in Greece: Rescue Stories of the Holocaust.* Several of her stories, recounting her family's rescue by righteous Greek Gentiles, have been included in *Flares of Memory: Stories of Childhood During the Holocaust,* published by Oxford University Press in 2001.

Index

A

B

C

D

E

F

G

H

O

P

R

S

T

U

Y